MILLIONS OF GIFTS FOR THE GODS

Hopi Sichomovi Polychrome eagle motif jar and macaw tail feathers
(Marlin Roos, Illinois State Museum photographer).

MILLIONS OF GIFTS
FOR THE GODS

THE FEATHER
DISTRIBUTION PROJECT

Jonathan E. Reyman

UNIVERSITY PRESS OF COLORADO
Denver

© 2025 by University Press of Colorado

Published by University Press of Colorado
1580 North Logan Street, Suite 660
PMB 39883
Denver, Colorado 80203-1942

The University Press of Colorado is a proud member of
Association of University Presses.

The University Press of Colorado is a cooperative publishing enterprise supported, in part, by Adams State University, Colorado School of Mines, Colorado State University, Fort Lewis College, Metropolitan State University of Denver, University of Alaska Fairbanks, University of Colorado, University of Denver, University of Northern Colorado, University of Wyoming, Utah State University, and Western Colorado University.

ISBN: 978-1-64642-753-6 (hardcover)
ISBN: 978-1-64642-776-5 (paperback)
ISBN: 978-1-64642-754-3 (ebook)
https://doi.org/10.5876/9781646427543

Library of Congress Cataloging-in-Publication Data

Names: Reyman, Jonathan E. author
Title: Millions of gifts for the gods : the Feather Distribution Project / Jonathan E. Reyman.
Description: Denver, Colorado : University Press of Colorado, [2025] | Includes bibliographical references and index.
Identifiers: LCCN 2025021939 (print) | LCCN 2025021940 (ebook) | ISBN 9781646427536 hardcover | ISBN 9781646427765 paperback | ISBN 9781646427543 ebook
Subjects: LCSH: Feather Distribution Project—History | Applied anthropology—Southwest, New— Case studies | Feathers—Religious aspects | Pueblo Indians—Religion | Pueblo Indians—Rites and ceremonies | Pueblo Indians—Social life and customs | LCGFT: Case studies
Classification: LCC E99.P9 R39 2025 (print) | LCC E99.P9 (ebook) | DDC 978.9004/974—dc23/eng/20250925
LC record available at https://lccn.loc.gov/2025021939
LC ebook record available at https://lccn.loc.gov/2025021940

COVER ILLUSTRATION CREDITS. Front (clockwise from top left): Gringoann.art /Shutterstock; Alexander Francis Lydon / Rawpixel, L. Prang Co./Rawpixel; Rawpixel /Shutterstock. Back cover: Francois Levaillant / Shutterstock.

Contents

Figures

Unless noted, all photographs and figures are by Jonathan E. Reyman.

Tables

MILLIONS OF GIFTS FOR THE GODS

Introduction

During the years I taught anthropology at Illinois State University (1972–1991) and later at the University of Illinois, Urbana-Champaign (1994–1995), students often asked what anthropologists did or could do to solve problems among the peoples with whom they worked. The Feather Distribution Project (1982–2015) was one example of an applied anthropology program that attempted to solve four problems. It was somewhat unusual in terms of applied anthropology projects in that it was informed by a heavy reliance on data from archaeology, ethnography, and ethnohistory and the author's field experiences among the Pueblos, and combined this knowledge with Sol Tax's (1952, 1975) concept of "action anthropology."

But what is "action anthropology?" Sol Tax, the late Chicago anthropologist, coined the term, and in an article describing a conversation he had with Tax, Robert Rubinstein (1991) wrote:

> Action anthropology is an approach that seeks to develop the understanding of social and cultural life while helping communities address the challenges they face. In contrast to applied anthropology, when seeking to help the communities with whom they work, action anthropologists facilitate the communities' own decision making about what actions should be taken to address those challenges rather than implementing decisions made outside of the community or for the community by the anthropologist. In seeking new theoretical understanding, action anthropologists work on problems identified in collaboration with communities, rather than only

https://doi.org/10.5876/9781646427543.c000

pursuing questions that emerge independently from social theory, in contrast to basic research. Action anthropology originated in the work of Sol Tax and his students in the Fox Project, conducted with the Meskwaki Indians in the 1950s. It has since been used with communities throughout the world to promote social change and develop anthropological theory.

Through time, the term "action anthropology" has become less common, and such programs are now subsumed under the more comprehensive discipline of applied anthropology.

The Feather Distribution Project, originally an "action anthropology" project, was directed toward the solution of four problems that affected Native Americans in general and, at first, the Pueblos of the American Southwest. It must be noted that the Project was created in 1982 as a direct response, albeit belatedly, to an earlier (1970) request for macaw feathers from Fred Cordero, a Cochití Pueblo man (see below) who had been introduced to me the year before by one of my mentors, Professor Charles H. Lange. The Project's original purpose was to provide the Pueblos with macaw, parrot, and wild turkey feathers required for traditional religious practices in order to help the Pueblos secure their Constitutional First Amendment right to freedom of religion. The Pueblos had difficulty obtaining the feathers they needed for their ceremonies, and the Project helped to resolve this. Their difficulty was due to factors discussed below.

Archaeological evidence in the American Southwest demonstrates that the Pueblos, and their Ancestral Pueblo forebears, used wild turkey, macaw, parrot and other feathers over more than a thousand years (McKusick 2001) for a wide variety of ceremonial purposes including specialized clothing such as katsina masks, headdresses, turkey feather robes, and macaw feather ceremonial aprons or kilts (Canby 1982:573; Lekson 1997:55). However, the loss of habitat had diminished wild turkey populations in the Southwest, and the Pueblos no longer kept large numbers of domestic turkeys as they once did (see McKusick 2001). Furthermore, fewer Pueblo men hunted wild turkeys (or other animals), and so the Pueblos had to rely on other sources for wild turkey feathers, which, as discussed later, are the single most important feather for traditional cultural practices.

Three unplanned but positive consequences developed during the thirty-four years of operation of the Feather Distribution Project, all of which related to factors in the difficulties the Pueblos had in obtaining feathers: first, the program apparently helped to reduce the smuggling of live birds and feathers from Latin America into the American Southwest, though it was difficult to assess accurately the degree to which this had occurred; this, in turn, alleviated some of the stress on the native bird populations and their habitats in Latin America. Therefore, the second, express purpose (or problem) was to reduce the smuggling of birds and feathers, and the third problem, which followed from the second, was to lessen the destruction of native bird populations and habitats, especially in the rainforests of Latin America. In this context, a colleague once suggested that the Feather Distribution Project was also a conservation biology program.

How did this last occur? At the outset of the Feather Distribution Project, Pueblo men paid from 25¢ for a small macaw or parrot body feather, up to $100 for a long, perfect, Scarlet Macaw tail feather. Many of these feathers probably came from illegal imports, though I believe that the Pueblos likely were unaware of this.

Advertisements offering to buy macaw feathers appeared, and *still* appear, in some bird magazines; it *is* legal to buy and sell feathers from captive bred and raised bred macaws in the United States. Based on prices that the feather dealers originally charged, the approximately 4.5 million macaw and parrot feathers that the Project distributed free of charge could have had a market value as high as $18 million to $20 million. Wild turkey feathers, by contrast, have no significant monetary value despite their immense ceremonial importance.

By distributing millions of feathers free of charge, the Project apparently reduced the number of commercial dealers, or at least the size of their operations. Pueblo individuals still purchased feathers, but many (most?) obtained them from the Project.[1] The average price of Scarlet Macaw center tail feathers, for example, dropped by about 75–85 percent, and there were far fewer buyers than previously. Advertisements in bird magazines to buy macaw and parrot feathers also decreased.[2] The diminished commercial market meant fewer birds and their habitats were exploited and destroyed to provide feathers for Native Americans such as the Pueblos. Nevertheless, smuggling birds and feathers across the United States–Mexican border remained a commercially viable business in some parts of the Southwest.

Starting about 1990, the Project focused on a fourth problem: the elimination of the plucking of those macaws and parrots kept by Pueblo individuals. Plucking live birds had a long history that extended well back into antiquity. More recently, Judd (1954:plate 75, 263) depicted and discussed a Military Macaw that he gave to the Macaw Clan at Zuni in 1924, and it lived in a heavily plucked state until its death in 1946; I have seen a few plucked birds in other villages.

Plucking hurts birds and makes them more susceptible to infections, diseases, and skin maladies. Birds regulate their temperature, in part, through their feathers, and a plucked bird is more vulnerable to problems of excessive heat and cold. Plucking also angers birds, and an angry macaw is *not* to be trifled with; its beak can do serious damage. I know this from our female macaw, Chip, who has badly hurt both Laura and me while ostensibly "playing" with us. I dread what she might do if angry. While conducting my 1967 ethnographic fieldwork among the Chachi Indians in the Ecuadorian rainforest, I watched a pair of Scarlet Macaws, guarding their nest and newborn chicks, use their beaks to literally "unzip" an eighteen-foot-long Rainbow Boa in less than a minute. The speed of the macaws and the power of their beaks were remarkable and frightening.

The Project provided larger numbers of feathers to Pueblo bird owners specifically to encourage them *not* to pluck their birds and to use only their naturally molted feathers; for example, if a Pueblo individual had an Amazon parrot, we provided twice as many feathers as the bird molted in a year—a greater number of Amazon parrot feathers given to that individual than we would usually have provided—in exchange for a promise not to pluck the bird and to allow us to see the bird when we visited the village. We told the owner that there was another benefit for not plucking: the bird would likely live longer, ensuring more feathers available as time passed. The same was true for someone who had a Scarlet Macaw or other species. We had some success with this approach; some birds appeared less bedraggled and healthier on subsequent visits.

There was no way, however, to monitor this situation as closely as we would have liked, because we could not visit Pueblo homes on a frequent or regular basis; the 1,200 miles that separate Illinois from the Southwest were a formidable barrier to truly effective monitoring. We also had no accurate count of the number of macaws and parrots kept by Pueblo individuals, but it was probably not a high number, because of the purchase price of a bird: for example, as much as several thousand dollars for a Scarlet Macaw.

For those who might think that our behavior was patronizing, it is well to remember that the Project began in response to an initial request for macaw feathers from a Cochití elder, and not on my initiative as a way to gain "favor" or special treatment from the Pueblos.

Feathers were provided to any Pueblo individual or Native American Church member who requested them, and were intended for religious and cultural use—to help the Pueblos and the Native American Church members maintain their traditional practices. However, in about a dozen cases since the founding of the Project in 1982, we learned that individuals used the feathers for decoration on native crafts sold commercially, and in a couple of instances, directly sold to others the feathers they had received gratis from the Project. One of the worst instances occurred more than two decades ago: eighteen Hyacinth Macaw tail feathers had been requested supposedly for a special katsina mask. The feathers had to be matched in width and length for proper placement and display on the mask. It took many months to acquire these tail feathers from donors, but eventually we had the necessary eighteen tails to be mailed to the man who requested them. Within a few days of mailing them, we heard from five men in one afternoon: the recipient had set up a table outside a Pueblo-owned shop that sold jewelry, pottery, and artwork, and he was offering the feathers for sale. One man even sent me a digital photograph, taken with his cell phone, of the man offering the Hyacinth Macaw feathers for sale. The men of this Pueblo were monitoring themselves.

I wrote the offender a letter in which he was told he would receive no more feathers. He never responded, but I was later informed he still sold feathers, though I didn't know where he obtained them. I regretted having sent feathers to him for several years.

In all cases, the distribution of feathers to people who we learned sold the feathers we provided immediately ceased. The feathers were for religious use only; they were too culturally important to give to someone for profit-making ventures, which ran counter to the Project's goal to reduce or eliminate the commercial market for feathers. The Project neither bought nor sold feathers, and we expected those who received them not to sell them either. This was our agreement. Some Pueblo and other Native American individuals requested feathers specifically for their craftwork, but we refused such requests explaining that our feathers were for religious purposes.

Greed occasionally occurred in other ways. Sometimes requests for feathers far exceeded what any individual could possibly use at the time. For example, two men, cousins, each requested 144 Scarlet Macaw center tails and 144 Blue-and-Yellow (sometimes called Blue-and-Gold) Macaw center tails—twelve dozen of each. We usually provided three to six center tails per request. Their requests were not filled, and an accompanying letter explained why each of them would receive only four center tails from each of the two species.

In another instance in a different village, a man to whom we had supplied feathers for several years sent a large envelope containing copies of our request form—seventeen copies with identical requests for feathers, all at the same address, which included names of women as well as men. I was surprised by this, not only by the number of requests but also by requests made by women in this Pueblo where women did not directly receive feathers from us and, furthermore, also customarily left the room when I arrived at homes to distribute feathers to the men.

"Feathers are men's work," one man explained. I made a call to a Pueblo member and tribal official who I trusted to ask about this, an unusual thing for me to do since it involved breaking confidentiality. Nevertheless, I thought the risk worth it because the seventeen requests were excessive and came within weeks of a large shipment of feathers to the very individual who sent the seventeen requests (including feathers for himself). During the course of our conversation, the tribal official asked me if the person who had sent the forms was someone whom he then named.

I confirmed this, and he told that the names on the list were his wife, children (several under the age of ten), and his older children and their spouses. He further said the man had bragged that he would receive hundreds of macaw and parrot feathers and at least a thousand wild turkey feathers. He boasted publicly within the village of his attempt to "game the system." His plan failed; not only did we not fill the seventeen requests, but he was told that in the future, he would not receive any more feathers. He had, effectively, "killed the goose that laid the Golden Eggs."

One final example of greed stands out. I made it a practice at one village to visit the home of a clan mother to distribute feathers en masse to members of her clan and the religious society to which her son belonged. I had done this four or five times without incident. On this occasion, however, after I had laid thousands of macaw, parrot, and turkey feathers on the floor—tails in one group, wings in another, body feathers, etcetera, in others—calls were made to the society members, or children were sent to the houses of those without telephones (this was before the advent of cell phones), telling members that feathers were available. About fifteen men arrived, and after introductions, they were told to choose the feathers they wanted.

Two men immediately tried to scoop up all the macaw center tails, which started a heated argument. This seemed especially remarkable to me because *all* the men were in the same clan or religious society. Apparently, another call was then made during the argument by the clan mother, and within a couple of minutes, an elderly man arrived and entered the house. There was immediate silence. He made a brief statement in his native language, and all feathers were put back in place. He then instructed the men, one at a time, to choose a certain number of each type of feather—"only what you need"—and then to leave the house. Thereafter the distribution proceeded in an orderly fashion, and within fifteen to twenty minutes, all these feathers had been distributed. I later learned from the homeowner (the clan mother) that the elderly man was the head religious official for the village, and his statement in the Pueblo language included an admonishment against greed. He took no feathers himself, but I asked the clan mother, in whose house I was staying for a few days, what feathers he might need. She told me and then walked with me to his home, where I delivered a large bundle to him. He accepted them, inhaled a breath from them to absorb their power, offered the customary prayer, and then asked us to join him for a meal.

I have since learned that this event has apparently entered the local village lore—the story of the tall white man who laid out feathers only to have a couple of men attempt to take them all, necessitating that the head priest come to take charge of the distribution.

On another occasion at the same village, we had arranged ahead of time to distribute more than 200,000 wild turkey feathers. Some three hundred people showed

TABLE O.I. Chronology of Southwestern Pueblos receiving feathers

Year	Village
1982	Cochití
1982	Zia, Acoma, Hopi (Hotevilla, Bacavi, Mishongnovi, Polacca, Walpi, Sichomovi, Shungopovi, Sipaulovi, Oraibi)
1989	Zuni, Pojoaque, Santa Ana
1990	Santa Clara, San Felipe, Santo Domingo
1992	Tesuque, Taos
1993	Jemez, San Ildefonso
1995	Okay Owingeh (San Juan)
1997	Picuris
1999	Sandia
2000	Laguna
2001	Isleta
2007	Nambe, Hano
2010	Kykotsmovi
2012	Upper and Lower Moencopi

up, and several religious leaders were present to instruct each person to take a large paper grocery bag and to pick the feathers they wanted, which were laid out on tables—one handful of each type. Under the watchful eyes of the religious officers, the distribution went smoothly and without incident. Ironically, the woman janitor who cleaned up afterwards obtained the most feathers, by collecting those that fell to the floor during the distribution; she took them home to her family. These two events suggest that McGuire and Saitta's (1996) paper is incorrectly titled, and that its premise and content need rethinking.

By the end of its thirty-fourth year of operation (2015), the Feather Distribution Project had provided approximately 15 million wild turkey, macaw, and parrot feathers to all thirty-two Pueblo villages in New Mexico and Arizona[3] (table 0.1), for use in traditional religious ceremonies.

An additional 200,000 feathers had been distributed to members of the Native American Church in a dozen or so states. Finally, some 300,000 wild turkey feathers were distributed to the Seneca (New York) and Wyandotte (Oklahoma) to make traditional headdresses, to the Cherokee in Tahlequah, Oklahoma, for arrow fletching, and to Pomo groups in California for feather screens (see figures 0.1–0.4). A limited number of wild turkey feathers were provided to other tribes and to Native American prison inmates. Except for macaw center tails, we did not count the

Figure 0.1. Wyandotte traditional headdress (*kus-to-wa*).

Figure 0.2. Seneca traditional cap (*gus-to-weh*).

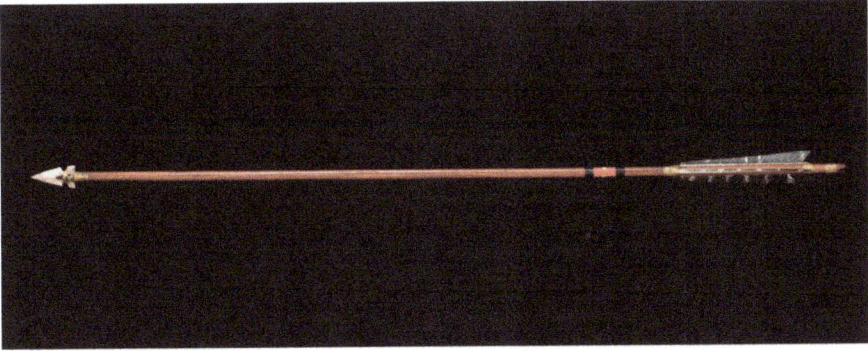

Figure 0.3. Cherokee traditional arrow made by Joe "Red Buffalo" Adams.

Figure 0.4. Pomo wild turkey feather screen.

feathers sent to recipients but weighed them beforehand. For example, seven hundred wild turkey back body feathers six inches in length weighed about one ounce, as did twelve to fifteen Scarlet Macaw center tail feathers. My worst nightmare was counting feathers—41,201, 41,202, 41,203 . . . Then the phone rings, I answer it, lose my count, and must start over. "Damn!" (and then I awake).

All feathers were provided free of charge, as gifts. We asked nothing in return. The Project neither bought nor sold feathers, but we did reimburse donors' shipping costs, if requested. The Pueblos and others sometimes reciprocated with gifts of jewelry or other items. These, in turn, were given to feather donors or those who otherwise helped with the work: bird club members, breeders, people with companion birds, turkey hunters, bird keepers in zoos and aviaries who collected molted feathers, and Project volunteers. The Project itself did not operate for financial or other material gain.

When the Project first began, I traveled alone to distribute feathers among the Pueblos. The Pueblos are family-focused, however, and I was repeatedly asked why I didn't bring my wife with me. I gave various explanations—excuses, really—about having different schedules, amounts of vacation time, and such, but it eventually became clear that Pueblo trust and hospitality were dependent, in part, on my having my wife with me, at least on some of the trips to the Southwest. Thereafter, I did so whenever possible. This resulted in improved relations between me and Pueblo families, and Laura was privy to information from Pueblo women that I was not.

Once, a woman graduate student in anthropology at an Arizona university requested to come along when I distributed feathers. I told her this might be possible, but only to a degree; I explained that she could not be present at most Rio Grande Pueblo homes when the distributions were made. She questioned this, and I further explained that in these villages, feathers were men's work from which women were excluded. She replied that this was sexist, and she was not going to be excluded. I explained this was Pueblo cultural practice, *their* villages and homes, and if she couldn't accept the reality of it, then she should stay home. She stayed home. Apparently, she had missed the basic lesson in anthropological ethnographic fieldwork about respect for and cultural acceptance of the views with whom one works.

As an archaeologist and anthropologist, I was deeply interested in Pueblo religious and ceremonial life. I was particularly interested in how feathers were used by individuals, religious societies, and the Pueblos in general, both today and in comparison with post-contact and Ancestral Pueblo times. However, the Project did not operate to obtain information about Pueblo religion and ceremonial practices nor about Native American Church practices. No questions were asked about sacred matters. Nevertheless, over the past thirty-four years, a great deal of information was freely given about Pueblo religious practices, individuals' clan and religious society affiliations, and the uses of feathers. Furthermore, Laura and I were regularly afforded the privilege of watching ceremonial activities, and, on occasion, I was asked to help make ceremonial objects when no other Anglos or non-Pueblo persons were present. The information received was never published nor discussed with anyone outside the Pueblo, and no specific information not already part of the existing anthropological literature and general knowledge is published herein. No sacred information was ever released for research or other purposes. This reinforced the fact that feathers were an outright gift and not a means to acquire sacred knowledge for dissemination to other anthropologists or to the public. This maintained the trust on which the Project depended for its acceptance by Pueblo peoples and Native American Church members.

Anthropologists generally do not like to make "all" statements about cultural behavior. Humans are sufficiently diverse that almost nothing one can say about individual or group behavior pertains to all peoples. However, it *is* fair to say that all groups throughout the world, to one extent or another, have special relationships with birds. Many nations have a national bird; ours is the Bald Eagle (*Haliaeetus leucocephalus*). Each state has a state bird: for Illinois, it's the Northern Cardinal (*Cardinalis cardinalis*), while for New Mexico it's the Greater Roadrunner (*Geococcyx californianus*) and for Arizona it's the Cactus Wren (*Campylorhynchus brunneicapillus*). More recently, China chose the Red-crowned Crane (*Grus japonensis*) as its national bird.

Judeo-Christian belief states that birds were created on Day 5 (*Genesis* 1:21, Old Testament). For the Pueblos, who recognize more than 220 species of birds (see Tyler 1979:xiii and 272–277 for a list of these birds and the Pueblos that use them), these birds play an essential role in daily life and are fundamentally important to them: in much of Pueblo oral history and in many Pueblo origin tales, birds guided Pueblo peoples from the Underworld into this world. (Those migratory species used by the Pueblos are indicated with an "**X**" in appendix C.) Therefore, the Feather Distribution Project filled a basic need in the preservation and continuation of traditional Pueblo life. For more than a thousand Pueblo people (see below), the Feather Distribution Project was their primary source of feathers.

1

The Archaeological Context

As noted above, the Feather Distribution Project was based, in part, on archaeological data from the American Southwest. No macaws were indigenous to the American Southwest; only the Thick-billed Parrot (*Rhynchopsitta pachyrhyncha*) was present; it resembles, somewhat, a small Military Macaw (*Ara militaris*). The Thick-billed Parrot is now extirpated in the Southwest, and efforts failed to reintroduce it in the 1980s and early 1990s. Although found at a few archaeological sites in the Southwest, including Chaco Canyon (McKusick 2001:9), the Thick-billed Parrot was neither widely nor frequently used ceremonially. At the time I wrote this manuscript, only thirteen specimens had been found in the Southwest and two at Casas Grandes (now more properly called Paquimé) in the northern Mexican state of Chihuahua (McKusick 2001:88). The White-fronted Parrot (*Amazona albifrons*) and the Lilac-fronted Parrot, also called the Lilac-crowned Parrot (*Amazona finschi*), rarely occur in Southwestern archaeological sites (McKusick 2001:9), and like the Thick-billed Parrot, also seem to have been of minor importance, judging from the meager archaeological evidence.

Therefore, macaws and all parrots, except for the Thick-billed Parrot, found at archaeological sites in the Southwest are prima facie evidence for ancient Mesoamerican-Southwest trade, trade that extends back more than a thousand years. Skeletal remains of over four hundred macaws and a number of whole and fragmentary macaw feathers are found at Southwestern archaeological sites. Macaw, and a lesser number of parrot, depictions are present on both ancient and

https://doi.org/10.5876/9781646427543.c001

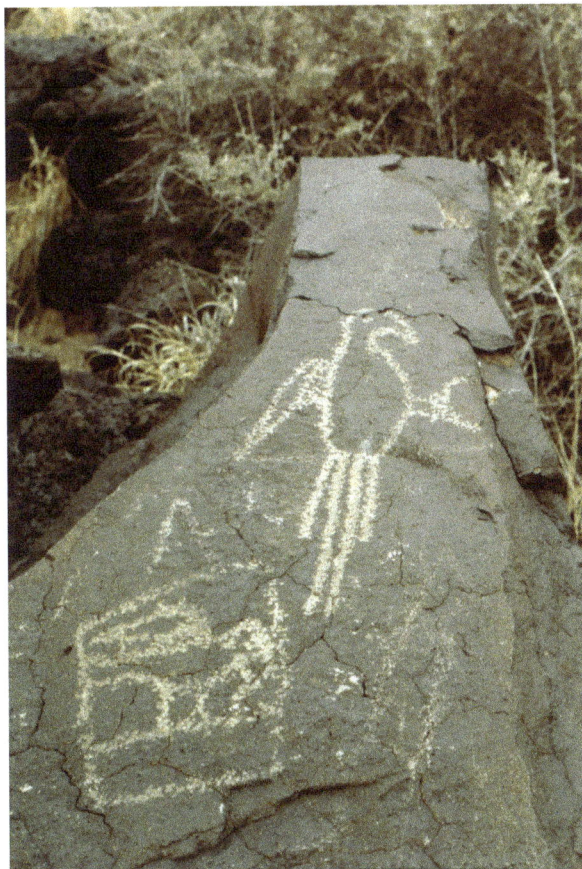

Figure 1.1. Macaw and caged parrot petroglyphs, Petroglyph National Monument, New Mexico.

post-contact pottery, on pre- and post-contact murals, and on rock art (see figure 1.1). In fact, birds are the most frequently depicted life-forms on kiva wall murals at Awatovi, Kawaika-a, Pottery Mound, and at Mesa Verde, and macaws are the most frequently depicted birds, more frequently than eagles, turkeys, and other species. Curiously, although the murals at Pottery Mound depict large numbers of macaws (Hibben 1975), *no* macaw remains were found during the archaeological excavations at the site (Emslie 1981; Clark 2007). Emslie (1981:853) identified fifty species of birds, and Clark (2007:215), with a much smaller sample size than Emslie, identified twelve species. In both analyses, the turkey (*Meleagris gallopavo*) was overwhelmingly the most common species. Similarly, despite the frequency of macaw and parrot motifs in the Awatovi and Kawaika-a murals (Smith 1952) and the prominence of macaw and parrot feathers in Hopi rituals, neither Hargrave

(1970) nor McKusick (2001) reports any macaw or parrot remains from the two sites or from the Hopi area in general.

One of the petroglyphs in figure 1.1 is especially interesting because it depicts a macaw or parrot in a cage, providing visual evidence of how live birds were transported into and within the Southwest. It is important to note again that macaws were never indigenous to the Southwest: live macaws and feathers were imported from Paquimé in northern Chihuahua, and possibly from Sonora and Sinaloa. The three species found at Southwestern sites are first, foremost, and overwhelmingly the Scarlet Macaw (*Ara macao*) and occasionally the Military Macaw (*Ara militaris*), and the Blue-and-Yellow Macaw (*Ara ararauna*), respectively. To the best of my knowledge, the Blue-and-Yellow Macaw is known only from a few rare finds of feathers, but Schroeder (1968:110) cites the use of Blue-and-Yellow Macaw feathers at San Ildefonso Pueblo circa 1880 in the post-contact period.

McKusick (2001:6) writes:

Scarlet Macaws, the only parrots traded into the Southwest in economically important numbers, were [originally] brought from the humid tropical lowlands below Mexico City. The first peak in macaw trade centers around ca. 1100. A secondary peak of macaw usage occurs in the 1300s, and is often found in conjunction with heavy buteonine hawk usage [e.g., Red-tailed Hawk (*Buteo jamaicensis*), Harris's Hawk (*Parabuteo unicinctus*), Swainson's Hawk (*Buteo swainsoni*), and others]. Like hawks, macaws usually occur as burials in areas where humans are buried in connection with ceremonial structures such as kivas or dance platforms. Burials of macaws, buteonine hawks, and eagles are characteristic of Western Pueblo sites during the late 1200s and 1300s.

McKusick (2001:76–78) later notes:

The live macaw trade was rather quiet during the early 1200s, but a sudden flurry of activity occurred between 1275 and 1300. Sites of this period include Kiet Siel, Houck, Pollock's Ranch, Turkey Creek, Point of Pines, and Gila Cliff Dwellings. It seems like a very remote and inconspicuous site to be included in the macaw trade. However, there was a beaver dam during its occupation . . . which made the immediate vicinity more suitable for raising crops. Manipulation of water from the beavers' pond may have been the reason for a desire to propitiate Quetzalcoatl by obtaining a Scarlet Macaw.

The revival of the macaw trade during the late 1200s and early 1300s draws attention to the relationship between Grasshopper Pueblo and Point of Pines in east central Arizona and Paquimé to the South. Both Grasshopper and Point of Pines had reservoirs. Point of Pines also had an elaborate system of agricultural terracing on the slopes above the site. Paquimé had complex water control devices ranging from simple check dams to indoor plumbing.

Another possible association of Scarlet Macaw occurrences with water control devices may be found at Arroyo Hondo Pueblo which is located about five miles south of Santa Fe, New Mexico. The occupation of Arroyo Hondo stretches from about 1330 to shortly after 1420, with population peaks at about 1335 and in the very early 1400s. The Scarlet Macaw material from Arroyo Hondo is among the best dated in the Southwest. Of the two well-documented burials, one dates to the late 1320s and the other to the early 1330s, and are thus coincidental with Arroyo Hondo's period of highest population and most active commerce. Both burials of 11 to 12 month old macaws were in Plaza G, which was also used for human burials. . . . A single quadrate bone from a third bird was deposited in Plaza C in the 1380s, but may have originated in an earlier stratum. [cf. Crown 2016a, 2016b].

During the late 1320s and early 1330s, when the two well-preserved macaws were buried, there was also a noticeable increase in water-dependent birds. . . .

In historic Pueblo religion, the Scarlet Macaw is associated with the Sun Deity, which in turn is associated with turquoise. The predominant color of the Scarlet Macaw is red, the historic Pueblo color for south and southeast. Further, parrots are associated with summer and such summer aspects as the rainbow, the Corn Maidens of Pueblo myth, and the "Germinator" or *Muyingwu*, an underworld supernatural who served as Lord of the Crops. The historic Pueblo association of Scarlet Macaws and turquoise parallels the early historic Pima [*Akimel O'odham*] custom of raising Scarlet Macaws for feathers to trade for turquoises far to the north (Hargrave 1979:1).

The third greatest concentration of macaws in the prehistory of the Southwest Culture Area north of the international border [between Mexico and the United States] was found at Point of Pines. The recovery of 29 macaws is noteworthy by itself, but the circumstances of the recovery are even more illuminating. The large site at Point of Pines, AZ W:10:50 had a dual population. The main part of the pueblo was occupied by local people. Once section, however, was occupied by a Kayenta Anasazi [Ancestral Pueblo] contingent. The macaw remains in the Kayenta section were closely concentrated, usually buried under room floors. The macaw remains in the main portion of the pueblo were more scattered, most often buried in trash dumps like humans, suggesting a difference in macaw usage. . . .

Apparently macaws were traded to Point of Pines in exchange for the enormous Large Indian Domestic Turkeys which were raised only at Point of Pines.

The Mimbres aviculturalists were gone by this time. Juvenile macaws were now being raised to a marketable age primarily at Paquimé, in four sections of the city set aside for that purpose. From Grasshopper Pueblo come the fragile remains of the only juvenile macaw recovered at an archaeological site north of the international border. It is too young to have been imported from the tropical Mexican lowlands where Scarlet Macaws occur wild. It was probably bred at Paquimé, but it is possible that it was bred at Grasshopper Pueblo. During the peak of the Southwest trade in live macaws one adult macaw was found at each of three sites, Pueblo Bonito, Wupatki, and Old Town in the Mimbres area. During the late 1200s and early 1300s revival of the macaw trade, two adult Scarlet Macaws were recovered from Point of Pines and three were found at Grasshopper Pueblo. Whether the increase in adult birds represents an attempt to breed macaws locally or not, it is certainly a variation in the customary pattern of usage. Macaw breeding in Arizona is possible, but extremely unlikely. First, the adult macaws may not have been present at the sites where they were found at the same time. Second, macaws are not easily sexed unless they happen to lay an egg. Third, even if a pair is correctly sexed, they may have to be associated for as much as five or six years before they mate. Fourth, and probably most important, human-imprinted birds often do not recognize members of their own species as potential mates.

The post-1400 macaws present quite a contrast in that all seven specimens complete enough to age are in the 11–12 month Newfledged age stage associated with sacrificial use.... It is probable that the worship of Tlaloc was much more important than the worship of Quetzalcoatl at Gran Quivira as evidenced by the presence of 944 Small Indian Domestic Turkeys to only two Scarlet Macaws. However, the presence of a human bone artifact, a disc made from the right parietal with two perforations like a button, similar to one from Pecos [Pueblo] which was incised with the four-pointed Morning Star pattern . . . points to the presence there of the Quetzalcoatl Cult.

Presumably macaws were originally captured and transported to Paquimé, or to another as yet undiscovered location, and from Paquimé they were distributed into the American Southwest—presently Arizona, New Mexico, and Utah (see note 4). In time, Paquimé itself became a breeding center for the Scarlet Macaw and, to a much lesser extent, for the Military Macaw, and apparently was the primary source for both species found in the Southwest (Di Peso et al. 1974). Although a Blue-and-Yellow Macaw (*Ara ararauna*) feather and a feather bundle possibly made from Blue-and-Yellow Macaw feathers have been found in the Southwest (see table 1.1), no Blue-and-Yellow Macaw feathers or skeletal remains have been discovered at Paquimé, nor has any other possible source for the species been identified so far. Where Blue-and-Yellow Macaws were traded from into the Southwest, and the route via which they were traded, are both unknown. In terms of the distribution of Blue-and-Yellow Macaws, the closest locations to the Southwest are the southeasternmost tip of Panama and the northernmost area of Colombia, neither of which, at a minimum of 2,670 miles (4,296 kilometers) to southern Arizona, can be considered close to the Southwest. It is possible that Blue-and-Yellow Macaws were found closer in pre-Columbian times, but as yet, we have no evidence they were.

TABLE 1.1. Prehistoric macaw, parrot, and turkey feather objects from the Southwest

Object	Site	Species	Date (all AD)
ARIZONA			
Atlatl darts	NE Arizona Basketmaker and early Pueblo sites	*Meleagris* sp. (?)	700–800
Feather*	Tonto Lower Ruin	*Ara macao*	1100
Arrows	Tonto Lower Ruin	*Meleagris* Sp. (?)	1100
Feather	Ridge Ruin	*Ara macao* (?)	c. 1120
Feather in basket	Ridge Ruin	*Ara macao* (?)	c. 1120
Ceremonial arrows	Ridge Ruin	*Meleagris* sp. (?)	c. 1120
Corn ear fetish	Antelope House	*Ara macao*	1050–1250
Feather bands	Antelope House	*Ara macao*	1050–1250
Feather cordage	Antelope House	*Meleagris* sp.	1050–1250
Feathers	Kiet Siel	*Ara macao*	1250–1275
COLORADO			
Feather cloth	Step House	*Meleagris* sp.	620–825
Headdress	Ruin 9 (Mesa Verde)	*Meleagris* Sp.	650–850
Arrows	Long House	*Meleagris* sp.	1180–1275
Feather cordage	Cliff Palace	*Meleagris* sp.	1210–1275
NEW MEXICO			
Feather	Pueblo del Arroyo	*Ara ararauna*	1060–1100
Feather	Aztec Ruin	*Ara macao*	C. 1150
Feathers	Water Canyon Cave	*Ara macao*	750–1150
Feather cordage	Water Canyon Cave	*Ara macao*	750–1150
Feather	Pinnacle Cave	*Ara macao*	1150–1400
Feather	Tularosa Cave	*Ara macao*	unknown
Feather bundle	Tularosa Cave	*Amazona* sp.	unknown
Feather	Gila Cliff dwelling	*Ara macao*	late 1200s
Feather cordage	Gila Cliff dwelling	*Ara macao*	late 1200s
Feather circlet	Gila Cliff dwelling	*Ara macao*	late 1200s
Feather-lined bag	U-Bar Cave	*Ara macao*	1150–1400
Feathers	Chetro Ketl	*Ara macao*	1100
Arrows	Pueblo Bonito	*Meleagris* sp.	900–1150
Ceremonial sticks	Pueblo Bonito	?	900–1150

continued on next page

TABLE 1.1—*continued*

Object	Site	Species	Date (all AD)
Feather bundles	Pueblo Bonito	*Ara ararauna* (?)	c. 1050
Feather "stockings"	Pueblo Bonito	*Meleagris* sp.	1060–1150
Wrapped feather	Pueblo del Arroyo	*Meleagris* sp.	1060–1100
UTAH			
Feather	Lizard Alcove	*Ara* sp.	750–900
Feather bundle	Allen Canyon in Grand Gulch	*Ara macao* and *Ara ararauna* (?)	1015–1155
Feather apron	Lavender Canyon	*Ara macao*	1080–1110
Feather	Westwater Ruin	*Ara* sp.	1150–1275
Feather-cord robes	Numerous sites throughout the Southwest	*Meleagris* sp.	700–1300

* The use of the word "Feather" indicates the feather had a fragment of cordage or some other material attached, which would have secured it to an object that is no longer extant.

One can raise the question of why there was an apparent hiatus in the macaw trade between about 1200 and 1275, which seems coterminous with an increase in turkeys at Paquimé. There is no definitive answer, but there are several possibilities. First, the evidence for the macaw trade depends upon the findings made at archaeological sites, and the period from 1200 to 1275 saw a population decline in several areas—Chaco Canyon became virtually deserted after about 1150–1175, although there was a small repopulation at about 1230. Mesa Verde and the general Four Corners Area started to experience a significant population decline in the early 1200s—and much of the Ancestral Pueblo area was undergoing a period of social, religious, and political discord and upheaval, which could have contributed to a decline in the demand for macaws; with people moving about so much, the "trading market" for macaws collapsed. Reestablishing socioeconomic and cultural stability took precedence over all else.

A second possibility is that given that seventy-five years is not a long time in the archaeological record of a large area, the lack of sites with macaw remains could simply be a sampling error of the archaeological fieldwork. For example, it took twelve years of research and the discovery of a charred log near Show Low, Arizona—the famous "Show Low Log"—to allow the astronomer, A. E. Douglass, to complete the initial master chronology for dendrochronology ("tree-ring") dating in the Southwest. Archaeologists simply may not yet have found the sites with evidence for macaw trade in the 1200–1275 time period.

Another possibility is that Paquimé may have had problems with its macaw breeding populations that led to a decline in the availability of birds for trade. One must remember that although we have a great deal of information about Paquimé (Di Peso et al. 1974), only about 40 percent of the site has been excavated. We have much more to learn about the history of Paquimé, both through further analysis of existing excavated materials and through new excavations. As for the increase in turkeys at Paquimé, this may reflect greater demand for them by trading partners, possibly in conjunction with an expansion of the Tlaloc Cult (McKusick 2001:46–49), or it could be that the people at Paquimé increased the numbers for their own consumption, especially if there was a decline in the export of macaws and they needed to replace lost "income" and to have sufficient food. The perceived decline in the macaw trade may be real or it may be an "artifact" of the archaeological research, and whichever it is, there may be no connection to the increase of turkey production at Paquimé.

It's worth noting how pre-contact macaws in the Southwest compare in frequency to Pueblo macaw preferences today, as indicated by the thirty-four-year history of the Feather Distribution Project. In the ancient Southwest, the only three macaw species at archaeological sites were the Scarlet Macaw (*Ara macao*), the Military Macaw (*Ara militaris*), and the Blue-and-Yellow Macaw (*Ara ararauna*). The Scarlet Macaw was the most common by a wide margin, followed by the Military Macaw and a tiny number of Blue-and-Yellow Macaws represented only by feathers. Today the Blue-and-Yellow Macaw is the most popular species among macaw owners in the United States, but among the Pueblos and among Native American Church members, Scarlet Macaw feathers were the most frequently requested, specifically the long center tail feathers. The next most frequently requested tail feathers were from the Blue-and-Yellow Macaw and the Greenwing Macaw (*Ara chloroptera*), with the latter species absent at pre-contact sites as far as we know. The center tails from the Military Macaw were the fourth most commonly requested, and the center tails of the Hyacinth Macaw (*Anodorhynchus hyacinthinus*) were the fifth most requested. The Hyacinth Macaw was absent in the pre-contact Southwest, which is not surprising given that the species is native to the west central portion of South America and Amazonia (Juniper and Parr 1998:416), the most distant species from the Southwest of the five main large macaws. Neither the Greenwing Macaw nor the Hyacinth Macaw is mentioned in ethnographic accounts, and it's unclear when their feathers were first used by the Pueblos. It's almost certainly post–World War II and probably no earlier than the 1960s and 1970s. The Feather Distribution Project first provided Pueblo recipients with feathers from these two species in the 1980s, and as discussed later in this volume, the provision of the Greenwing Macaw tail feathers was my mistake due to a misunderstanding about a mural painted by Alex Seotewa that I saw several times in Our Lady of Guadeloupe, the old Zuni mission church.

Center tails from other, smaller species of macaws, sometimes called mini-macaws, were requested only infrequently: for example, the Blue-winged Macaw, also known as Illiger's Macaw (*Primolius maracana*), and the Red-shouldered Macaw, also referred to as either Hahn's Macaw or Noble Macaw (*Diopsittaca nobilis*). Again, these two species and the other mini-macaws have not been recovered from archaeological sites in the Southwest, nor are they mentioned in ethnographic and ethnohistoric documents. What has become apparent in recent years is that Pueblo men with access to the internet searched for macaw feathers, sometimes found species with colors that appealed to them, and then requested the feathers even though they were not traditional. One Pueblo recipient regularly requested center tail feathers from the Harlequin Macaw, a hybrid cross between a Blue-and-Yellow Macaw and a Greenwing Macaw, a macaw that does not occur in the wild. I once saw Harlequin Macaw center tails on the back of a Zuni *Sha'lako* mask, a decidedly nontraditional use. Furthermore, although Amazon parrots are uncommon in the pre-contact Southwest (see McKusick 2001), Amazon parrot tail feathers were frequently requested by both the Pueblos and Native American Church members, and Amazon parrot wing feathers were also requested, though much less often than tail feathers.

As noted, macaws are far more common than parrots at archaeological sites within the Southwest, despite the indigenous presence in the past (until the late 1920s to the mid-late 1930s) of the Thick-billed Parrot (*Rhynchopsitta pachyrhyncha*) in southern Arizona. The long tail feathers of the Scarlet, Military, and Blue-and-Yellow macaws are visually more spectacular in comparison to the significantly shorter tail feathers from Thick-billed and Amazon parrots. Or it may reflect the greater importance of macaws in Pueblo oral tradition and ritual behavior (see, for example, Tyler 1979:16–45). Whatever the reason, macaws and macaw feathers predominated in ancient times, continued to be more important than parrot feathers through the Spanish period starting in 1539, and remain more important to the present day.

Figure 1.2 shows a partial distribution, as of the mid-1980s, of macaw remains found at archaeological sites in the Southwest. It includes the location of Paquimé in northern Chihuahua, Mexico, a pre-contact macaw breeding and distribution center until its destruction around AD 1450 according to the revised chronology for the site (table 1.3).[4] The remains of 322 Scarlet Macaws, 81 Military Macaws, and 101 macaws of unidentified species were recovered from Paquimé, and McKusick (2001:73) further states, "Current dating indicates that the trading center of Paquimé took commercial advantage of an already existing trade in macaws, rather than initiating it."

Figure 1.2. Mid-1980s map of macaw remains in the Southwest (Doug Carr map).

A recent paper (Watson et al. 2015), using AMS ^{14}C dating of macaw skeletal remains from Pueblo Bonito and the Old Town and Mitchell sites in the Mimbres area, produced clusters of dates in the AD 900–975 and AD 1015–1155 range for Chaco Canyon and AD 1025–1155 for the Mimbres sites. These ranges all pre-date the revised Medio Period chronology for Paquimé, the period when macaws were bred at and exported from the site, but the authors offer no source for the macaws other than speculation that "the acquisition of scarlet macaws likely required lengthy trips between the northern SW and the lowland tropical forests of Mesoamerica."

I discuss below in "The Concept of Value in Mesoamerican-Southwestern Trade" Pueblo long-distance journeys south for trade, especially in the immediate pre-contact and post-contact period, but as far as I am aware, there is no empirical evidence for such trading journeys between the Southwest and lowland Mesoamerica. Scarlet Macaws in the Southwest could have come from the lowland tropical rainforests of Mesoamerica, but there is no evidence at present that they did. Furthermore, my comments on the problems with the revised chronology for

TABLE 1.2. Mesoamerican-Southwestern architectural parallels

| | American Southwest | | | |
Mesoamerican Trait	ANCESTRAL PUEBLO	HOHOKAM	MOGOLLON	SINAGUA
Rubble core masonry	+	+	?	+
Platform mound	+*	+	+	?
Great sanctuary (Great kiva)	+	–	+	–
Ballcourt	–	+	–	+
Square column	+	–	–	–
Column-fronted gallery	+	–	–	–
Tower observatory	+	?	–	–

* Includes tri-wall and bi-wall structures. Note: This is based on the original survey by Edwin Ferdon (1955), with later additions by J. Charles Kelley and Jonathan E. Reyman.

Medio Period Paquimé (note 4) are also germane to this issue. For me, and I may be alone in this opinion, the possibility that Paquimé was the source of these birds at the earlier date is not foreclosed. Finally, recent research examined the possibility of a macaw breeding colony being present in the Southwest (George et al. 2018) but concluded there is no evidence for its location at this time, though they did not foreclose on the possibility that a breeding colony site might be found at some future date (George et al. 2018:8744).

Scholars have long debated the questions of when macaws (and parrots) first entered the Southwest and the context(s) for their appearance. So few parrots have been found that their earliest presence at sites is problematical, but the archaeological evidence now indicates that macaws are found in the Hohokam area, perhaps in the AD 500s during the Estrella Phase, and are certainly present during the 600s in the Sweetwater Phase (McKusick 2001:74). McKusick (2001:6) states that the first peak in macaw trading occurred around AD 1100. She further states (2001:80) that with these two Mesoamerican deities (Tlaloc and Quetzalcoatl) the association and use of macaws and turkeys was with these deities: "From the avian and iconographic evidence at hand, I believe the full pan-Southwestern socio-politico-religious complex was in place by not later than 1000, and continued into the historic period in areas not invaded by the Pueblo Katsina Cult."

It is worth noting, however, that the use of macaw feathers and, to a lesser extent, Amazon parrot feathers is widespread among the post-contact Pueblos for katsina masks and other ceremonial paraphernalia. For example, as reported below, several

TABLE 1.3. Casas Grandes (Paquimé) revised Medio Period chronology

	Di Peso et al. (1974)	Ravesloot et al. (1995)	Braniff (1986)	Lekson (1984)	LeBlanc (1980)
1600					
		Tardio Period			
1500			1450	1450	
1400		Medio Period	Medio Period	Medio Period	Medio Period
		[1350]			
1300					
		Medio Period			
1200					
			[1150]	[1150]	
1100					
		[1060]			
1000					
		Viejo Period			
900					
800					
700		[700]			
600					
500		Plainware Period			
400					
300					

continued on next page

TABLE 1.3—*continued*

	Di Peso et al. (1974)	Ravesloot et al. (1995)	Braniff (1986)	Lekson (1984)	LeBlanc (1980)
200					
100					
AD	[50]				
0					
BC					
100					

years ago the Feather Distribution Project provided some 2,200 macaw center tail feathers to Hotevilla for a single Parrot Dance that involved about seventy masked participants.

Scholars have also had greater disagreements over the question of context, but a general consensus seems to be forming that macaw feathers appear with the development of more advanced farming techniques including more productive varieties of maize, beans, and squashes, and various forms of irrigation, specifically canal irrigation among the Hohokam and later irrigation ditches among the Chacoans. I have long argued (Reyman 1971, 1976b) that macaws and parrots were part of ancient Southwest farming technology—the ceremonies for which the feathers (and additional Mesoamerican objects such as copper bells) were considered essential to the successful growing of corn, beans, squash, and other cultigens.

The association of macaws and parrots with farming ceremonialism has a logic in terms of visual symbolism. Ethnographically, Pueblo cosmologies have strong systems of color-direction symbols and similarly strong color associations with other elements of their culture (Riley 1963). The flame-red tail feathers of the Scarlet Macaw are equated, in part, with the sun's rays. Furthermore, most Scarlet macaws found in the Southwest archaeological sites for which age can be determined were "newfledged" at the times of their death, that is, eleven to twelve months of age (Hargrave 1970:53; McCusick 2001:72), the age at which they develop their first set of long red tail feathers. One might argue that ancient Southwestern peoples should have waited for the first molting of tail feathers and subsequent growth, since the second set would have been longer and probably a richer red color because the birds were older. However, what they *should* have done and what they *did* do not coincide. They sacrificed the birds when newfledged, at around the time of the spring equinox (McCusick 2001:67). The time is significant because it is when the Ancestral Pueblos started to prepare for spring planting, and so do the present-day Pueblos. The green bodies of the Military Macaw and the Thick-billed Parrot refer to the green of new plant growth, especially corn, and the Amazon parrot's tail feathers can be viewed as symbolic of corn leaves, and are used to symbolize leaves on a corn plant (despite its green body, Military Macaw tail feathers are not green but red and blue with yellow undersides). The Blue-and-Yellow Macaw has the colors of sunrise and East (yellow), and sunset and West (blue), among other associations. These color-direction and other color associations were well established when the Spanish first arrived in the Southwest and undoubtedly extend far back into antiquity (e.g., Riley 1963; McKusick 2001). Macaw and parrot feathers are visually prominent in Pueblo ceremonies, both masked (katsina) dances and nonmasked dances (e.g., Feast Day dances among the Rio Grande Pueblos). For example, at Zuni, bundles of macaw tail feathers adorn the backs of the six Sha'lako masks. The Sha'lakos are giant birds, one from each of the six Zuni kivas, which are associated with the six directions. Feathers from various bird species also adorn Sha'lako masks, clothing, other katsina masks, and fetishes such as the *mili* and ritual paraphernalia (e.g., Stevenson 1904:419–420) used in the Sha'lako ceremony. Furthermore, archaeologists have found macaws, like turkeys, associated with human burials (e.g., Hargrave 1970; McCusick 2001), though the significance of this practice is not understood. Unlike turkeys, however, macaw burials were not accompanied by valuable or high-status grave goods.

There are further associations of mainly macaw feathers and, to a lesser extent, parrot feathers in conjunction with farming activities. The kiva murals found at Pottery Mound (Hibben 1975) and Awatovi and Kawaika-a (Smith 1952) make abundantly clear the importance of these feathers to farming. For example, figure 52 from Pottery Mound (Hibben 1975:72–73) depicts feathers with other water and rainmaking symbolism surrounding stylized corn plants. This is not a unique representation but is found again and again among the surviving murals. Also, as Hibben (1975) notes throughout his book on the Pottery Mound kiva murals, the macaws, parrots, other elements, and ceremonialism are examples of Mexican influence at these Southwestern sites in the pre-Columbian images found at them.

The same sorts of associations are present in the kiva murals from Awatovi and Kawaika-a. Indeed, Hibben (1975:71) noted the similarity in some of the curvilinear motifs found at Pottery Mound to those found among the Hopi. This is readily apparent in plate H from Awatovi, and plate I, also from Awatovi, which depict macaws in conjunction with rain and corn symbolism, and other motifs (Smith 1952). Although Awatovi was destroyed in 1700–1701 by the Hopi themselves, the murals pre-date the Spanish presence at the town, that is, they are Ancestral Pueblo in time and context. Smith (1952:127) notes the presence of macaws and parrots among the Southwestern Pueblos in prehistoric times, and once again the presence of these birds in northern Arizona connects the area with Mesoamerica. Furthermore, because corn and other cultigens originated in Mesoamerica, as did macaws and associated commodities, and because these are all found in the murals as part of farming depictions, it is clear that they are part of the ancient "technology" used to produce crops.

It is generally agreed that maize arrived in the Southwest around four thousand years ago, but it was not cultivated until some two thousand years later, in the vicinity of Bat Cave in southern New Mexico. At first it was probably not a significant crop but merely one of many plants people grew for food. As it spread throughout the Southwest, the technology for growing maize also spread, including water control systems, planting calendars, cosmological ideas such as color-direction symbolism, the use of certain feathers and other ritual paraphernalia, and more. Turner and Turner (1999:3) provide a succinct description of the Mesoamerican-Southwest connection:

> As was the case in Mesoamerica, where the actual and figurative seeds of Southwestern agriculture originated, prehistoric Southwestern Indians both evolved and borrowed elements for their cultural and economic system—a system similar to but simpler than that of their Mesoamerican counterparts. The system emphasized year-round community ritual observances, ancestor idolatry, social conformity, priestly authoritarianism, communalism, intellectual conservatism, animal and human sacrifice, warrior societies, rainfall magic, and fertility rituals for nature, crops, and by humans. These features were present in the Greater Southwest wherever environmental conditions permitted some semblance of an agricultural and sedentary lifeway.

In Mesoamerica, from which maize and other cultigens diffused, Quetzalcoatl—the Plumed Serpent—was associated with farming, and the Scarlet Macaw (*Ara macao*) was a sacrificial bird to him (McKusick 2001:18). In the Southwest, every Pueblo has a Plumed Serpent (Reyman 1995a), the plumes being Scarlet Macaw and other feathers. The Hopi story about *Pala'tkwabi*, "The Red Land of the South" (see below; Seowtewa 2022 gives the Zuni equivalent), provides a detailed discussion of these cultural connections. There is no specific time connection, however; maize and the things which accompanied it did not necessarily arrive everywhere in the Southwest at the same time, and thus the chronology varies with location. McKusick (2001:17–23) provides some examples of this, but it is not an all-inclusive discussion. Furthermore, it will change as more archaeological field research is done and as existing collections and excavation data are restudied. It's the nature of the discipline, and of science. Change is "built in" to the system.

Perhaps this is a good point for an overview of my general thoughts about how the ancient system worked, based on both the archaeological record and the ethnographic and ethnohistoric accounts for the post-contact Pueblos.

Farming success is not simply a matter of putting seeds in the ground, watering them, and waiting for the plants to grow. One must know when to prepare the ground and when to plant the seeds. The system requires a "tool kit," starting with basic observational or "naked eye" astronomy (see table 1.4). Watching the sky and noting the changes in the positions of the celestial bodies throughout the year, such as the positions of the sun at sunrise and sunset, allows one to develop a calendar, which, in turn, allows one to plan and implement farming activities and their accompanying rites and rituals. As I have argued (Reyman 1976a:959), astronomical observations, done correctly, give the group a strategic adaptive advantage in managing their farming system. When such observations are the responsibility of a designated observer—a sun watcher—and are incorporated into architecture such as at Pueblo Bonito (Reyman 1976a) or the Flint Ku-ShaLi House at Cochití Pueblo (C. Lange 1959:fig. 8b), one outcome is often the "Predictive Dimension of Priestly Power" (Reyman 1980).

Ruth Benedict (1935:66–67) provides one of the best accounts of how sun watching developed among the Zuni:

The man who went to the Sun was made *Pekwin*. [Note in original text: *Pekwin* "cares for the sun." He observes its movements to determine the ceremonial dates.] "When you get home, you will be *Pekwin* and I will be your father. Make meal offerings to me. Come to the edge of the town every morning and pray to me. Every evening go to the shrine at Matsaḵa and pray. At the end of the year when I come to the south, watch me closely; and in the middle of the year in the same month, when I reach the farthest point on the right hand, watch me closely." "All right." He came home and learned for three years, and he was made *Pekwin*. The first year at the last month of the year he watched the Sun closely, but his calculations [note in original text: for the winter solstice] were early by thirteen days. Next year he was early by twenty days. He studied again. In eight years he was able to time the turning of the sun exactly. The people made prayersticks and held ceremonies in the winter and in the summer, at just the time of the turning of the sun.

Cushing (1883:40–41) provides a complementary account from his time at Zuni:

Each morning, too, just at dawn, the Sun Priest [*Pekwin*], followed by the Master Priest of the Bow, went along the eastern trail to the ruined city of Ma-tsa-ki, by the river-side, where, awaited at a distance by his companion, he slowly approached a

TABLE 1.4. Mesoamerican-Southwest Puebloan astronomical parallels

Astronomical Feature	Mesoamerica	Pueblos
SOLAR CALENDAR	+	+
Observance of solstice rise and set points	+	+
Directions based on rise and set points	+	+
New fire ritual associated with winter solstice	+	+
New fire ritual associated with vernal equinox	+	+
LUNAR PHASES / LUNAR CALENDAR	+	+
TIMING STARS AND CONSTELLATIONS		
Aldebaran	+	+
Cassiopeia	+	−
Castor and Pollux	+	+
Galaxy (Milky Way)	+	+
Orion's Belt	+	+
Pleiades	+	+
Polaris	+	+
Procyon	−	+
Scorpio	+	−
Sirius	+	+
Ursa Major (Big Dipper)	+	+
Ursa Minor (Little Dipper)	+	+
Venus as Morning Star	+	+
Venus as Evening Star	+	+

Note: This list is limited to those astronomical features that can be definitely identified for both areas. Thus, Central Mexican constellations such as Mamalhoatzli ("Fire Drill") and the Zuni A'chiyala'topa ("Knife Wing") are not included, because they have not been defined in terms of specific stars or other celestial features.

square open tower and seated himself just inside upon a rude, ancient stone chair, and before a pillar sculpted with the face of the sun, the sacred hand, the morning star, and the new moon. There he awaited with prayer and sacred song the rising of the sun. Not many such pilgrimages are made ere the "Suns look at each other," and the shadows of the solar monolith, the monument of Thunder Mountain, and the pillar of the gardens of Zuñi, "lie along the same trail." Then the priest blesses, thanks, and exhorts his father, while the warrior guardian responds as he cuts the last notch in his pine-wood calendar, and both hasten back to call from the house-tops the glad tidings of the return of spring. Nor may the Sun Priest err in his watch of Time's slight; for many are the houses in Zuñi with scores on their walls or ancient plates

Figure 1.3. Zuni Harvest Day dance, 2006 (Troyden Chavez photograph, used with permission).

imbedded therein, while opposite, a convenient window or small port-hole lets in the light of the rising sun, which shines but two mornings in the three hundred and sixty-five on the same place [spring and vernal equinoxes]. Wonderfully reliable and ingenious are these rude systems of orientation, by which the religion, the labors, and even the pastimes of the Zuñis are regulated. Each day whole families hastened away to their planting pueblos, or distant farm houses [Upper and Lower Nutria, Pescado, and Ojo Caliente].

If one goes to Zuni today and visits the site of Matsakia, the stone structure mentioned by Benedict and Cushing is no longer extant. Indeed the site is now little more than a large mound covered with ancient building debris, pottery shards, and other artifacts. The stone pillar (actually more of a slab) described by Cushing is still extant, though not at Matsakia. It was removed long ago and is today stored in the home of a family, who bring it out on occasions, as needed, for use in ceremonies.

Note that in Benedict's account, the pronouncements of the *Pekwin* result in making prayer sticks that require feathers. As noted below (Ladd 1963, 1972), Zuni prayer sticks incorporate a wide variety of feathers, some of which include macaw feathers. Macaw and parrot feathers are used in many, perhaps most, Pueblo ceremonies and individual rituals connected to farming. One need only attend Pueblo ceremonies such as masked katsina dances at Zuni and Hopi and nonmasked harvest and Feast Day ceremonies at Zuni (figure 1.3), Acoma, and the Rio Grande Pueblos to see first-hand the importance of macaw and parrot feathers in farming-related ceremonial activities (see also figure 1.3). Feathers are also used (among many other materials) to decorate ceremonial clothing, altars, rattles, dance wands, and numerous other ritual objects seen both publicly and only by the initiated, in kivas and elsewhere that are restricted to Pueblo or religious and medicine society members (religious and medicine societies are sometimes, but not always, synonymous).

The relationship of macaw and parrot feathers to ancient Southwestern farming practices is more tenuous and circumstantial, largely because macaw and parrot feather artifacts are not often preserved except in a few dry caves and rock-shelters, and occasionally in sites such as Aztec Ruin and possibly Pueblo Bonito (Judd 1954:266). Other feather artifacts are also sometimes found such as a feather bundle from room 298 at Pueblo Bonito (Judd 1954:267). While the ethnographic literature abounds with examples of how macaw, parrot, and other feathers are used in conjunction with farming ceremonies (e.g., Stevenson 1904:plates 13 and 14), and as noted above, one can witness the relationship of macaw and parrot feathers to farming when attending Pueblo ceremonies (see figure 1.3), evidence for such in ancient contexts is more difficult to identify. However, if we look at nonfeather artifacts that represent or symbolize feathers, such as the kiva murals at Pottery Mound, Kuaua, Awatovi, and Kawaika-a, cited throughout this volume, the relationship becomes readily apparent. Ancient ceramics such as Mimbres Pottery (Brody 1977; Brody et al. 1983) offer numerous examples of macaw motifs in a wide variety of contexts, and if one adds to these the numerous wooden and other material artifacts from ancient Southwestern sites that depict, represent, and symbolize macaws, parrots, and other birds, the relationship is even stronger. A major example is from Chetro Ketl in Chaco Canyon where a cache of carved and painted wooden ritual bird heads, tails, bills, feathers, and probably bird effigies were excavated in 1947—more than two hundred objects in all (Vivian et al. 1978:4–8, 63–72). The original excavator, Gordon Vivian (Gwinn Vivian's father), "postulated that the wood represented an altar that had been left assembled in the room and was crushed by the collapse of the roof" (Vivian et al. 1978:59). However, Gordon Vivian further conjectured on the basis of the evidence that before the roof collapsed, the "intact altar had been vandalized while the room was vacant and that parts of the paraphernalia had been removed" (Vivian et al. 1978:60). In contrast to Gordon Vivian's ideas, the report's authors "suggest storage of ritual artifacts as an alternative to the intact altar hypothesis" (Vivian et al. 1978:60).

For my purposes, the important point is not whether this was an intact altar that was vandalized or the storage of ritual artifacts, but rather that the finds provide a clear example of ritually important macaw and parrot images from Chetro Ketl, a major Chacoan Ancestral Pueblo great house, seemingly associated with Chacoan farming practices and, further, which seem related, through time, to post-contact Puebloan ethnographic objects and farming activities.

Finally, Ridge Ruin near Flagstaff, Arizona (figure o.2), a site with one of the richest burials (a male individual) found in the Southwest, yielded two elaborate mosaic turquoise and shell bird objects plus the remains of four macaws, three Scarlet (*Ara macao*) and one *Ara* sp. (McGregor 1943; Hargrave 1970:40). The macaw remains were found in a different room from that of the buried man, who was apparently a high-ranking ceremonial practitioner, with grave goods still recognizable to McGregor's Hopi informants (McGregor 1943:295–298).

Although the emphasis here is on macaw tail feathers, especially center tail feathers (the longest and most visually conspicuous feathers) and parrot tail feathers, wing feathers and body contour feathers are also used. Among the most important feathers are Scarlet Macaw shoulder coverts, specifically the yellow feathers with blue tips, used atop or on the front of certain katsina masks. The use of small, body contour feathers extends well back into antiquity. Perhaps the most elaborate and certainly the most visually striking pre-contact feathered artifact found to date in the Southwest is a skirt or apron from Lavender Cave (c. AD 1080–1110), southeastern Utah, in which 2,336 Scarlet Macaw body contour feathers were attached to cords (see Canby 1982:573; Lekson 1997:55).

It is worth noting that feather colors required for ceremonies and ceremonial objects are not necessarily what one might expect. Both the Military Macaw and the various species of Amazon parrots have beautiful body contour feathers in a wide variety of greens, from bright, almost chartreuse, yellow green, to darker rich greens like a shamrock and a pine tree. Because young and growing corn and bean plants have green leaves, one would think that green feathers would be of primary importance. Green feathers are important, but we rarely had a shortage of them to fill requests. By contrast, the number of requests for red, yellow, blue, and multicolor body contour feathers always exceeded those for green, and these other colors *were* often in short supply to the extent that we refrained from shipping feathers until we had sufficient numbers of them on hand. I saw prayer sticks and some other ritual objects with red, yellow, blue, and multicolor macaw and parrot body contour feathers on them, but I never saw green body contour feathers used for them. Admittedly, my personal observation sample is small, and green body contour feathers may have been used in ceremonies that I didn't observe.

The most conspicuous use of Amazon parrot green and multicolor green, red, and yellow tail feathers is in ceremonial head bundles worn by men, especially among the Rio Grande Pueblos and perhaps most often at Feast Day dances. If one looks at the Zuni Harvest Dance image (figure 1.3), the absence of green feathers is remarkable. The feathers are overwhelmingly red, blue, and white (eagle fluffs). The yellow visible is the underside of Blue-and-Yellow Macaw tail feathers.

The late Charles Di Peso suggested that macaws and other Mesoamerican-derived commodities were associated with the worship of Tezcatlipoca, the ruler of the surface of the Earth and also known as the God of the Smoking Mirror (the mirror was probably made from grey or black obsidian). Like most Mesoamerican deities, Tezcatlipoca came in various guises, each with a specific color-direction association. There were four, the best known of which was probably the Black Tezcatlipoca (North)—evil whisperer, witchcraft, and the dark arts; Yellow Tezcatlipoca (East)—rising sun and maize; Blue Tezcatlipoca (South)—midsummer sun and the blue color of Huitzilopochtli (a sun deity and the Blue Hummingbird or "Hummingbird on the Left"); and Red Tezcatlipoca (West)—the red of Xipe Totec ("Our Lord the Flayed One") symbolizing suffering and sacrificial blood (Vaillant 1950:88; Burland and Forman 1975:55–56). Various feathers, including macaw feathers, are an essential part of Tezcatlipoca's appearance, and in one guise, he appears in a turkey costume festooned with feathers (Vaillant 1950:184); a turkey-foot censer is also associated with Tezcatlipoca. Skin-covered turkey legs with spurs and claws attached were common symbols for Tezcatlipoca (Burland and Forman 1975:61) and were probably components of the items offered at the worship of the deity. Other animals and commodities associated with the worship of Tezcatlipoca might have included black bear (*Ursus americanus*) and mountain lion (*Felis concolor*) bones and artifacts, eagle, owl, and hawk feathers and artifacts, obsidian, perhaps turquoise, pseudo-cloisonné decorated materials, pectorals, and more (McKusick 2001:91–93).

McKusick (2001:73–93, 104–106) develops this argument further and with greater specificity: she links the Military Macaw and the Thick-billed Parrot to the worship of Chalchihuitlicue, the Scarlet Macaw to the worship of Quetzalcoatl; links these three birds along with sacrifices of the Large Indian Domesticated Turkey (Scarlet Macaws were also sacrificed) to the worship of Tezcatlipoca; and considers all these as elements in the later development of the Katsina religion. The Spanish observed, recorded, and reported elements of this large, complex, and widespread system of cultural practices that is glossed as "Pueblo religion," but clearly the Spanish neither fully appreciated nor understood its significance beyond what most of them considered devil worship, which they frequently attempted to suppress by destroying sacred Pueblo objects and punishing Pueblo individuals.

Finally, unlike the situation with the wild turkey, the pre-contact Southwest peoples (Hohokam, Mogollon, Sinagua, Ancestral Pueblo) never developed breeding populations of macaws and parrots. McKusick (2001:77–78) briefly discusses this and provides possible reasons for it, which focus on the lack of a suitable number of adult birds and the problems associated with human-imprinted birds. I suggest there is a more basic underlying economic factor in this situation: macaws and their feathers were an extremely valuable trade commodity, so valuable that the Mesoamericans wanted to maintain control of the trade. Therefore, they never permitted the residents at any Southwest site with whom they conducted trade to acquire enough adult birds of both sexes to allow for the creation of a breeding population. Although the remains of several hundred macaws have been recovered from sites in the Southwest, these finds span a huge area and some one thousand years in time. Even at sites where relatively large numbers of macaws were found, such as Wupatki (41) and Pueblo Bonito (31), there are few, if any, birds of breeding age: one at Wupatki, and none at Pueblo Bonito. The Mesoamericans kept tight control of the macaw supply, not unlike that control maintained today by De Beers and other diamond producers. It seems likely that, although live birds were exported to Southwest sites, greater numbers of feathers were sent. If the ethnographic context is any guide, feathers much more than live birds are needed for ceremonies. Furthermore, export of feathers was a much easier task than exporting live macaws.

Mesoamerican-Southwest trade for macaw feathers (and other precious commodities) is noted in early Spanish records (see Bandelier 1890, 1890–1892, 1892; Reyman 1995a, 1995b, 2008). For example, based on Spanish sources, Bandelier (1890:61, 1890–1892:1, 39–40) writes:

> On account of the demand for animal products, commerce existed in the Southwest over much greater expanses than might be supposed. . . . The inhabitants of the Colorado river shores, the Seris of Sonora, exchanged bivalves for the turquoises of Zuñi, or the tanned hides and rabbit of Moqui [Hopi]. The same took place with parrot feathers. The large green parrot [*Ara militaris*] is very common . . . and Cabeza de Vaca tells us that the Jovas . . . exchanged its plumes for green stones farther north. . . . All these objects were not necessities of life in the strictest sense, they were luxuries, and constitute to-day what the Southwestern Indian regards as his specific "treasure." Still, the possession of these was regarded as essential, because they formed an accessory to religious rites, or to the magic processes with which their religion is so intimately linked.

Bandelier (1892:3–5) further writes:

> There existed in 1539, and prior to it, quite an intercourse between Zuñi and the land-tilling aborigines south of the Gila River. That intercourse took the form of journeys

made by the Opatas, the Southern and Northern Pimas, and possibly the Endeves and Jovas, to Cibola-Zuñi for the purpose of acquiring turquoises and buffalo hides, in exchange for which they gave parrots' feathers, and probably sea shells, or which they earned by working for the Indians of Zuñi. . . . The information which Fray Marcos [de Niza] gathered among the Opatas proved quite trustworthy; it embraced the Moqui or Totonteac, and Acoma or Hacus [see also Riley 1974].

Bandelier (1890–1892:1, 63–64) also notes that the Opatas obtained turquoise and turquoise ornaments from the Zuni, to whom they traded parrot skins and feathers. He states (1890–1892:64), "Aboriginal commerce, slow and irregular, contributed to modify these ideas and customs, by creating new desires, and furnishing the means of satisfying them."

Furthermore, another Spanish cleric, Padre Luis Velarde, wrote in 1716: "At San Javier del Bac and neighboring rancherias, there are many macaws, which the Pimas raise because of the beautiful feathers of red and of other colors . . . which they strip from these birds in the spring, for their adornment" (Wyllys 1931:129).

Henderson and Harrington (1914:45) write: "The ceremonial use of macaw feathers continues today among the Pueblos of Arizona and New Mexico. In one ethnographic report, Pueblo informants stated that the feathers of the *Tañí* (macaw), are highly prized by the Tewa for ceremonial purposes." Henderson and Harrington further state, "the feathers and also live *tañí* were obtained from Mexico in former times. Their informants also stated that a *tañí* is at present time kept in a cage at Santo Domingo Pueblo." Probably the best example of this, as noted earlier, is Neil Judd's 1924 gift of a Military Macaw to the main priest at Zuni, which the priest used for feathers until the macaw's death in 1946. The bird was not replaced by Judd.

The importance of macaws and parrots is also reflected in the fact that many Pueblos have parrot or macaw clans, for example, the Zuni Múlakwe (Macaw) Clan (Hodge 1896). Today, the Macaw Clan is the largest clan at Zuni (Seowtewa 2022), and it was the 1970 request for macaw feathers by the late Fernando (Fred) Cordero of Cochití Pueblo that eventually led to the 1982 creation of the Feather Distribution Project.

A full discussion of Pueblo use of feathers in ceremonial life would require a separate book, but the evidence for their importance lies with the millions of feathers provided by the Feather Distribution Project to the thirty-two Pueblo villages in New Mexico and Arizona. Figure 1.3 provides a clear example from Zuni with hundreds and perhaps thousands of feathers visible in the photograph. At every Corn Dance among the Rio Grande Pueblos, a pole is carried at the front of the lines of dancers, on the top of which is a large "ball" with macaw tail feathers inserted into it. The dancers themselves wear a variety of feathers: feather-bundle head ornaments for the males and feathers on the *tablitas* (head ornaments) worn by women and girls. The Feather Distribution Project regularly provided thousands of macaw and parrot feathers for Corn Dances, and even more wild turkey feathers.

At the Zuni Sha'lako, almost every deity and personage represented, and especially the Sha'lakos themselves, are adorned with feathers, and the religious officers who often accompany them carry prayer sticks and other bundles of feathers. The Feather Distribution Project regularly provided thousands of macaw and parrot feathers for the Zuni Sha'lako, and thousands more wild turkey feathers. The same is true for Zuni and Hopi Katsina dances that are open to the public, which feature *katsinam* wearing thousands of feathers.

Several years ago, macaw tail feathers were requested by the Hopi for a Parrot Dance at Hotevilla. Over a two-year period, for two dances held in June of each year, the Feather Distribution Project provided more than 2,200 macaw tail feathers from all five large species, the majority of which were the long center tails.

ARCHAEOLOGY

The place names below in the Chaco Canyon vignette all post-date the Spanish entradas into New Mexico and the greater American Southwest, of which the entrada made by Alvar Nuñez Cabeza de Vaca (1536) may have been the earliest; he possibly reached what is now eastern New Mexico. The first confirmed entrada was that of Fray Marcos de Niza in 1539, whose party reached Hawikku, one of the ancestral villages of modern-day Zuni. Francisco Vázquez de Coronado (1540–1542) followed into New Mexico and ventured east onto the plains of Kansas in an unsuccessful search for Quivira, one of the "Cities of Gold." However, most of the place names post-date 1800, or are even more recent. Archaeologists do not know the ancient name of the site in Chaco Canyon, New Mexico, we now call Pueblo Bonito ("beautiful town" in Spanish, see figures 1.4 and 1.5). Nor do archaeologists know the names by which the Ancestral Pueblo inhabitants of Chaco Canyon and New Mexico referred to these places, or even what the Ancestral Pueblos called themselves. Archaeologists formerly referred to the Chacoans as the "Anasazi." *Anasazi*, however, is a Navajo term, sometimes translated as "ancient ones" or "ancient enemies," and the Navajo had not yet arrived in the Southwest from their Athabascan homeland in the interior of northwestern North America when Chaco was inhabited by Ancestral Pueblo peoples during the time the first part of this vignette takes place. Indeed, the Navajo did not migrate into the Southwest until late in the fifteenth century, long after Chaco had been abandoned by Pueblo peoples. By general consensus among Pueblo peoples and archaeologists, the term *Ancestral Pueblo* has now replaced *Anasazi*. Finally, archaeologists do not know by what term the ancient inhabitants of Chaco Canyon referred to the winter solstice, or even if they named or numbered the years.

What archaeologists do know is this: Over several hundreds of years, one or more groups of people with similar cultures built Pueblo Bonito and eleven other large apartment-like communal structures, sometimes called towns, sometimes called "great houses" or "great pueblos," within Chaco Canyon and on the surrounding mesa tops. They also built hundreds of smaller sites in the canyon and its immediate environs, and a hundred or so large towns ("outliers") and numerous smaller settlements in the surrounding area.

Archaeologists also know the Chacoans and other Ancestral Pueblo peoples worshipped the sun and used its apparent movements along the horizon[5] to create a solar calendar by which they planned and implemented the religious, economic (farming, collecting, hunting), and political activities that structured their lives. We further know they kept and used macaws and parrots for ritual activities. The remains of more than four hundred macaws have been found at archaeological sites in the American Southwest. As noted earlier, objects with macaw feathers still preserved have also been found, and macaws and parrots are the most common animals depicted in murals discovered at Pottery Mound, New Mexico, Awatovi and Kawaika-a, Arizona, and at other ancient towns and villages such as in several kivas at Mesa Verde.

Anthropologists know from Pueblo oral histories and other accounts that birds were important to these peoples in the distant past, as well as today. For example, the Hopi of northeastern Arizona recount how birds helped guide them from the Underworld into this world, the Fourth World (Nequatewa 1936:7–23). Contemporary reports and the existence of the Feather Distribution Project together demonstrated that these birds, today, are still important.

Archaeological excavations confirm the importance of birds in ancient Pueblo life. The Pueblos domesticated turkeys from wild turkeys perhaps 1,500 years ago. Turkey burials in which the (now) skeletal remains are accompanied by turquoise and other grave goods (e.g., Roberts 1932, 1933, 1939, 1940a, 1940b) attest to the importance of the turkey, as do the remnants of turkey-feather robes and numerous artifacts made from turkey bones.

Most birds—eagles, hawks, ducks, and a wide variety of others—were obtained locally, but macaws and parrots were imported. The Military Macaw (*Ara militaris*) was indigenous to northern Mexico in the Sonora area (Hargrave 1970:10), and the Thick-billed parrot (*Rhynchopsitta pachyrhyncha*) was indigenous in what is now southern Arizona. Curiously, these two species were less utilized than more distant species such as the Scarlet Macaw (*Ara macao*). The Military Macaw (*Ara militaris*) is rarely found in the Southwest, and feathers from the Blue-and-Yellow Macaw (*Ara ararauna*) are very rarely found at Ancestral Pueblo sites.

Paquimé, in northern Chihuahua, Mexico, a large, urban site that was destroyed in the mid-fifteenth century, was a major breeding and distribution center for Scarlet Macaws and Military Macaws (*Ara militaris*). The remains of at least 322 Scarlet Macaws, 81 Military Macaws, and 101 macaws of unidentified species were recovered from Paquimé (McKusick 1974; 2001:73); Paquimé was not completely excavated, and the number could be much higher. Skeletal remains of at least one Lilac-crowned Amazon parrot (*Amazona finschi*) and a White-fronted Amazon parrot (*Amazona albifrons*) have been excavated in the Southwest. These last two might be the most distant imports. Birds and their feathers were critical resources for Pueblo ceremonial life and still are today. As Ladd (1972:12) notes: "Macaws, traded up from Mexico from prehistoric to modern times, were kept for their plumage. In 1940, there were four macaws in Zuni, including one given to the Sun Priest (*pequinne*) by Neil Judd in 1924 . . . it spoke Zuni."

WINTER SOLSTICE AT PUEBLO BONITO, CHACO CANYON, NEW MEXICO
The following is my imagined scenario of the winter solstice morning at Pueblo Bonito in the tenth and eleventh centuries.

Shortly before daybreak, the old man, wrapped in a turkey-feather robe, stands in the rear corner of a small, third-story room in the southeastern section of the town and gazes out through the diagonal window in the wall (figures 1.4–1.8). He is the Sun Priest, and he waits patiently for Father Sun to climb above the horizon. Sun Father's appearance today marks the winter solstice sunrise that signals the start of the New Year, as Sun Father begins his journey back toward the north and the warmth of summer. If the year has a number, it is lost in time; but this winter solstice sunrise occurs some five hundred years or so before an Italian sailor known as Cristoforo Colombo, in service to the Spanish royal court, discovers the "New World," where the Sun Priest's community had thrived for hundreds of years, and where his descendants still live. This winter solstice sunrise occurs about 550 years before the first Spanish entrada into this part of Nueva España that they call Nuevo Méjico. By our calendar, the year is probably sometime between AD 950 and 1000, and the day is December 21.

Father Sun arrives in a green flash followed by a burst of brilliant light (figures 1.3 and 1.4). Father Sun has kept his promise and returned to start the New Year. His son, the Sun Priest, is pleased. The priest offers his prayers of welcome, pulls his robe tightly around himself for warmth, and then turns to begin a short walk to the north section of Pueblo Bonito. Here he enters a room where several Scarlet Macaws perch. Sun Father needs to be welcomed and thanked properly in ceremonies from

Figure 1.4. Pueblo Bonito from atop the mesa, 1896 (George Pepper–Richard Wetherill photograph, Hyde Exploring Expedition).

Figure 1.5. Pueblo Bonito from atop the mesa, 1974.

Figure 1.6. Pueblo Bonito, southeast section with corner windows: Room 228 (*left*) and Room 225 (*right*), 1973.

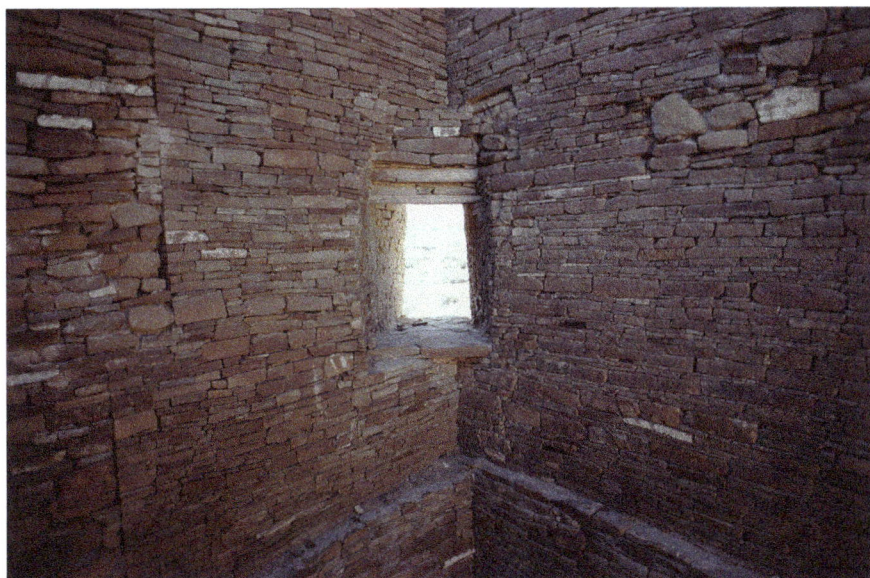

Figure 1.7. Pueblo Bonito: Room 228's corner window from inside, 1973.

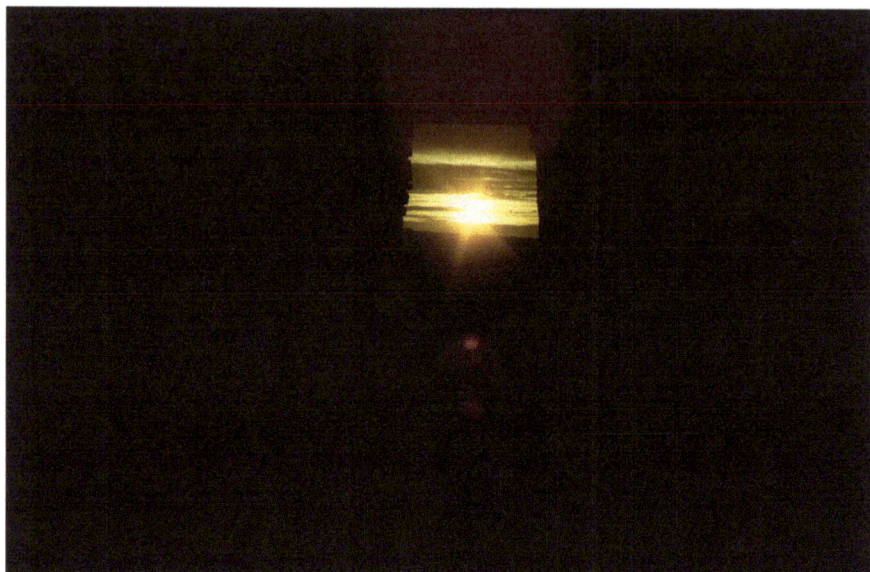

Figure 1.8. Pueblo Bonito Room 228, winter solstice sunrise, 21 December 1973.

now until the summer solstice in June, and the beautiful red-orange tail feathers of the Scarlet Macaw are required for this. Their long tail feathers are especially prized, and the Sun Priest collects several to prepare for his ritual to thank Sun Father.

THE CONCEPT OF VALUE IN MESOAMERICAN-SOUTHWESTERN TRADE

As noted earlier, pre-contact Mesoamerican-Southwestern trade is indicated by the presence of Mesoamerican-derived commodities and ideas at Southwestern archaeological sites.[6] Archaeologists generally agree that these and other items are of Mesoamerican origin, for example, macaws, copper bells, marine shells, shell artifacts such as shell trumpets, some of the basic cultigens such as maize and cotton, and architectural features such as ball courts and platform mounds, though there is disagreement over whether specific examples such as the "ball court" at Wupatki and the "platform mound" at talus unit number 1 behind Chetro Ketl at Chaco Canyon can be interpreted as such (see Vivian and Hilpert 2012:261). Fewer archaeologists accept the argument that certain *other* commodities, traits, or features present in the Southwest are ultimately, in fact or in concept, of Mesoamerican origin: for example, pseudo-cloisonné decoration (see Pepper 1920:264–267) and other decorative investment techniques; mosaic pyrite mirrors; ceremonial canes;

architectural features (table 1.1) such as great sanctuaries (great kivas), column-fronted galleries at Chetro Ketl and Bc-51, rubble-core masonry, Classic Period Hohokam compounds; Katsina religion; Plumed Serpent deities[7] (Quetzalcoatl); and the major components of Puebloan astronomical and calendrical systems (table 1.2). In short, although archaeologists accept that pre-contact and contact period Mesoamerican-Southwestern trade occurred, there are sharp disagreements over the amount and significance of that trade. The debate is not new but has taken place for more than a century.

Part of the debate centers on methodological issues: "Until the *pochteca*[8] model is framed in such a way as to make refutation possible, it is not a testable hypothesis" (Cordell 1984:274). Wilcox (1986:30) states, "The strong thesis of pochteca merchant-priests ... may be untestable archaeologically." However, Kelley (1980:53) previously argued in a paper (overlooked by both Cordell and Wilcox) that the accumulated data was precisely what would be expected from the "*pochteca* model." In fact, testable hypotheses have been proposed and evaluated on a preliminary basis (e.g., Reyman 1971, 1978, 1985; Nelson 1986), although the Nelson 1986 and Reyman 1985 papers appeared after Cordell and Wilcox published theirs.

As the late Daniel Patrick Moynihan reportedly said, "Everyone is entitled to his own opinion, but not to his own facts." Therefore, regardless of the argument over whether or not there were actual Mesoamerican traders or trading groups in the pre-contact Southwest, the facts are that Scarlet, Military, and Blue-and-Yellow macaws, the White-fronted Parrot, and the Lilac-fronted Parrot, all birds which were not indigenous to the Southwest but which originated in Mesoamerica, were present in the Southwest and are evidence of trade between the two regions. The birds did not fly free-ranging from Mesoamerica to the Southwest. Furthermore, the *value* of the macaws, both live birds and feathers, is the critical factor and has been overlooked. Rather, the argument has been framed solely in terms of *quantity*, which is precisely the wrong measure. Lange (1986:167–168) writes:

> While we cannot be dependent on quantities to measure *contact* we must depend upon some level of quantification to measure *impact*. Thus, the quantification of exotic goods, correlated where possible with the results of instrumental analyses, is an important step in understanding Mesoamerican-periphery interaction. ... For the present, all categories of Mesoamerican artifacts found on the peripheries, or vice versa, occur in relatively small quantities.

The emphasis on quantity of goods (Plog et al. 1982:228) overlooks other non-material factors. Nevertheless, they stress quantification over all, arguing, for example, that the weight of the imported items found at Southwestern sites is minimal and that relatively little effort was needed to transport the material; or, as Haury (1976:357) states, "barely enough [quantity of material] to make it worth a trader's time and effort." As will be made clear, Haury also erred in his assessment.

These arguments that the quantities of goods exchanged were minimal or insignificant ignore several important factors, most notably *value*. For items such as turquoise and macaws, *value* and *not* gross weight or number of specimens is the more important criterion. The quotation from Bandelier cited above is evidence for this. Turquoise was highly valued in both pre-contact and post-contact times and still is. It was the "god stone" among many Mesoamerican and Southwestern cultures, especially among the Ancestral Pueblo peoples and their descendants and the later Navajo. Macaws and their feathers were similarly prized (Henderson and Harrington 1914:45).

To understand the importance of value, consider this: on any given day, at any particular diamond exchange in the world (for example, New York City or Antwerp), the volume of gem-quality diamonds available is probably no more than a bushel or two (.35–.70 hectoliter); and the gross weight of these diamonds could easily be carried by two or three people. The volume and weight of the diamonds might possibly equal all the turquoise found at Ancestral Pueblo, Hohokam, and Mogollon sites. The value of these diamonds, however, is hundreds of millions of dollars, or more. In recent years, for example, the market price for a one-carat, grade D IF, investment-quality diamond has been as high as $58,000. Even lesser-grade one-carat diamonds cost thousands of dollars. One carat is approximately 0.02 grams in gross weight. Finally, these diamonds would be sold over a period of years; indeed, they are deliberately sold in relatively small, limited quantities to preserve their high monetary and prestige values.

Clearly, the value of diamonds is so disproportionate to their gross size and weight that trading even a handful of high-quality diamonds is immensely profitable. A single handful or two of investment-quality diamonds would be enough to ensure one's lifetime financial security. The same is true, if on a somewhat more modest scale, for other gems such as emeralds, rubies, and sapphires.

To a lesser extent, this was probably the case for turquoise in the ancient Southwest. Great value was embodied in relatively little volume and weight, so traders need not have transported huge quantities of turquoise to make a trip profitable. Large quantities of turquoise were excavated legally by archaeologists and illegally by looters, from ancient sites throughout the Southwest and especially in and around Chaco Canyon. The quantity of turquoise was substantially greater than generally reported or recognized (e.g., Pepper 1905, 1909, 1920; Judd 1954, 1959) and so was its corresponding value. It is not unreasonable to assume that those who mined and distributed turquoise in ancient times would have tried to control the amount produced and exchanged in order to maintain its high value in much the same way as today's diamond production and distribution are controlled by a relatively few corporations.

The emphasis on value, not weight, can also be applied to other exotic or precious commodities such as macaws and their feathers. I noted earlier McKusick's (2001:6) statement: "Scarlet Macaws [were] the only parrots traded into the Southwest in economically important numbers." Hargrave (1970) summarizes the data, which indicate that both live birds and feathers were exported from Mesoamerica into the Southwest, an example of "creating new desires, and furnishing the means of satisfying them" (Bandelier 1890–1892:1, 64). Excluding the 504 macaws recovered from Paquimé, and recognizing that any listing is necessarily incomplete, it is likely that more than four hundred macaws, mostly Scarlet Macaws, have been excavated at sites throughout the Southwest. The sites of Wupatki (41), Pueblo Bonito (31), and Point of Pines (28) had especially large numbers of macaws. Macaw feathers were also recovered from some of the same sites as well as from Aztec Ruin in New Mexico and Lizard Alcove (42Ka276) and Westwater Ruin (42SA14) in Utah where no macaw skeletal remains were found. Earl Morris found a Scarlet Macaw (*Ara macao*) feather at Aztec Ruin and wrote (1919:44):

> For the sake of completeness there may be mentioned here one macaw feather, still retaining its brilliant colors of red and blue [probably a blue-tipped Scarlet Macaw tail feather]. This feather is one more proof of commerce with the tribes of Mexico.

As noted earlier, perhaps the most spectacular find is the dance apron found in a small cave in Lavender Canyon, Utah (Canby 1982:573; Lekson 1997:55), made from 2,336 red and blue Scarlet Macaw body feathers tied to cordage that led Hargrave to conclude it had been made by a "Mexican" Indian (Hargrave 1979:5).

The number of macaw feathers in the apron skews the data in that it alone far exceeds the number of macaw feathers found in the Southwest. The number of feathers found at other sites is minuscule, largely because feathers are perishable and rarely survive long in the ground, although they may survive in a dry cave setting as in Lavender Canyon, unless they are destroyed by insects. Furthermore, one macaw may provide anywhere from dozens to a thousand or more feathers, depending on which feathers are used and how long the bird lives. Therefore, we have no accurate estimate of the number of macaws that existed in the Southwest at any given time period or for the entire pre-contact period. The same is true for the parrot remains at Southwest sites. The total number for both macaws and parrots (excluding Paquimé) was certainly in the hundreds and may well have been more than a thousand. And if the prominence of macaws and parrots in extant murals and rock art is an indicator, the number could even have been in the thousands. There are thousands of unexcavated sites including at least several hundred large sites, many or most of which potentially contain macaw and parrot remains.

Table 1.1 is a partial listing of macaw, parrot, and turkey feather objects found at pre-contact sites in the Southwest. It is a partial listing because not all such finds are reported in the archaeological literature. There are also feather objects from other birds, such as Hopi altar objects made from eagle feathers (see, e.g., McKusick 2001:fig. 26) and feather bands containing Northern Flicker (also known as the Red-shafted Flicker [*Colaptes auratus*]) from Pueblo Bonito (Pepper 1920:30), but they are not included in table 1.3, because the focus is on macaw, parrot, and turkey feathers. And although the skeletal remains of the Thick-billed Parrot (*Rhynchopsitta pachyrhyncha*), White-fronted Parrot (*Amazona albifrons*), and Lilac-fronted Parrot (*Amazona finschi*) have been found at archaeological sites in the Southwest (McKusick 2001:9), objects that incorporate their feathers have not been recovered. Surely there must have been objects with feathers from these birds, but they have not survived or possibly have not yet been found. Preservation is often serendipitous. Although evidence of feather robes is widespread at Southwestern archaeological sites, all the finds are fragmentary. For example, Moorehead (1906:34) states:

> Under the floor of the small room near the northwest corner of Pueblo Bonito was found a splendidly preserved skeleton of a young woman [later analysis proved this to be a male] wrapped in a large feather robe, which was originally 1.3 by 2 meters....
>
> Unfortunately, of the feather robe nothing remains but the cords on which the feathers were strung.

Feather-related objects such as a possible ceramic feather box from Pueblo del Arroyo (Judd 1959:161) are not included in the table. Finally, table 1.1 does not include "feather" objects made from wood and other materials, such as the possible altar pieces discussed earlier that were found at Chetro Ketl in Chaco Canyon, nor the hundreds of depictions of macaws, parrots, and turkeys in murals from sites such as Pottery Mound, Kawaika-a, Grand Quivira, Kuaua, some of which are discussed elsewhere in this volume; nor does it include depictions of macaws, parrots, and turkeys on Mimbres and other pottery or bird-effigy vessels found in the Southwest. I have included some arrows in the table, which are usually fletched with turkey primary and secondary wing feathers. Occasionally, a goose or other feather such as a primary Golden Eagle (*Aquila chrysaetos*) wing feather might have been used, though an accurate identification is often impossible because what is left of the feather is so fragmentary that DNA testing is not feasible.

Value, however, is another matter, and here some recent data from the Feather Distribution Project are relevant. Under provisions of the United States Endangered Species Act (ESA) and the Convention on International Trade in

Endangered Species of Wild Fauna and Flora (CITES: http://www.cites.org/eng
/disc/text.php), it is illegal to import most macaws, parrots, and their feathers into
the United States without a special permit. Specifically, CITES is an international
agreement among governments. Its aim is to ensure that international trade in specimens of wild animals and plants does not threaten their survival. Authorization
for the Endangered Species Act expired in 1992. Although the prohibitions and
requirements of the Act still remain in force, appropriations must be sought yearly.
Since 1992, the Act has been the focus of attacks from interest groups bent on
relaxing species protections to allow increased development. Nevertheless, the
Feather Distribution Project operates in full compliance with the provisions of the
Endangered Species Act, as well as CITES and the Migratory Bird Act.

Nevertheless, the ancient requirements for feathers for traditional cultural practices persist among the Pueblos. The Feather Distribution Project was created in
1982 to meet this need for feathers, to combat the illegal market for feathers, and to
help preserve the native bird populations and habitat in Latin America.

During the thirty-four years (1982–2015) of the Feather Distribution Project,
through cooperation with zoos, bird clubs, veterinary clinics and hospitals, rehab
facilities, private businesses, breeders, and individual owners, the Project distributed approximately 4,500,000 macaw and parrot feathers (and more than 10 million wild turkey feathers) free of charge to more than a thousand Pueblo individuals
in all thirty-two villages in New Mexico and Arizona. This total included all feathers,
from the longest center tails to the smallest body contour feathers. Pueblo recipients
reported that, during the ten to fifteen years preceding the creation of the Project,
most macaw feathers were purchased from traveling feather merchants and vendors
at ceremonies such as Pueblo Feast Days—modern-day equivalents of the "mobile
merchants" of the past—for $1 to $100 each depending upon species, size, color,
and condition: the long center tails of the Scarlet Macaw (*Ara macao*) regularly cost
$45 to $100 each (Reyman 1990a, 1990b), and sometimes still did cost that when
in short supply and if the buyer was desperate to obtain them. Smaller feathers cost
proportionately less, but even a bag of fifty to one hundred body contour feathers
might have brought $25 to $45. Using this information, as noted above, the market
value of the feathers distributed free of charge by the Project might have been as
high as $18 million to $20 million. Yet, the total weight of these feathers sent (we
have also delivered hundreds of thousands in person), excluding packing for shipment by parcel post, was approximately one thousand pounds (±454,000 grams).
By comparison, macaw feathers were more valuable per ounce or gram than most
illegal street drugs. Simply in terms of weight, a dozen or so merchants could have
carried all the feathers distributed by the Project, in a single trip. Furthermore, it
was certainly possible that the Project distributed more feathers in its thirty-four

years of existence than were imported by the Ancestral Pueblos and other ancient peoples in the Southwest over hundreds of years, or even a millennium or more. For one thing, the majority of feathers distributed were wild turkey feathers, to which the Ancestral Pueblos and their post-contact descendants would have had ready access through domestication and hunting.

The transportation of live macaws and parrots would not have presented ancient traders with an insurmountable problem in terms of weight. Creel and McKusick (1994: fig. 3, 516–517) discuss the transportation issue in the ancient Mimbres area. Although the "macaws in the Classic Mimbres sites are part of the first large group of macaws known to have been imported into the American Southwest" (Creel and McKusick 1994:516), they conclude that the total number of birds is not great and would not have required a large contingent of people to transport them (Creel and McKusick 1994:517). For example, a Scarlet Macaw generally weighs between 1,060 and 1,123 g (2.3–2.5 pounds), not much weight for the value of the bird. It can be easily carried in a crate, as seen in the petroglyph (figure 1.1); tethered to a burden basket, as depicted on Mimbres Pottery and a Pottery Mound mural; or even carried on one's arm or shoulder without difficulty. The macaw was easily portable. Great value was contained in little weight.

As with turquoise, it is fair to assume that because of the high value of birds and feathers, traders could have carried a few birds profitably, thousands of feathers, or both, neither of which would have weighed much or required more than a couple of porters. With their light weight and high value, transporting large numbers of macaw feathers would have been relatively easy and extremely profitable. For example, on trips to the Southwest, I regularly carried fifty to a hundred thousand macaw and parrot feathers in a crushproof case that measures 125 cm × 75 cm × 25 cm. Packed, it weighs less than 10 kg; most of the weight is in the case itself. Macaw feathers are so valuable that, even with mortality rates of 85 percent (Nilsson 1981), smugglers who attempted to bring in illegal birds still found it profitable to pluck the dead birds and sell the feathers (Reyman 1990a, 1990b).

The fragility of the feathers; their use in offerings such as prayer sticks (*pahos*) and in other disposable contexts, including sacrifice; and the inability of pre-contact peoples in the American Southwest to establish viable breeding colonies or even sizable populations (Hargrave 1970; McKusick 2001) meant that constant supplies of birds and feathers were needed. Profitable trade was thus ensured, trade that continued late into the post-contact period and still continues today, both legally (e.g., on eBay) and illegally.

Value, not weight or raw numbers, then, is the most important criterion for determining whether certain economic activities such as long-distance trade were profitable, specifically trade in precious commodities such as macaws, macaw feathers, turquoise, and other exotic items such as copper bells and shell trumpets. Those who argue that Mesoamerican-Southwestern trade had a minimal impact on the course of ancient Southwestern economic and cultural development use the wrong criterion when they emphasize *only* either quantity or weight rather than *value* as the measure of this significance. Finally, as is demonstrated later in this volume, when the importance of feathers in the context of Pueblo life is understood, the explanation for the high value of feathers becomes clear.

2

The Ethnographic and Ethnohistoric Context

As noted in the last chapter, the earliest Spanish entradas into the American Southwest—led by Alvar Nuñez Cabeza de Vaca (1536), Fray Marcos de Niza (1539), and Francisco Vázquez de Coronado (1540–1542)—provide the first written records of trade in feathers and live birds between Mesoamerica (now Mexico) and the American Southwest. These records, written by those who accompanied Fray Marcos de Niza, Francisco Vázquez de Coronado (Hammond and Rey 1940; Winship 1896), and also later expeditions, are invaluable sources of information about the macaw and parrot trade on the cusp of the moment in time when life in the Southwest was about to change drastically. To be sure, other economically important commodities traveled along these trade routes and through the trade networks, including bison and deer hides, cotton textiles, "emeralds" (malachite?) and turquoise (perhaps the same thing), salt, shells, and enslaved people. The focus here, however, is on birds and feathers, and primarily on turkeys, macaws, and parrots, though other avian species are briefly mentioned.

Several points are noteworthy about the Spanish *relaciones*. As scholars such as Riley (1974) have noted, the Spanish were accompanied by Mexican Indians who apparently could communicate with various Indigenous peoples along the routes of the entradas, including with Pueblo peoples such as the Zuni (Cibola) in what is now the American Southwest. Hammond and Rey (1940:178) specifically note the presence of a lad from Petetlán [a city in Guerrero, Mexico] who served as an interpreter and accompanied Esteban as part of the Fray Marcos de Niza entrada in

https://doi.org/10.5876/9781646427543.c002

1539. He was captured by the Zuni when Esteban was killed, and a year or so later was released to Francisco Vázquez de Coronado. This, in turn, indicates that the trade routes were well established and of considerable antiquity: as discussed below, when the Spaniards first arrived in the Southwest, the trade for feathers and birds had already been in place for at least 1,000 to 1,100 years. It began at the Hohokam site of Snaketown in southern Arizona circa AD 500 (McKusick 2001:74) and later spread throughout the rest of the Southwest. The trade the Spanish noticed and reported was an ancient, widespread economic and cultural activity: one account, for example, states that "this Indian said he was the son of a trader who was dead, but that when he was a little boy his father had gone into the back country with fine feathers to trade for ornaments" (Winship 1896:472). The Spaniards also partook of turkeys, food given them by the Pueblos (Winship 1896:491), and noted the Indians wore long feather robes (Winship 1896:517). Various early Spanish writers noted the presence of turkeys at Zuni, Acoma, and the Rio Grande Pueblos, raised both for feathers and, as later archaeological fieldwork demonstrated, for food (Hammond and Rey 1940:171, 218, 255).

Schroeder briefly reviewed early and later Spanish documents and found substantial evidence for Pueblo use of turkey feathers to make robes (1968:98, 100, 103). He also found evidence for the use of macaw feathers: for example, trade of macaw feathers by Mexican Indians to peoples in Arizona, as far as we know, for use in "feather crests" (98), and a gift of "two bonnets made of many macaw feathers" to a member of the Rodriguez-Chamuscado expedition of 1581–1582 (99). Centuries after, in the Early American Period (1840–1880), Schroeder (1968:109–110) cites reports of macaw feathers at a number of Pueblos (west to east: Zuni, Acoma, Laguna, San Felipe, Santo Domingo, Sandia, Isleta, San Juan [now Ohkay Owingeh], Santa Clara, San Ildefonso, Pojoaque, and Nambe) and also the use of cedar boxes to hold the feathers, a practice I've seen that continues today in the Pueblos. One noteworthy point of Schroeder's essay (1968:109–110) is that San Felipe and several other Pueblos during this period obtained live macaws directly from Sonora, Mexico. There is no mention, however, of whether the Pueblos traveled to Sonora to obtain them or whether traders from Sonora traveled to the Pueblo area. Perhaps both were the case.

It would be difficult to overstate the importance of feathers in Pueblo cultural and especially ceremonial life. Reading Schroeder's (1968) brief survey, it is clear the Pueblos bury large numbers of turkey feathers in their fields—feathers which are not generally seen, as are those used in public ceremonies such as the Cochití Feast Day in July. Furthermore, consider that since 1982, when the Feather Distribution Project[9] was created in response to a request for macaw feathers by the late Fred Cordero of Cochití Pueblo, the Project provided almost 15 million feathers free of charge to all thirty-two Pueblo villages, mostly wild turkey (10 million), followed by macaw and parrot feathers (4.5 million). About one thousand of the approximately seventy thousand Pueblo people received feathers from the Project, yet the Project did not provide all the feathers needed by the Pueblos for ceremonial use; for example, eagle, hawk and other raptors, jay, cardinal, magpie, roadrunner, and dozens of other protected bird species whose feathers the Pueblos use (e.g., Henderson and Harrington 1914; Ladd 1963, 1972; Tyler 1979) were not collected, accepted, or distributed by the Project. Furthermore, the feathers provided did not meet the total Pueblo Indian need for wild turkey, macaw, and parrot feathers.

Two points must be made: first, we know that we did not provide all the macaw, parrot, and wild turkey feathers required for Pueblo ceremonial life, because requests for feathers were continuous throughout the year. In some cases, a man may have asked for a dozen Scarlet Macaw center tails but we sent only six because supplies were low, or he requested seventy Amazon parrot tail feathers for a ceremonial head bundle but we did not send more than three or four dozen. In other words, the number of requests and the number of feathers requested frequently were greater than our ability to provide that number. As many feathers as the Feather Distribution Project provided, we did not provide all the feathers needed, and we *always* had a backlog of requests, both first-time and repeat. A second aspect of this was that many feathers, especially wild turkey feathers, were used only once and needed constant replacement. Prayer sticks and prayer plumes usually required multiple feathers (see, e.g., Stevenson 1904:plates 25 and 41; Ladd 1963; McKusick 2001:11–13), and these objects were used only once—planted at a shrine or placed in a field—where they deteriorated through time. Replacement was necessary for the next occasion of use, so more feathers were required. Feathers used for ceremonial clothing and for head bundles and other paraphernalia last longer, but they, too, must be replaced from time to time. The long macaw center tails used on katsina masks frequently broke from the force of wind, and the Feather Distribution Project was often asked to provide new center tails—the longer, the better—for masks. Yet we could not replace all feathers requested, when requested, and so we did not provide all the feathers needed. Men sometimes borrowed them from other Pueblo members, but they also bought feathers from various commercial sources such as the Hopi-owned Tsakurshovi Trading Post on Second Mesa, eBay, and traveling vendors who showed up at the villages, such as the Four Corners at Zuni, and at Pueblo public dances.

Second, the Feather Distribution Project provided wild turkey, macaw, parrot, and to a much lesser extent, duck feathers to the Pueblos. But the Pueblos' ceremonial requirements for feathers included many feathers we did not and could not legally provide: eagles, hawks, other raptors, passerine ("perching birds" such as jays, cardinals, woodpeckers and flickers, and so forth), and migratory birds. Again, we did not provide sufficient feathers for Pueblo needs. Where did the Pueblos obtain these? Zuni Pueblo has the Zuni Eagle Sanctuary that houses disabled birds and others that, for various reasons, cannot be returned to the wild. The Zuni obtain most of their eagle feathers from the Sanctuary. Other Pueblos can apply for eagle feathers from the National Eagle Repository operated by the US Fish and Wildlife Service and located at the Rocky Mountain Arsenal National Wildlife Refuge northeast of Denver, Colorado (http://www.fws.gov/eaglerepository/index.php). To apply for eagle feathers or parts, one must fill out an application form, submit it, and then wait. Pueblo men told me it could take up to two or three years to receive the requested feathers, depending on what is requested and the supply at the repository.

Pueblo men, however, and many other Native Americans, are permitted to own eagle, hawk, and owl feathers and can obtain them by other means than from the National Eagle Repository. Traditionally, Hopi, Zuni, and Keres-speaking villages took eagles from nests, and Hopi, Zuni, Taos, and Jemez snare eagles from pits (Parsons 1939:1, 28–29). A pit is dug deep enough for a man to crouch in, then overlaid with branches. Bait, usually a rabbit, is tied to a branch, and when an eagle arrives to take the bait, the man reaches through the branches, grabs the eagle's legs, and subdues the bird. He then takes it home and tethers it to the roof of his house-top (Hopi) or cages it on the roof or ground. As needed, loose feathers are picked up or plucked from the bird. After plucking, the Hopi choke the eagle (Parsons 1939:29) to release its spirit back to the sky. Ellis (1968:65) provides another account of eagle plucking:

> Eagles, formerly captured by reaching out to grab the legs when the bird settled on a piece of meat tied at the edge of an opening in the roof of a brush shelter, were kept captive and annually plucked to a state of nakedness in the fall when the feathers naturally loosened. A designated man held the bird, with a cloth over its head, while another removed the feathers. Should even a drop of blood appear, the medicine man was summoned at once.

Although Pueblo people and other Native Americans are permitted to possess eagle feathers, capture eagles, and even sacrifice them, they are not permitted to sell eagle feathers or parts of eagles. The same pertains to other federally protected species. Yet, over the years, the news media have carried stories of Native Americans who have been arrested, tried, fined, and in some cases imprisoned for selling or attempting to sell eagle feathers and bird parts (wings, tails, etc.) and those from other raptors and passerines.

Hawks and owls are captured or hunted, and the same is true for passerines ("perching birds")—jays, cardinals, magpies, woodpeckers and flickers, and so on—and migratory birds (see, e.g., Ladd 1963; Tyler 1979; and McKusick 2001:7–10 for a full listing of bird feathers used by the Pueblos). Pueblo men also obtain feathers from all these birds during walks around the villages and their environs, when they encounter molted feathers, birds killed by cats and other predators, and birds that have flown into buildings. Roadkill is another source of feathers as well as for the skins of foxes and other animals.

The Greater Roadrunner (*Geococcyx californianus*) is an important bird, notably for Pueblo prayer plumes. The Greater Roadrunner is neither a passerine nor is it currently a federally protected species, so there are few restrictions on the capture or killing of roadrunners. The Pueblos do both to obtain Greater Roadrunner feathers. Nevertheless, although we received frequent requests, the Feather Distribution Project did not provide Greater Roadrunner feathers to the Pueblos. Few zoos seemed to have roadrunners, and we didn't request them from those that did. Macaws, parrots, wild turkeys, ducks, and geese were sufficient to keep us busy. Zoos do have protected passerines (e.g., jays, cardinals, magpies, woodpeckers and flickers) and various migratory birds, the feathers of which the Pueblo use, but again, we neither requested them nor distributed them; both were illegal activities for the Feather Distribution Project.

Birds and feathers were similarly important in pre-contact times and continued in importance after the Spanish entradas and in the centuries following. Some evidence for this comes from murals found at sites such the Hopi villages of Awatovi and Kawaika-a, villages destroyed by the Hopi themselves in 1700–1701 (Smith 1952, 183–189), and sites such as the pre-contact pueblo of Pottery Mound west of Las Lunas, New Mexico (south-southwest of Albuquerque), and the pueblo of Kuaua (Dutton 1963), currently known as Coronado State Monument, near Bernalillo, New Mexico. Kuaua lasted into post-contact times and apparently was abandoned late in the sixteenth century. At the two Hopi villages (Awatovi and Kawaika-a), birds are the most common life-forms depicted in the murals, more common than either humans or *katsinam* (masked figures, male and female), and the *most* commonly depicted birds are macaws and parrots (Smith 1952:183–189). What makes this especially interesting is that, except for the Thick-billed Parrot (*Rhynchopsitta pachyrhyncha*) in southern Arizona (now extirpated), macaws and parrots were never indigenous to the American Southwest. The Scarlet Macaw (*Ara macao*), Military Macaw (*Ara militaris*), Blue-and-Yellow Macaw (*Ara ararauna*), White-fronted Amazon parrot (*Amazona albifrons*), and Lilac-crowned Amazon parrot (*Amazona finschi*)—found at archaeological sites in the Southwest—were all imported from Mesoamerica. Although no comparable research has been done for Pottery Mound and Kuaua, nor for any other site that I am aware of where murals have been found such as Gran Quivira, examination of the publications for

Pottery Mound (Hibben 1975; Emslie 1981; Clark 2007) and Kuaua (Dutton 1963) indicates that birds were common and important mural depictions; macaws and parrots were especially common at Pottery Mound. Curiously, however, although macaw depictions are notably common in the murals from Pottery Mound, where birds are the second most common taxonomic group of faunal remains, no macaw skeletal remains have been identified at Pottery Mound (Clark 2007). The same is true for parrots, several of which are seen in the Pottery Mound murals. Furthermore, macaw and parrot images, and those of many other birds, are also common on Mimbres pottery (McKusick 2001) and are found on the pottery from the Zuni ancestral (and post-contact) site of Hawikku, as seen in exhibits at the A:shiwi A:wan Museum and Heritage Center at present-day Zuni.

Macaws and parrots are depicted in Southwestern rock art, especially from the Ancestral Pueblo area. The two petroglyphs (figure 1.1) at Petroglyph National Monument on the western edge of Albuquerque, New Mexico, are from the pre-contact period, though no specific date can be assigned. The top image, a macaw, is now the logo for the monument. The bottom image, of a macaw or parrot[10] in a cage with a handle, is significant because it provides information on one means by which macaws and parrots were transported into the Southwest. Figure 98 in *Kiva Art of the Anasazi at Pottery Mound* (Hibben 1975) depicts a second technique: a parrot tethered to the rim of a V-shaped burden basket carried on the back of a woman. This mural is also noteworthy because, prior to its discovery, the general assumption was that women did not participate in long-distance trade. This assumption is obviously false, though the degree to which women participated is unknown. Nor do we know how feathers, as opposed to live birds, were transported—we have neither archaeological nor ethnographic evidence—but it is likely feathers were packed in baskets or wrapped in textiles or hides and then carried on one's back or perhaps carried in a basket or strapped to a basket or other type of pack.

What is curious, and has long struck me as so, is that the Spanish apparently never viewed the feather trade as an important economic activity, at least not one worth pursuing. As cited above, they recorded the trade for feathers in the various *relaciones* that survive from the sixteenth century and later. They actively sought gold and silver (and later copper, lead, and turquoise); farmed, bred, and raised animals they had brought with them such as horses, cattle, sheep, goats, and chickens; hunted; encouraged Pueblo, and later Navajo, textile production for trade; and engaged in a wide variety of other economic activities. For example, given the Spanish appreciation of Zuni salt (Hammond and Rey 1940:181) and the importance of salt in their diet, the Spanish may have pursued the salt trade in addition to searches for other commodities. However, they seem never to have considered that the feather trade or trade in other precious commodities such as shells might be economically profitable.

Such would have been profitable had the Spanish been able to control the bird and feather trade outright, or even to have participated in it to a significant degree. The Feather Distribution Project neither bought nor sold feathers; all were given as gifts to the Pueblos. Nevertheless, as noted earlier, the feathers had substantial economic value: there was a widespread commercial market for them evident, for example, in the presence of individuals selling feathers at villages during ceremonial occasions and in the number of feathers for sale on eBay on any given day.

The following email request (2015) reflected the high cost of feathers from commercial sources:

> I am a spiritual leader of the Louisville Native American community. We as a community are looking for feathers that we can use in the making of ceremonial items that we use for prayer, dance fans, and ceremonial regalia. These are hard for us to find because they are sold due to their beauty. We was [sic] wondering if you could as your group to please donate feathers for a short time to our cause. I have given my cell number in case you have further questions.

I noted earlier that the estimate of the commercial value of the several million macaw and parrot feathers given away by the Feather Distribution Project was in the millions of dollars in terms of this market. The Spanish, of course, would have been involved in a more basic trade or bartering exchange system, but given the importance of the long-distance trade for feathers, the lack of involvement by the Spanish is indeed curious. What makes it perhaps more so is that when the Spanish entered the Southwest and for two hundred years afterwards, the number of Pueblo villages and the size of the Pueblo population were substantially greater than today. Therefore, it is reasonable to assume that the demand for feathers and the consequent trade for them were also substantially greater than today. In retrospect, the feather trade clearly represents an economic opportunity the Spanish failed to exploit, for reasons unknown.

TURKEYS

Although much is made, and rightly so, of the importance of eagles, hawks, ravens, macaws, parrots, and other birds in Native American life and lore, both ancient and post-contact, the fact is that, wherever it occurred, the wild turkey (*Meleagris gallopavo*) and its domesticated descendants were and are the single most important bird in American Indian ceremonialism. More turkey feathers were and are used than from any other species. Parsons (1932:274), for example, noted the preeminence of turkey feathers over all other feathers at Isleta Pueblo. Isleta, located in the Rio Grande Valley about a dozen miles south of Albuquerque, just off current

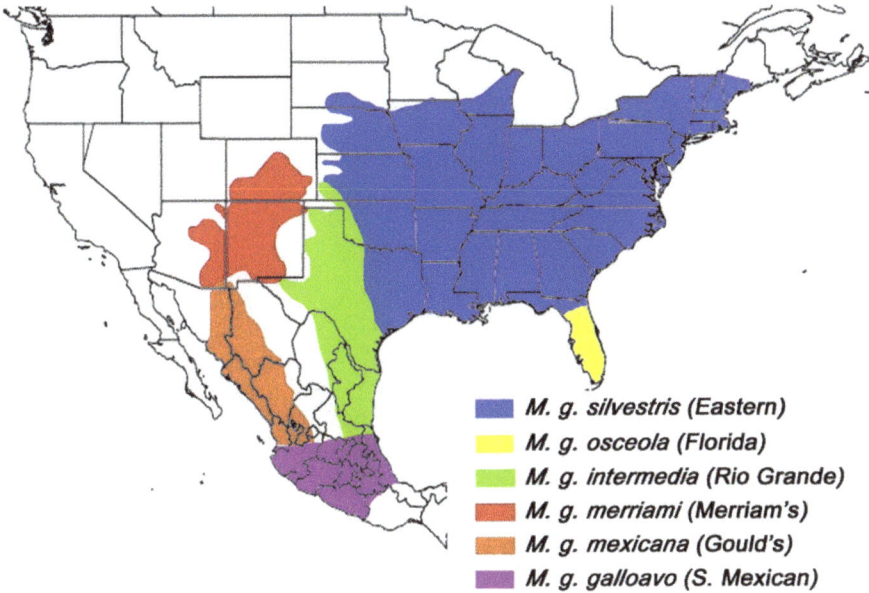

Figure 2.1. *Meleagris gallopavo* sp. distribution map for the United States and Mexico.

Interstate 25, is one of the larger New Mexico Pueblos, with more than three thousand residents.

The same preeminence of wild turkey feathers was true at the other Pueblo villages, as our Project experience demonstrated. We distributed about 10 million wild turkey feathers, compared with some 4.5 million macaw and parrot feathers. Furthermore, although wild turkeys were important throughout their North American habitats, the wild turkey became domesticated only in the Southwest and Mesoamerica. Indeed, at archaeological sites in the Southwest, there is a clear distinction between the skeletal remains of the wild turkey and its domesticated descendants (McKusick 2001:8, 46–49, 109–125). We do not know with certainty when the wild turkey began to be domesticated in Mesoamerica, but the archaeological data suggest that sedentary life, including turkeys, occurred by 1500 BC (Borhegyi 1965:8). At the El Mirador site in the Mayan lowlands, recent research suggests the turkey was domesticated as early as 300 BC (Thornton et al. 2012). However, because the turkeys at El Mirador seem to have been imports (Thornton et al. 2012), an even earlier date for domestication in the lowlands is certainly possible.

At present, three subspecies of wild turkeys are found in the Southwest (see figures 2.1–2.3): *Meleagris gallopavo intermedia* (Rio Grande Wild Turkey; figure 2.2), *Meleagris gallopavo merriami* (Merriam's Wild Turkey; figure 2.3), and Gould's

Figure 2.2. Rio Grande Turkey (*Meleagris gallopavo intermedia*).

Wild Turkey (*Meleagris gallopavo mexicana*). The current range of the Rio Grande Turkey extends into Oregon and California, and that of Merriam's Turkey extends into Montana and Idaho, in part because of introductions to repopulate areas with turkeys for hunting. Two of the subspecies are depicted in figures 2.2 and 2.3. Of the three subspecies, only the Merriam's is found at archaeological sites in the Southwest (McKusick 2001:8).

As cited above, the accounts written during the Spanish entradas into the Pueblo area note the presence and importance of turkeys for food and clothing. The earliest Southwest occurrences of turkey domestication date to long before 250 BC at Canyon del Muerto in the Four Corners area, where a natural mummy of a sacrificed Small Indian Domestic gobbler was recovered from a Basketmaker II deposit (McKusick 2001:44) dated to about 250 BC at Tularosa Cave in western New Mexico. By AD 100–300, domesticated turkeys appear in Basketmaker II Lolomai Phase sites on Black Mesa (McKusick 2001:113). McKusick (2001:47) further states, "The Southwest is marginal at best for the survival of turkeys, and *there were no wild turkeys before the introduction of domestic breeds*" (emphasis added). Furthermore, "the SID [Small Indian Domestic] is the only turkey in the Southwest from 250 BC to AD 500, a period of 750 years. The SID is found only in association with human settlements" (McKusick 2001:113).

Figure 2.3. Merriam's Turkey (*Meleagris gallopavo merriami*).

McKusick (2001:47–48) summarized the data for the Small Indian Domestic Turkey as follows:

> The Small Indian Domestic was completely dependent upon human husbandry. Its very presence implies a surplus of corn and/or beans which could be used for turkey feed. It did not have the genetic diversity to survive in the wild, and needed to be fed by its keepers. One does not independently invent a fragile turkey breed in the hinterlands where there are no turkeys at all. Therefore, I believe it is reasonable to suppose that the presence of Small Indian Domestic turkeys, plus turkey sacrifices, indicates the presence of at least a few people who knew how to produce a luxury item like a specialized ceremonial turkey breed, and the food to feed it. The simplest explanation is that this phenomenon was a complex involving improved seed corn, the songs to sing to make it come up, a patron supernatural to oversee its growth and productivity, and a suitable sacrificial bird to keep the supernatural happy.

McKusick (2001:44–46, 111) sees the introduction of the SID as likely of Mexican origin, possibly from Paquimé or extreme northeastern Mexico, or perhaps even Southwestern Texas. A Mexican origin fits with my argument herein that Mesoamerican exports to the Southwest included better varieties of corn and other cultigens plus the astronomical knowledge, ceremonialism, and commodities needed for successful farming. However, elsewhere McKusick (2001:113) states she agrees with Schorger (1966) "that the most probable source for the LID [Large Indian Domestic Turkey] and *M. g. merriami* [*Meleagris gallopavo merriami*: Merriam's Wild Turkey] is *M. g. silvestris* [*Meleagris gallopavo silvestris*: the Eastern Wild Turkey, but a western variant of it] in Oklahoma."

Shaw (2002:75–76) is more or less neutral on the Indian Transplant Hypothesis (ITH), but writes:

> To this day, ponderosa pine stringers extend well down the Canadian river toward the Llano Escatado. The presence of birds in these various drainages, extending from both the eastern forests and western forest into the plains, gives strong support to an origin of Merriam's turkey from natural expansion of eastern wild stock. Intuitively, I prefer this hypothesis to the ITH but cannot assign a relative likelihood to either. The ITH is based on negative data—the lack of fossils or artifacts prior to a specific period. But many potential fossil sites undoubtedly remain unexplored, perhaps unknown; and hundreds of ruins throughout Merriam's historic range remain undug. A finding of an early to mid-Holocene turkey from either source could place the ITH in doubt.

It seems, then, that taxonomy, archaeology, paleo-ornithology, and paleobotany combine to give *Meleagris gallopavo merriami* an uncertain history. Nonetheless, a wild turkey existed in the Southwest when the first naturalist arrived and classified it as something different. It has retained this distinction for nearly one hundred years, and modern genetics supports the existence of the bird in a discrete historic range and a characteristic habitat: Southwestern ponderosa pine forests. Still, Merriam's turkey had not expanded into the entire range of that particular tree species by the time Anglos arrived.

Shaw (2002:76) concludes:

> In summary, I believe the evidence suggests strongly that *Meleagris gallopavo* made a post-Pleistocene arrival in the Southwest. It probably arrived after the first humans came to the area. At present, we cannot be sure that it has been here for more than about 1,500 years. For the present, the Indian Transplant Hypothesis cannot be discounted. But it is also far from proven.

Therefore, the ultimate origin(s) of the SID, LID, and the Merriam's—if there is *one* ultimate origin—remains an open question despite the research that has been done (e.g., Schorger 1966; Olsen 1968; Lang and Harris 1984; Breitburg 1988; and Shaw 2002). Further complicating the problem is that motifs on Mimbres bowls offer clear evidence that the SID, LID, and Merriam's apparently coexisted at the same time in the ancient Southwest (see McKusick 2001:figure 22). However,

Shaw's time frame for the introduction of the Merriam's turkey is generally in agreement with McKusick's.

There is yet another complication, in the argument put forth by the late archaeologist Jean Pinkley (1965), who noted fifty years ago: "To say that the Indian domesticated the turkey is 'putting the cart before the horse.' The Indian had no choice; the turkey domesticated him." Pinkley's research at Mesa Verde demonstrates that wild turkeys were attracted to food scraps in Basketmaker III sites, and once they adapted to this ready source of sustenance, they could not be driven off. It only remained for the site inhabitants and their descendants to pen up the birds, thus providing themselves with a steady supply of feathers, food,[11] and bones and other body parts for tools and musical instruments. Pinkley argues that wild turkeys existed in the Southwest before domestication, and that domestication might not have happened as usually assumed. McKusick (2001:47), by contrast, states, "The Southwest is marginal at best for the survival of turkeys, and there were no wild turkeys before the introduction of the domestic breeds." This strikes me as perhaps overstated given the original forested habitat around Mesa Verde, and Shaw's (2002:76) contention that pine forests were a natural and characteristic habitat for the Merriam's turkey. What is also curious is that McKusick doesn't refer to Pinkley's paper, which she surely must have known about. Nevertheless, once domesticated—by whatever means and whenever it occurred—the turkey remained an important element of Pueblo life throughout the Spanish period and on past World War II. Parsons (1939:29) notes, "Turkey feathers are the commonest of all feathers used on prayer sticks or as prayer feathers" (see also Parsons 1939:275, 290–291). This is still true, yet today there are relatively few turkeys in the Pueblos. I've been told they are vulnerable to predation by Pueblo dogs, foxes, coyotes, raccoons, opossums, and even cats, the last of which prey on the poults, but except for the last, these predators existed in ancient and post-contact times when domesticated turkeys seem to have thrived in the villages. I suspect the decline has more to do with fewer people in constant residence to watch for and guard against predators than with the presence of predators, per se. It could also be that people have much less time to care for turkeys because of work outside the pueblo, but one would think that children and the elderly could be given this task. I know one Santa Clara woman who keeps a few turkeys in her yard outside her front door, but in most cases of which I was aware, those who kept turkeys penned them up at some distance from their houses. This increases their likelihood of loss from various predators, as well as from theft by humans.

Finally, it's worth noting that some Pueblo men were willing to accept feathers from entirely domestic varieties of turkeys, such as the Royal Palm Turkey (*Meleagris gallopavo* sp.). The apparent reason was the spectacular black-and-white coloration of the bird's feathers, with the tail feathers occasionally used as a possible substitute for Bald Eagle (*Haliaeetus leucocephalus*) tail feathers if eagle feathers were unavailable. This was the same reason given when men substituted African Grey Parrot (*Psittacus erithacus*) tail feathers for Northern Cardinal (*Cardinalis cardinalis*) tail feathers (see below). A few men also accepted feathers from other domestic turkey breeds such as the Blue Slate and Bourbon Red, though to a much lesser extent, because their coloration was not as dramatic as that of the Royal Palm.

The ethnographic data suggest several reasons for the importance of turkeys in the Southwest, of which two are of particular importance: first, turkeys live on the ground during the day but roost in trees at night. Therefore, they symbolically connected Mother Earth with the Upper World. Second, aside from whole capes, fans, and wings, which, with proper care, were used for years, most turkey feathers were generally used only once, and therefore, new turkey feathers were constantly required for ceremonial use. For example, the Pueblos used turkey feathers to make prayer sticks and prayer plumes that were deposited at shrines, springs, and other sacred places along with prayers for rain, fertility, good health, and other blessings. These feathered objects quickly disintegrated, and new ones needed to be made whenever prayers were contemplated. Zuni prayer sticks and prayer plumes usually required a minimum of three turkey feathers (and perhaps feathers from other birds as well). Ladd (1972:12) states that five feathers per prayer stick is the norm, and Stevenson (1904:plates 25 and 41) supports this, or even a larger number. Plate 25 specifically shows prayer plumes made from feathers of the turkey, flicker, Red-tailed Hawk, other species, and eagle plumes. Ladd (1963:chapter 4; 1972:12) notes that seventy-two species of birds were used ceremonially at Zuni, and Stevenson (1904:419–420) describes a *mili*, an especially elaborate object with almost ninety feathers from ten species of birds.

Ladd writes: "Feathers are used in the annual seasonal public and special ceremonies performed by the masked gods and in the ritual making and offering of prayer-sticks involving the entire tribe" (1972:12). Ladd (1963:28, 1972:12) further states that depending on the individual's religious position, each Zuni must "plant" prayer sticks from 4 to 20 times each year, using 16 to 80 prayer sticks annually, and incorporating approximately 80 to 400 feathers of various kinds. Bunzel (1932a:501) notes:

> Prayer sticks are especially male offerings. Although women frequently offer prayer sticks they never make them. Their male relatives (actual or ceremonial) make them for them. So also, although men offer food and corn meal, it is always prepared for them by the women.

By contrast, at Acoma, both men and women make prayer sticks; they are made by the person who will plant them (White 1932:125–129).

Based on the above statement by Ladd, if "each Zuni must 'plant' from 16 to 80 prayer sticks annually," and each prayer stick or plume required a minimum of three turkey feathers, then each Zuni man required a minimum of 48–240 turkey feathers annually for one-time use. The current Zuni population is about 9,000, of which about 5,000 men and women are sixteen or older, old enough to take part in traditional ceremonial activities. If we assume 4,000 of these 5,000 people were ceremonially active during the course of the year and each required 16–80 prayer sticks, then some 192,000–960,000 turkey feathers were needed each year for basic ceremonial obligations. Still more were necessary for special ceremonial occasions, to use for part of katsina masks and clothing, and the same was generally true at other villages. A visit to a Hopi village during a ceremony such as Powamû (Bean Dance) revealed shrines overflowing with prayer plumes of turkey feathers. A visit to a dance, masked or not, quickly demonstrated the importance of turkey feathers, as well as other feathers (see below). Bird katsinam are found among many Pueblos such as the Parrot (Macaw) Katsina (Kyaro) and Turkey Katsina (Koyona) at Hopi, where Crow Mother (Tumas) is considered the mother of all katsinam. And lest we forget, the six Zuni Sha'lakos are giant birds (see Stevenson 1904:plate 64). Finally, at Cochití, the Híshta-kats (Hitter) Katsina throws turkey eggs filled with corn smut to punish those persons who appear excessively proud of new clothes (C. Lange 1959:487–489).

As cited, turkey feathers were also used in both ancient and post-contact times to make warm blankets or robes (figure 2.4). Few such robes are made today, but one example is on exhibit at the visitor's center at Giusewa, also known as Jemez State Monument. Remains of turkey feather blankets or robes have been recovered from archaeological sites at Chaco Canyon, Mesa Verde, and elsewhere. Turkey bones were used to manufacture flutes and, ironically, to produce turkey calls for turkey hunting, as well as for awls and other tools. Turkey bones were sharpened to make scarifiers, and dried turkey tendons served the same purpose in the Eastern Woodlands. Turkeys were a food source throughout their range in North America, including the Southwest, and especially in Mesoamerica, where turkey *mole* (chocolate sauce) is recorded in Spanish records.

One of the more interesting aspects of turkeys in the Southwest is evident in the archaeological record. At Ancestral Pueblo sites in the Whitewater District of eastern Arizona, for example, Frank H. H. Roberts Jr. excavated more than thirty turkey burials, most beneath stone slabs and accompanied by various grave goods, including shell and turquoise necklaces (1939:figure 44; 1940:134–135). In three reported instances, the turkeys were buried with infants and children, leading Roberts to infer that perhaps they were pets sacrificed to accompany the children's spirits to the afterlife. In some cases, the turkeys had so many grave goods interred with them

Figure 2.4. Turkey feather robe. Giusewa Pueblo, Jemez State Monument.

that, had they been human, one could have inferred they were high-status individuals. Turkey burials—all young female turkeys (Roberts does not identify the sex of the Whitewater specimens)—have also been excavated at the site of Gran Quivira in New Mexico and at kivas at Tseh So (Bc 50) in Chaco Canyon. The five turkeys at Tseh So were buried in front of the kiva ventilator shafts, one each in Kivas 1–3 and two in Kiva 4. All five were female, complete, articulated postcranial skeletons, and all were missing their heads (Brand et al. 1937:101). McKusick (2001:43–48) discusses turkey sacrifices at Southwestern sites in conjunction with the worship of the rain god, Tlaloc, and an instance of the use of a turkey head as a fetish at a Basketmaker II site in Canyon del Muerto.

Pottery from the Whitewater District sites spans the Basketmaker III through Pueblo III period, Tseh So dates to circa AD 900–950, and Gran Quivira was occupied prior to the Spanish entradas and was not abandoned until 1672 as a consequence of a prolonged drought. The turkey burial at Gran Quivira is not specifically dated but is probably from the middle to late period of occupation. What is significant is that, to the best of my knowledge, there are no ethnographic data for turkey burials among the Pueblos either today or in the nineteenth and twentieth centuries. I have spoken with dozens of Pueblo individuals from various villages, including religious officers, and none has indicated an awareness of the practice of turkey burials; indeed, they were surprised to learn that the practice existed in ancient times. Whatever the reasons for it, the practice of interring turkeys does not seem to have survived into the post-contact period and almost certainly does not seem to exist today. Parsons (1939:29) briefly notes turkey sacrifice in her encyclopedic *Pueblo Indian Religion* but does not mention ethnographic examples of either turkey sacrifice (cf. McKusick 2001:3–4, passim) or turkey burial among the Pueblos. Bunzel (1932a:677n19) notes the deposit of turkey feathers in a hole with food and the use of turkey feathers on prayer sticks for the dead, but she does not record turkey sacrifice or burial at Zuni. Finally, Ellis (1968) reviews ancient and post-contact Southwestern death practices and makes no mention of either turkey burials per se or turkeys buried as grave goods with human burials.

Moreover, although wild turkey populations are still found on Pueblo lands, often the result of a reintroduction or stocking program by a state agency or by an organization such as the National Wild Turkey Federation, few domesticated turkeys are found among the Pueblos; Jemez and Santa Clara are two villages that still have a few domesticated turkeys. Given the ongoing importance of turkey feathers for ceremonial purposes, this seems surprising. As noted earlier, Pueblo colleagues say the presence of cats is partly to blame—they kill turkey poults—and wild animals such as foxes, coyotes, raccoons, and opossums are also at fault because they eat both birds and turkey eggs. Nevertheless, one would expect the Pueblos to take preventative measures to protect their turkey flocks. Although cats were not present in ancient times, coyotes, foxes, raccoons, and opossums were, and cats were present once the Spanish arrived with them. Yet subsequent Spanish reports note the presence of turkey flocks in the villages. Furthermore, domesticated turkey populations are reported as common among the Pueblos up through World War II. Clearly another factor—a recent one—seems operable in the decline of Pueblo domesticated turkey populations. Perhaps this is an aspect of the general post–World War II decline in Pueblo farming and animal husbandry activities in favor of wage labor. For example, Parsons (1939:29) notes, "There are flocks of turkeys in several towns"; however, Lange (1959:112) notes there were no turkeys in Cochití in 1946, but there were a few in 1947, 1948, and 1951.

MACAWS AND PARROTS

The presence of macaws and parrots in the Southwest, both birds and their feathers, is well documented at archaeological sites, as is their presence, to a lesser extent, in post-contact Pueblo villages ethnographically and ethnohistorically. Perhaps the best-known relatively recent example is the Military Macaw given to the Zuni Macaw Clan by Judd in 1924. Judd visited Zuni in 1939, and the bird "was still alive, but it had been pretty thoroughly plucked" (Judd 1954:plate 75, 263). Judd writes:

The macaw had been presented because . . . most of the Zuñi we took to Chaco Canyon [as excavation workmen] were Macaw, and they told me a live macaw had not been seen in Zuñi within the memory of their oldest men. The feathers they annually needed for prayer sticks and other purposes had been purchased from Santo Domingo[12] where two macaws were privately owned. After plucking feathers, the owners professed to control the new growth by rubbing over the empty follicles "paint" of the desired color. The Macaw group has long been numerically important at Zuñi. (cf. Seowtewa 2022)

Judd (1954:263n56) further writes: "A sequel to my 1939 visit to Zuni: Under date of March 21, 1946, the Sun Priest sent me an airmail, special delivery letter reading, 'Yesterday my parrot fell over dead. Please think it over and see if you can get me another one.'"[13]

Another early example is Bourke's (1884:26–27) report from Santo Domingo, the only Pueblo he visited that had live parrots.

A youngster named "Trinidad" told me that there were parrots kept in cages by his people. "There is one in my house; come and see it."

There it was in a little cage of willow saplings. The poor bird was in a fearful state of demoralisation, nearly every one of its fine blue, red, and yellow feathers [apparently a Scarlet Macaw] having been plucked to make wands for the dancers or to decorate the sacred standards.

There were several other parrots in the Pueblo utilised for the same object. The value ascribed to the plumage of the eagle and parrot by all the sedentary Indians of Arizona and New Mexico is doubtless based on some considerations graver than those of commerce. The feathers of the parrot, which have been brought up from the interior of the neighboring Republic of Mexico, are treasured by all the Pueblos as far north as Taos and Picuris, and west to Acoma, Zuni, and Oraybe [*sic*]. They will always be found carefully preserved in peculiar wooden boxes, generally cylindrical in shape, made expressly for this purpose . . . but in no Pueblo except Santo Domingo have I ever come across live parrots.

Ellis (1968:65) provides another, more recent, example from Santo Domingo Pueblo: "For the last several years Santo Domingo Pueblo has kept a macaw, purchased from a pet shop, and similarly has plucked its feathers for use in costumes and ceremonial paraphernalia, after which the bird must spend some weeks tethered behind a warm wood stove while his plumage replaces itself."

Bandelier (1890:36) notes the Cochití eagerly sought "Plumas de Guacamayo" (macaw feathers), and throughout his classic ethnography on Cochití Pueblo, Lange (1959) discusses at length the traditional Cochití use of macaw, parrot, and other feathers. More generally, Parsons (1939:34) writes: "Through a Havasupai-Walapai-Mohave trade route to the Yumans of the Lower Colorado the Pueblos got their abalone and haliotis shells, also some of the parrot feathers [that] now [have] become so scarce."

At Cochití, Amazon parrot (all species) tail feathers are used in "tufts" (I prefer the term "bundles") worn on the top of dancers' heads (Lange 1959:345), and the same is true for most Rio Grande Pueblos, at Acoma, and at Zuni, as anyone who attends a public dance can easily see.[14] Judging from how few Amazon parrot remains are found archaeologically at Southwestern sites, it seems their feathers have become more important in recent times—post-1900—than was the case in pre-contact or even the early post-contact period.

The above information on Pueblo feather-plucking witnessed by Judd and Bourke during the post-contact period is not unique; I saw examples of plucked Amazon parrots, though I never saw a plucked macaw. Plucking is mistreatment, and it is not limited to the ethnographic period; there are archaeological data that are evidence macaws were not well cared for at sites in the Southwest. In terms of the archaeological reports of where the skeletal remains of the Scarlet Macaw occurred at Pueblo Bonito, Pepper (1920) and Judd (1954) usually found them in the dark interior and often semi-subterranean rooms, locations far from ideal for the keeping of macaws—"birds of the sun"—which require sunlight. As Judd (1954:264) wrote,

That ventilator, and the ceiling hatch when open, supplied such light as reached the upper chamber. From the latter a floor hatchway was the only means by which light and air filtered down into the lower chamber. And yet the lower chamber was designed and utilized as a cage for live macaws. Their excrement lay upon the floor and upon the remains of an adobe-surfaced shelf, 40 inches wide, which had extended across the east end of the room at a height of 3 feet 8 inches. Shelf, introduced floor, and the original first-story ceiling had all crashed down into the lower chamber with collapse of the second-story walls. Under this ruin . . . lay the four articulated skeletons of *Ara macao* and the skull of a fifth. . . .

That these tropical birds had been confined some time in their dark, ill-ventilated quarters, into which no ray of sunlight could possibly penetrate, is evidenced by the fact that their breast bones were deformed, the sternal keel being bent to one side. . . . From remains conspicuous among the room's debris, we know these captives were fed pinyon nuts, squash seeds, and roasted corn-on-the-cob. This fare could scarcely cause the deformity mentioned, but utter lack of sunlight might.

However, if most Scarlet Macaws were birds of sacrifice or intended as such, as McKusick (2001:4) argues, then keeping them in good avicultural conditions was relatively unimportant. They were sacrificed at about one year of age (McKusick

2001:4), an age supported by Hargrave's research (1970:table 10) where 83.7 percent of the macaws he studied, which could be classified by age, were between four months and twelve months old. And if one adds Hargrave's data for adolescents (one to three years old), listed in the same table, the number of young macaws at death is 96.6 percent. Hargrave (1970:table 9) notes pathologies in 46.9 percent of the macaws he studied, which, he states, "reflected either normal accidents or were attributed to dietary deficiencies" (Hargrave 1970:53). Again, macaws were not generally well cared for at archaeological sites in the Southwest.

One especially troubling example of mistreatment of a macaw, albeit speculative, comes from Pueblo del Arroyo in Chaco Canyon where Judd (1959:127) excavated "an incomplete skeleton of a gorgeous red-blue-yellow macaw (*A. macao*) in Room 44." Judd (1959:127) then states:

> This latter find (field No. 312) is of more than usual interest because it provides evidence of an apparent clash of tempers. We may imagine a sudden painful bite from an irritated beak and a sharp, angry blow in retaliation. Landing full on the bird's breast, the blow resulted in [a] permanent injury which A. Wetmore describes as follows: The lower end in both coracoids has been fractured and then has healed in such a way as to bring complete fusion at the normal area of attachment to the sternum, as well as the manubrial area. The free edge of the keel of the sternum also shows an old injury, being distorted to the side in subsequent healing. (Note: The coracoids were driven within the sternal apparatus; the keel distortion is due to lack of sunlight or calcium deficiency.)

To take this imaginary scenario a step further, one can imagine that the bite by the Scarlet Macaw was in retaliation for having a feather or feathers plucked. A macaw's jaw is powerful, and a hard bite, as opposed to when a bird is being playful in a manner similar to a puppy, can easily draw blood or even break a finger bone. I know from personal experience that if the bite is in the area between the thumb and forefinger, it can completely pierce the back of the hand through the palm. A friend of mine once kissed her Blue-and-Yellow Macaw (a behavior I would never recommend or do) of twenty-five years when for some reason, he bit her lip, piercing it, with the tip of his beak and penetrating so deeply into her gum that she required stitches and root canal surgery on a tooth. And they were playing! Whoever tried to pluck the Scarlet Macaw in the above imaginary scenario described by Judd wasn't playing, and the bird's reaction was both predictable and justifiable, in my opinion. Of course, we'll never know if this is what happened, although clearly the macaw suffered a hard blow. Wetmore's note is also important in this context; the macaw was not given access to the sunlight or the food it required for good health. The

Ancestral Pueblos considered these birds precious and may have even worshipped them, but they did not treat them well (see also McKusick 2001:1–2).

In another example noted earlier from Chaco Canyon, Judd (1954:plate 76) recovered the skeleton of a Scarlet Macaw (*Ara macao*) from Pueblo Bonito Room 249, where it had been killed when the ceiling collapsed. Room 249 was a first-floor room and presumably dark, not a good living situation for a macaw. In Room 19 at Pueblo Bonito, Judd (1964:97) excavated "the skeleton of a thick-billed parrot (*Rhynchopsitta pachyrhyncha*), imported from near the Arizona-Mexico border. While imprisoned, its sternum had become deformed by improper food or lack of sunlight, or both." Again, macaws and parrots (and presumably other species) were not treated well by the Ancestral Puebloans at Chaco Canyon.

This seemingly uncaring behavior toward important birds is not an isolated or even rare circumstance among the Ancestral Pueblo peoples. McKusick (2001:2) writes:

> No special treatment was given to the carcass, which generally ended up in the trash dump. Birds treated in this manner undoubtedly account for the vast majority of specimens which constitute avian collections from Southwestern archaeological sites, both as relatively complete skeletons or, scattered by scavengers, as random bones. If birds were taken far from the pueblo, while on long hunting expeditions, they were skinned in the field and discarded there. When the hunter returned home, the ritual was the same, except the skins were not plucked. They were draped over the beams of the house, to which they adhered as they dried, until needed.
>
> Since the bodies of birds of ceremonial and ritual use were of no importance, it is reasonable to suppose that, once they were plucked, other body parts could have been utilized. The bones from wings and legs could have been saved as raw materials for tube manufacture [e.g., for turkey calls]. If prehistoric bird use was similar to that at Zuni Pueblo in the early 1960s, the prehistoric inhabitants of the northern and eastern peripheries of the Southwest, where great numbers of tubes were manufactured for trade to Plains Indians, may have been using birds for ceremonial and ritual use for commercial purposes.

Parsons's 1939 classic, mammoth, two-volume *Pueblo Indian Religion* is a must-read for Southwest Pueblo ethnology, yet as one of my major professors the late Charles H. Lange told me, almost no one can read it from beginning to end, nor would one want to do so. It provides an extended synthesis and discussion of the uses of macaw, parrot, and turkey feathers (along with other bird feathers), though readers must work their way back and forth from the index through the 1,275 pages of the two volumes. It is a massive compendium, and although its organizational structure is apparent, it is so densely written ("thick description") that it does not yield easily to anything but selective reading on specific topics.

Following the preface, table of contents, and list of illustrations, there is the 111-page introduction and nine chapters, some with subsections:

1. "Ceremonial Organization"
2. "The Spirits"
3. "Cosmic Notions, the Emergence, and the Next World"
4. "Ritual"
5. "Calendar"
   Hopi
   Zuni
   Keres [San Felipe, Cochití, Laguna, Acoma]
   Jemez
   Isleta
6. "Ceremonies"
7. "Review, Town by Town"
   Walpi
   Zuni
   Acoma
   Laguna
   Santo Domingo
   Cochití
   Sia [Zia]
   Jemez
   San Juan [now Ohkay Owingeh]
   Hano
   Isleta
   Taos
8. "Variation and Borrowing"
   Contacts and Loans
      Interpueblo
      Foreign
         California
         Yuman Peoples
         Pima-Papago [now Akimel O'odham–Tohono O'odham]
         Mayo-Yaqui: Tarahumara
         Cora-Huicholes
         Aztec

These chapters are followed by bibliographical notes, the bibliography, an appendix titled "Research Desirable in Pueblo Culture, as Indicated in Foregoing Commentaries," and a sixty-page index that is indispensable to the use of the two volumes.

There is a wealth of information in *Pueblo Indian Religion* about birds and the use of their images and feathers in specific ceremonies and on ceremonial paraphernalia, as well as Pueblo attitudes toward birds, the care and feeding of captive birds, and the sacrifice of eagles and other species. However, without the index, the information would be very difficult to track down except by reading the volumes page by page. With the index, the task is made much easier. For example, if one looks up "Bird(s)," there are about thirty page and illustration references to topics such as summer, orientated by direction, ritual feathers, and more. These are followed by references to specific birds: for example, Blue-jay, Crow, Eagle, and Hawk (1939:1220). However, one cannot rely completely on the "bird" category in the index. For example, there is no reference to turkey under "bird." One must look up "Turkey(s)" and "Turkey feather(s)" on pp. 1268–1269 to find dozens of page references for these two topics.

If one looks up "feather(s)," one finds about two dozen page references to topics such as boxes to hold feathers, down, feathers sewed to cloth, prayer feathers, and more, followed by references to species such as bluebird, duck, eagle, hawk, parrot, and turkey. Turning to the pages cited, one finds a few words or a brief sentence or two, or several pages of information. Finally, Parsons provides references to the works of others, some of whom she directly cites, and others to whom she refers the reader for details and more information.

The following quotation from pp. 270–271 typifies the wealth of detailed information that one finds in Parsons. The topic is the prayer stick, and this is but one of the hundreds of topics she covers in her *Pueblo Indian Religion*.

There is no ceremonial, as far as I know, outside of Tiwan and Tewan towns in which, in some connection, prayer-sticks are not offered or used. Indeed, it can be said that Pueblo ceremonial consists of prayer-stick making and offering together with prayer and other ritual [see Ladd 1963]. Buried in field or riverbank or riverbed; cast under shrub or tree or into pits; sunk in water, in springs, pools, lakes, river, or irrigation ditch; carried long distances to mountaintops; immured in house or kiva wall or closed-up niche; set under the floor or in the rafters, in cave or boulder or rock-built shrine; placed on altar or around image or corn fetish, as in the case of War Brother images of Zuni or of the Walpi image of Dawn Woman or of the corn fetish of Sia [Zia]; held in hand during ceremonial or cherished at home for a stated period or for life, prayer-sticks are used by members of all ceremonial groups, and in the West, by "poor persons," even by children.

At Zuni, "poor persons" offer or "plant" prayer-sticks to the dead, after a death in the family, at Shalako and at the solstices when women plant to the Moon, and men to the Sun and kachina, all these solstice sticks being placed in the middle of one's cornfield. At Shalako, all the men "plant" to the kachina. In certain house walls and in the houses where they are entertained, the kachina themselves enshrine prayer-sticks. In every ceremony kachina impersonators plant to those beings they imper-sonate, and four days before a dance the kiva chief sends prayer-sticks to the kachina chief asking him to dispatch the kachina. Society members "plant" at the solstices and periodically throughout the year to deceased members, to their fetishes and patrons, to the War Brothers, the Ants, Rattlesnake, Spider, or prey animals.

We will cut prayer-sticks for our father, Yellow Wolf, says the boy in the tale of the abandoned children. It won't do to have him living near us here. We shall have to send him away. So he cuts prayer-sticks and takes them to Wolf's house. One prayer-stick he gives to father Wolf, one to mother Wolf, one to the Wolf sons, one to the Wolf daughters. Father Wolf he bids go to the north, mother Wolf to the west, the boys to the south, their two little sisters, to the east. That is why today wolves are in the hills in every direction.

About to take a journey of importance, a Zuni man might offer prayer-sticks, or they would be offered for him. Parsons's discussion of prayer sticks continues on through page 285 and is followed by almost fifteen pages about prayer feathers, sometimes referred to as prayer plumes. Parsons (1939:285–291) notes that prayer feathers are even more numerous than prayer sticks. Not only do these pages rein-force the importance of feathers among the Pueblos, but they also help explain why so many feathers are needed. As discussed above in this volume, large numbers of feathers are used only once: for example, to make prayer sticks and prayer feath-ers that are "planted" or placed at shrines and other sacred locations and left to deteriorate naturally, thus requiring that new feathers be obtained to make new prayer sticks and prayer plumes, a continuing process throughout a person's life. And while this long section on prayer sticks provides much detailed information, a check of "prayer-stick(s)" in the index (Parsons 1939:1254–1255) provides another hundred or so general and specific references to the topic. Feathers are at the core of Pueblo religious and other cultural activities.

Tyler (1979:16–45) devotes chapter 2 to "birds of the sun"—macaws, parrots, and parakeets[15]—a general synthesis of their use among the Pueblos. Tyler states, "There is never a single theme for any bird, but macaws and their relatives are first of all for the Sun. . . . The multicolored plumage of macaws is also directly related to the many colors found on ears of Indian corn" (1979:16). This color association, in turn, echoes what I wrote earlier, that the first imports of macaws probably occurred in conjunction with the early appearance of corn, another Mesoamerican import. Furthermore, the Scarlet Macaw has bright red (or red-orange) center tail feathers, and red is identified with the south direction and, notably for the Hopi, with "the Red Land of the South," which, in turn, is associated specifically with the Sun (Tyler 1979:24), and from which place many other Mesoamerican traits were derived (Reyman 1995a). What is more, among the late Alex Seowtewa's murals in the restored mission church Our Lady of Guadalupe at Zuni Pueblo, there is one painting showing the religious official in front of the Sha'lako figure and wearing a ceremonial shirt with the colors of the rainbow on his shoulder (figure 2.5), just as the Scarlet Macaw's shoulder covert colors are a rainbow (figure 2.6). The symbolic color association is obvious. Schwartz et al. (2022) devote an entire volume—*Birds of the Sun*—to this topic.

In summary, macaw and parrot feathers have been essential to Pueblo ceremonial for more than a thousand years and continue to be essential today. The same is true for wild turkey feathers. Bird feathers are ceremonial requisites—necessities—and were the basic reason for the creation of the Feather Distribution Project. Given the importance and high value the Pueblos place on macaw and parrot feathers, as demonstrated above, it is surprising, at least from my perspective, that they don't take better care of the birds they have by refraining from plucking them to the point that some birds are almost denuded of feathers. It is also surprising that the macaw given by Judd to the Zuni Sun Priest lived as long as it did under the highly adverse conditions in which it was kept. Perhaps if the Pueblos had more macaws and parrots, they would treat them better, but I doubt it. The feathers are so valuable, and the numbers they require are so large, that it's unlikely they would ever have enough to rely only on molted feathers. Feathers received from the Feather Distribution Project took pressure off Pueblo bird owners to pluck their birds, but the temptation was always there, especially as important ceremonial occasions approached for

Figure 2.5. The late Alex Seowtewa's Sha'lako mural, Our Lady of
Guadalupe Mission Church, Zuni Pueblo.

which more feathers were needed. In the past, such as when Judd gave the macaw
to Zuni, such a facility as outlined in appendix A was not feasible; today it was a
possible solution to the ongoing problem of not enough macaw and parrot feathers
to meet Pueblo needs for them. However, so far the Pueblos have not committed
the necessary resources to make it a reality, nor have they been willing to discuss
seriously the possibility of assuming responsibility for the operation of the Feather
Distribution Project.

Figure 2.6. Scarlet Macaw (*Ara macao*) shoulder covert feathers.

DUCKS AND GEESE

Although ducks and geese are well represented in both the archaeological and ethnographic literature for the American Southwest (e.g., Ladd 1963; C. Lange 1959; Tyler 1979; Hill 1982; McCusick 2001), the Feather Distribution Project distributed few feathers from these birds, probably not more than 1,500–2,000 and mostly Canada Goose (*Branta canadensis*). Nevertheless, we created a fact sheet for ducks, for distribution to duck-hunting groups, and also to zoos and wildlife parks, in an attempt to obtain more duck feathers (figure 2.7). It resulted in a few donations of duck feathers, all from zoos and wildlife parks.

Canada Goose feathers were distributed to only three Pueblos and were the only feathers we were told had been received in sufficient numbers, and we were asked not to send more until requested. The last request was several years before the Project ended in 2015, so however they were used, they were not used in large numbers. At Santa Clara, the Canada Goose (*ka^{n}gi*) was highly prized as food, and its feathers were used in arrow fletching (Hill 1982:55). I did not know if this was still the case, and we never distributed Canada Goose feathers to Santa Clara.

Duck katsina masks are present at several Pueblos such as among the Hopi, where the Duck katsina is called Pawik (Colton 1949:38; see also Stephen 1936). At Cochití, the *Waiyosh* (Duck Dance) was held often, and the Duck mask is a helmet type (C. Lange 1959:469, 498, fig. 32d). The information given the Feather

TABLE 2.1. Ducks and geese used by the Pueblos

Ducks (alphabetical order)

American Coot (*Fulica americana*; duck-like, but not a duck, although considered a duck by the Pueblos)

American Wigeon (*Anas Americana*)

Blue-winged Teal (*Anas discors*)

Bufflehead (*Bucephala albeola*)

Canvasback (*Aythya valisineria*)

Cinnamon Teal (*Anas cyanoptera*)

Common Goldeneye (*Bucephala clangula*)

Common Merganser (*Mergus merganser*)

Gadwall (*Anas strepera*)

Green-winged Teal (*Anas carolinensis*)

Hooded Merganser (*Lophodytes cucullatus*)

Mallard Duck (*Anas platyrhynchos*)

Northern Pintail (*Anas acuta*)

Red-breasted Merganser (*Mergus serrator*)

Redhead (*Aythya americana*)

Ring-necked Duck (*Aythya collaris*)

Ruddy Duck (*Oxyura jamaicensis*)

Wood Duck (*Aix sponsa*)

Geese (alphabetical order)

Canada Goose (*Branta canadensis*)

Snow Goose (*Chen caerulescens*)

White-fronted Goose (*Anser albifrons*)

Distribution Project was that most duck and goose feathers were used in prayer sticks and in other types of ritual paraphernalia such as feather bundles, as discussed by Ladd (1963) for Zuni. How they are used differed from one village to another, and there did not seem to be a general pattern. Pairs of whole duck wings were sometimes seen on the sides of katsina masks (the same is true for turkey wings). I've seen duck feathers used in head bundles worn by boys and men during dances, and I've noted them in a wide variety of ceremonial objects throughout the Pueblos, but again, we did not distribute large numbers of either duck or goose feathers.

Table 2.1 lists the species of ducks and geese most commonly used by the Pueblos, and figure 2.7 was a fact sheet provided by the Feather Distribution Project to hunters and zoos when duck feathers were requested. The species listed on both are incomplete listings (cf. Tyler 1979:272), but much of the literature that notes the use of ducks and geese does so without providing species names. Other water birds such as the Great Blue Heron (*Ardea herodias*) and the Sandhill Crane (*Grus canadensis*) are specifically recorded as important in the archaeological and ethnographic literature, but these are federally protected species, the feathers from which the Project neither collected nor distributed.

Ducks and geese habitats were probably a factor in why so few duck and goose feathers were requested by the Pueblos. If one checks Peterson (1990), it is clear that ducks and geese, except for the Mallard (*Anas platyrhynchos*) and, to a lesser extent, the Canada Goose (*Branta canadensis*), are not generally found year-round in the present-day Pueblo area. Despite the fact that the Hopi have a duck katsina (Pawik), ducks are uncommon in the Hopi area. A few may occasionally turn up around a spring, but the lack of ponds and lakes in the Hopi area means the generally arid environment is unsuitable for ducks and geese. It is possible that the duck katsina may have been introduced to the Hopi from outside the villages, just as the Hopi Sha'lako katsina is an introduction from Zuni, with whom many Hopi resided during nineteenth-century measles and other disease epidemics at the Hopi mesas.

The Zuni Reservation has lakes, and Acoma has a few, mostly seasonal, ponds at which ducks and geese are sometimes found. I don't know whether ducks ever visited the cisterns on the top of Acoma's mesa, but it is a possibility. Laguna Pueblo, to the east of Acoma, is named for a small nearby lake ("laguna" means "small lake" in Spanish), and the Eastern Pueblos along the Rio Grande River and its tributaries all have greater access to waterfowl, so it's not surprising that duck and goose feathers have been requested by most Pueblos, except the Hopi. However, the requests were infrequent, and as noted, the Feather Distribution Project provided a minuscule number of them in comparison to wild turkey, macaw, and parrot feathers.

OTHER BIRDS

Among the more commonly requested feathers by Native American Church members were those from the Anhinga (*Anhinga anhinga*), which is a prominently featured motif in peyote ritual paraphernalia. It, too, is federally protected by the Migratory Bird Treaty Act (see appendix C), so we neither requested its feathers from zoos and wildlife parks, nor would we have distributed the feathers if we received them. They would go into our Museum ornithological study collection. This is a moot point, however, because we never received any.

Perusal of the birds listed in appendix C reveals dozens not native to the Pueblo area and many which are native but whose feathers are of no interest to the Pueblos, past or present: for example, the Mexican Whip-poor Will (*Antrostomus arizonae*), though Tyler (1979:178–180) mentions the Whip-poor Will as a night bird, especially with regard to the Hopi. Other birds are of great interest for their feathers among the present-day Pueblos (see Tyler 1979:271–277), for example, the Scrub Jay (*Aphelocoma californica*), the Pinyon Jay (*Gymnorhinus cyanocephalus*), Steller's Jay (*Cyanocitta stelleri*), and the various flickers (*Colaptes auratus*) and woodpeckers (*Picoides* sp.), and especially the Greater Roadrunner (*Geococcyx californianus*), and all are found in archaeological sites in the Southwest (McKusick 2001:7–10). Therefore, their importance presumably extends back one thousand years or more. Because these birds are all protected species under the Migratory Bird Treaty Act, the Feather Distribution Project did not provide their feathers to the Pueblos or any other group, even though some Pueblo peoples have a right to possess and use them. Occasionally, feather donors collected such feathers from the ground and

FOUNDER: Jonathan E. Reyman, Ph.D.

ORIGIN DATE: 1982

PURPOSE: To provide duck wings and feathers to the Pueblo Indians of the American Southwest for traditional cultural practices. The Pueblos have used ducks for more than 1,000 years in these rituals. Zuni Pueblo in western New Mexico still uses the largest numbers of duck wings, tail feathers, and whole body carcasses (except for heads and feet), and with 11,000 people, there is a high demand for duck wings and feathers.

    Many duck species are used, especially Mallard and Wood Duck, but the following are also needed: American Wigeon; Black-bellied Whistler; Canvasback; Common Goldeneye; Common Merganser; Gadwall; Lesser Scaup; Northern Pintail; Northern Shoveler; Ruddy Duck; Bufflehead; and Teals (Blue-winged, Cinnamon, Green-winged).

FEATHER SOURCES: Hunters, zoos, rehab facilities.

PERSONNEL: Jonathan E. Reyman and volunteers.

RESULTS: Since 1982, the Project has distributed about 9,000,000 wild turkey, macaw, parrot, and duck feathers *free-of-charge* to all 31 Pueblos.

DONATIONS: For ducks, the need is especially for whole wings, preferably in pairs, and also feathers. Please dry the wing *thoroughly* before shipping. One method is, after removal, to place the joint end of the wing in borax for 30–45 days.

SEND FEATHERS TO: Dr. Jonathan E. Reyman
Illinois State Museum
Research & Collections Center
1011 East Ash Street
Springfield, IL 62703-3500
(217) 785-0069
E-mail: reyman@museum.state.il.us

THE PROJECT NEITHER BUYS NOR SELLS FEATHERS. Shipping costs are reimbursed unless otherwise directed.

Figure 2.7. The Feather Distribution Project duck fact sheet.

sent them to us, but these were placed in our study collections. The same was true if we received such feathers from a zoo or other institution. A number of zoos that donated feathers to the Project have Greater Roadrunners (*Geococcyx californianus*), but we specifically requested they not send the feathers to us.

    Macaws and parrots are not migratory and are not listed under the Migratory Bird Treaty Act, but they are listed in the Convention on International Trade in Endangered Species of Wild Fauna and Flora (CITES) as protected species. The

Feather Distribution Project had a permit from the US Fish and Wildlife Service, so we could distribute macaw and parrot feathers received from zoos and other organizations.

One interesting feather substitution among several Pueblos is worth noting. Many Pueblos used the tail feathers from the Northern Cardinal (*Cardinalis cardinalis*) for prayer sticks and for other ceremonial objects. Cardinal tail feathers became increasingly difficult to obtain, and several individuals at one Pueblo requested the tail feathers from the African Grey Parrot (*Psittacus erithacus*), which they used as a substitute for cardinal tail feathers. This is the only such example, of which I was aware, of a specific substitution. The use of cardinal tail feathers may also be a relative recent development, because cardinal remains are not reported from archaeological sites by McKusick (2001:7–10), nor are they depicted in murals at Awatovi, Kawaika-a, Kuaua, Pottery Mound, or elsewhere.

Of the species listed in table 2.1, the most commonly requested were the Mallard Duck (*Anas platyrhynchos*) and the Wood Duck (*Aix sponsa*), yet neither species was frequently asked for; we rarely received more than a half dozen requests a year, and then only for small numbers of duck feathers. The majority of duck feathers were sent to Zuni, where men especially prized Mallard Duck feathers because their blue-green color resembles the color of turquoise (Ladd 1963), the Pueblo godstone (Reyman 1995a).

The sharp contrast between the importance of duck and goose feathers in the literature and the low number of requests over the thirty-four-year history of the Feather Distribution Project might have reflected changing cultural patterns among the Pueblos. Like the discussion earlier about turkey burials in Ancestral Pueblo sites and the lack of knowledge about the practice among present-day Pueblo peoples, the few requests for duck and geese feathers could have signaled that the need for such feathers had diminished or was dying out. It could also have indicated a decline in local duck and geese populations, but this decline had happened with local wild turkey populations, especially in the area around the Hopi villages, without affecting the large number of requests for wild turkey feathers. Finally, the offer of whole duck wings at one village brought a quick response such that the many dozens of wings were completely distributed in a matter of minutes. Generally, however, that so few requests were made for duck and geese feathers was puzzling.

3

The Genesis of the Feather Distribution Project

As a graduate student at Southern Illinois University–Carbondale (SIUC), I was required to take the written general examinations, and later the oral special examination, for admission to candidacy as a doctoral student. I took and passed the general examination in the spring of 1968, and immediately thereafter left with one of my professors, the late Dr. Joel Maring, for a brief period of linguistic fieldwork at Acoma Pueblo. On our return trip to Carbondale, we stopped in Santa Fe to attend the annual meeting of the Society for American Archaeology. While there, Dr. Charles H. Lange, Chair of the Department of Anthropology, informed me that I had passed my exams and had done so well that the department was prepared to provide a graduate fellowship for me to study with Dr. Walter W. Taylor, in Santa Fe, concentrating on the archaeology and ethnology of the American Southwest. I accepted, though not without some reservations; Taylor was known to be a difficult graduate advisor (see various essays in Maca, Reyman, and Folan 2010) who, in his years at Carbondale, successfully mentored only three PhD students.

My first task, after moving to Santa Fe and installing myself in Taylor's library at his home, was to compile, as per his instructions, a bibliography of the archaeology, ethnology, ethnography, ethnohistory, linguistics, and social anthropology for the American Southwest. A couple of months later, I had done this and had entered all the archaeological sites I had found on a series of maps of the Southwest. Taylor then instructed me to read the approximately 2,200 bibliographic entries I had compiled and to take notes on them. I was also directed to visit as many

https://doi.org/10.5876/9781646427543.c003

archaeological sites as possible, to visit all the Pueblos, and to observe as many ceremonies as I could. Fortunately, the fellowship provided sufficient funds to do so.
Two other SIUC faculty, Dr. Charles H. Lange and Dr. Carroll L. Riley, who would
eventually become members of my doctoral dissertation committee, provided me
with introductions to several Pueblo individuals at Cochití, Santa Clara, and Zuni.
I made additional acquaintances on my visits to the Pueblos and during events such
as the Indian Market in Santa Fe. Of these, as will be discussed shortly, the most
important acquaintance, who later became a good friend, was the late Fernando
(Fred) Cordero of Cochití, to whom I had been introduced by Lange, and I also
met Fred's wife, Helen, the famed creator of the Storyteller figures, at their house in
the village during the annual Corn Dance.

During my attendance at Pueblo ceremonies from Taos to Hopi, the importance
of feathers was immediately obvious, and my reading of the archaeological reports
and the ethnographic and ethnohistoric accounts made it clear that the importance
of feathers had great antiquity; birds and their feathers had been essential for more
than a millennium and still were essential to Pueblo religious life. It also became
apparent, in the case of macaws and parrots, that trade with Mesoamerica and later
with what became Mexico was the source of these feathers. So I was not completely
unprepared for what was to come, though I was unprepared as to how to respond
and to comply with the request.

Let me reiterate what others have said or written: good science often proceeds
from good questions, and the role of imagination is also critically important. As
Albert Einstein once said: "Imagination is more important than knowledge. For
knowledge is limited to all we now know and understand, while imagination
embraces the entire world, and all there ever will be to know and understand."

FEAST DAY, COCHITÍ PUEBLO, NEW MEXICO: 14 JULY 1970

The Corn Dance at the annual Cochití Pueblo Feast Day is over.[16] Hundreds of
other people, Anglos and Indians alike, are still present. Scarlet Macaw (*Ara macao*)
and Blue-and-Yellow Macaw (*Ara ararauna*) tail feathers are prominently displayed,
proof that the Cochití (and other Pueblos as well) use these feathers in traditional
religious ceremonies, as they have for a millennium or more.

As I prepare to leave the pueblo, a short, wiry, late-middle-aged man approaches.
I know him: Fred Cordero had first been introduced to me a couple of years earlier
by one of my professors, Dr. Charles H. Lange. Fred and I talk briefly about the
dance and Feast Day, and then Fred asks me, "Can you get us macaw feathers?"

"No. I don't know where to get them. Sorry."

"It's okay. Possibly you will think of something."

The critical question had been asked—the impetus in 1970 to "action anthropology" (now called "applied anthropology") and the eventual creation of the Feather Distribution Project.

HILLSIDE PET SHOP, OTTAWA, ILLINOIS: 2 FEBRUARY 1982

I'm in the Hillside Pet Shop to buy rawhide chew bones for my Brittany Spaniel. In one corner of the shop, there's a sign, "Corby's Corner," and beneath it, behind a barrier, perches a gorgeous Scarlet Macaw. The floor is littered with feathers. Immediately, Fred Cordero's question from 1970 pops into my mind.

I pay for the bones, introduce myself to the shop owner, and ask, "What do you do with Corby's feathers?"

"Why?"

I explain that Pueblo Indians in New Mexico and Arizona use them and other feathers in their religious ceremonies and have for over a thousand years. Bob Streul, the shop owner, tells me he throws away Corby's feathers.

"Would you save them for me to give to the Pueblos?"

"Yes."

I leave the store with several dozen Scarlet Macaw and Amazon parrot feathers. Bob and his wife, Diane, also provide the names and telephone numbers of area macaw and parrot breeders they know from whom I might obtain additional feathers. I call and meet with them, and within a couple of months, I've acquired several hundred macaw and Amazon parrot feathers.

FRED AND HELEN CORDERO'S HOME, COCHITÍ PUEBLO: 24 JUNE 1982

In June 1982, while on a brief research trip to New Mexico, I visit Fred Cordero at his home in Cochití. He had first requested the feathers at Feast Day on 14 July 1970. His wife, Helen, the Pueblo potter who created the first Storyteller pottery figurines, is also home. After mutual greetings, much talk (I've learned nothing happens quickly on visits to Pueblo homes), and a meal of chile, Pueblo oven bread, and peach pie, Fred and I go into another room while Helen cleans up the dishes. She then leaves the house to visit her sister. This is to be men's work, and among the Keres Pueblos, women customarily are not in the room, and often not even in the house, during such activities. I hand Fred the long, brown-wrapped, lightweight package containing several hundred (±400) Scarlet Macaw, Blue-and-Yellow Macaw, and Amazon parrot tail and body contour feathers.

Fred opens the package, and his eyes widen at the contents. He exclaims "Ai-eeee" and takes a breath from the feathers to absorb their spiritual power. Then he thanks me, and says, as though the request had come only days before rather than twelve years earlier, "You thought of something."

The Feather Distribution Project has begun. It will remain the legacy of Fred Cordero's initial question for more than twenty years after Fred dies in 1994, shortly after Helen's death, also in 1994.

THE FEATHER DISTRIBUTION PROJECT

The Feather Distribution Project was founded in 1982. It was an applied anthropology program—"action anthropology" in Tax's (1952, 1975) usage, informed by both Ancestral Pueblo archaeology and Pueblo ethnology and ethnography. To the degree that archaeology is central to an understanding of the Project's basis for existence, it can also be considered an applied archaeology program. Indeed, when Fred Cordero's 1970 question, the original impetus for the Project, came to fruition in 1982 with the creation of the Feather Distribution Project, it's fair to say that the term "action anthropology" had fallen out of general usage, and that the Project was now subsumed within the field of applied anthropology.

One interesting aspect of the Project is that when I spoke at Pueblo villages about Ancestral Pueblo use of macaws and parrots, as understood through the archaeology, many Pueblo people in the audiences were generally unaware of the ancient context to their post-contact and current religious practices. They knew the use of macaws and parrots was old, that it had always been this way, and that it went back as long, or longer, than anyone alive could remember, but most were unaware of its great antiquity—the 1,000–1,500 years of use. This was made clear in a review of an earlier version of this manuscript by Dr. Joseph Suina of Cochití Pueblo (2024): "While we, I am Pueblo, have knowledge of our actual use of feathers, most of us do not know the origins of our practices." As such, Dr. Suina thought the book might find an audience among the Pueblos.

The Project had two main goals: first, to provide macaw, parrot, and wild turkey feathers to Pueblo Indians to help them maintain their traditional cultural practices and to help ensure their First Amendment right to freedom of religion under the United States Constitution (Native American Church members also received feathers for ritual use); and second, to eliminate, if possible, smuggling of endangered and threatened species of macaws and parrots, which in turn lessened destruction of native bird populations and habitats in Latin America. The Project did not distribute eagle or other raptor feathers. Eligible Indians may acquire these from the National Eagle Repository in Denver, and the Zuni have their own Zuni Eagle Sanctuary. As the Project evolved, a third goal developed: to eliminate the plucking of macaws and parrots by Pueblo people who own these birds. To foster

FEATHERS

BIRD	TYPE	COLORS*

MACAW: Tail: Red ___   Blue/Yellow___   Mixed Red & Blue/Red ___
                           Blue/Black ___   Mixed Red, Blue & Yellow/Yellow ___

                Wing: Blue/Red ___ Blue/Yellow ___ Blue/Black ___
                           Blue & Green/Red (small) ___
                           Blue & Green/Yellow (small) ___

                Body: Red ___ Blue ___ Yellow ___ Green ___ Multicolor ___

PARROT: Tail: Red ___ Green ___ Green & Green-Yellow ___ Multicolor ___

                Wing: Green & Black ___ Green, Black & Blue ___ Multicolor ___

* A split color combination (Blue/Red, Blue/Yellow, etc.) means that the top of the feather is blue, and the underside is red, yellow, or whatever color is indicated.

WILD TURKEY: Tail ___ Wing ___ Breast ___ Body ___ Beard ___

                    Other wild turkey feathers ___ (please specify below)

NOTES: If you have a special need for a particular macaw, parrot, or wild turkey feather, please let me know, and I'll try to obtain it. HOWEVER, IT IS ILLEGAL FOR ME TO SEND FEATHERS FROM EAGLES, HAWKS, OTHER RAPTORS, AND MIGRATORY BIRDS. I NEVER HAVE FEATHERS FROM THESE BIRDS.

         There is NO charge for feathers. They are a gift.

         NAME:

         ADDRESS:

         PHONE (OPTIONAL):

Figure 3.1. Feather request form: macaws, parrots, and wild turkeys.

this, as mentioned earlier, the Project provided twice as many feathers as the bird would molt in a year on the condition that the owner promised not to pluck the bird and to permit us to see the bird on visits to the house. During the Project's thirty-four-year existence, the bird owners—and only a few Pueblo people own macaws and parrots—who agreed to this provision kept their promises not to pluck their birds.[17] So though the Project benefited only a few birds in this regard, even a few was better than none.

Over thirty-four years (1982–2015), the Feather Distribution Project provided almost 15 million feathers free of charge to all thirty-two Pueblo villages in New

Figure 3.2. Turkey feather request diagram.

Mexico and Arizona (see note 3 and table 0.1 for the list of these villages). As stated on the feather request form (figure 3.1) and the Turkey feather request diagram (figure 3.2), the feathers were a gift; nothing was asked in return. If recipients provided us with ceremonial information, it was neither published nor otherwise disclosed, and the names of the recipients were confidential, even from other members of the same Pueblo, unless they allowed their names to be disclosed or there was some urgent reason to do so.

The Project neither bought nor sold feathers, and no macaws or parrots were plucked or killed to provide feathers; all macaw and parrot feathers were molted (or in two instances, the birds died and their feathers were removed). Zoos, bird owners, bird clubs, breeders, and rescue and rehabilitation facilities donated feathers (see acknowledgments). Hunters, particularly members of the National Wild Turkey Federation, donated wild turkey feathers, recycling a resource they would otherwise have discarded. Volunteers helped sort feathers for distribution. Almost all feathers were precious; even cut and damaged feathers were used. For example, the Sandia Pueblo man's head bundle (figure 3.3) is made entirely from cut macaw feathers. Conservation of resources was a key element in the Project.

The protection of birds extended to the relatively few macaws and parrots owned by Pueblo individuals. There are accounts cited above, and the photograph of the Military Macaw Judd gave to the Macaw clan at Zuni in 1924, of Pueblo-owned birds plucked for their feathers. This is painful to the bird and unhealthy because birds regulate their body temperature partly through their feathers. Indeed, it is possible that one reason there are so few adult macaws and parrots among the remains found in archaeological sites is that the birds became susceptible to disease and illness due to constant plucking and the lack of sunlight where they were housed.

Pueblo Indians applied to the Project and received forms to request feathers (figures 3.1 and 3.2). The earliest requests were made in person when I attended a dance or visited someone, as in the case of Fred Cordero. These were casual inquiries made before the Feather Distribution Project was established, and even after 1982, the requests were infrequent aside from Cochití. Later, as word of the Project spread, letters would arrive, more often written by women, who usually had clearer writing than men and often a better command of English; the women wrote on behalf of their husbands, sons, brothers, grandfathers, and other relatives, actual or ceremonial. Pueblo women rarely requested feathers for themselves.

The next development was requests for feathers via telephone calls. Then, as Pueblo individuals obtained computers and became increasingly internet-savvy, requests came via email, and the Project's web page was often the source for the initial contact. We then received more emails than written letters or telephone calls, from individuals requesting feathers, for the first time as well as for repeated requests, and smartphones were increasingly used. When we sent the request forms (see figures 3.1 and 3.2), to individuals, these were often photocopied and given to others, who then mailed them, faxed them, or scanned and sent them back to us with their specific feather requests. Modern technology served an ancient need.[18]

Because feathers were precious and valuable—as noted earlier, the feathers distributed without charge would have brought millions of dollars on the open market—some who received feathers as a gift, sold them. When we learned this, they no longer received feathers. This was an unfortunate consequence of the value of feathers, but it happened, and we became aware of a few instances. When this happened, we were always informed by other members of the Pueblo. It was instructive because it raised issues about how supply, demand, and value might have been mediated in ancient times as well as in the Spanish post-contact period in the Southwest. The ancient trade for feathers also raises questions—unanswerable for

Figure 3.3. Sandia Pueblo man's head bundle made from cut macaw and parrot feathers.

now—about what was traded for what (for example, turquoise for Scarlet Macaw tail feathers, salt, cotton textiles) and how the equivalencies were established, presumably through barter. Feathers were and are essential for Pueblo religious practices, and such a valuable commodity attracts interest and research, which will lead to a better understanding of Pueblo cultural history.

The Feather Distribution Project began slowly. In 1982 we provided about four thousand feathers, almost entirely macaw and parrot, to Cochití and then to Mishongnovi and Hotevilla. Each year, the number of feathers increased, and requests for wild turkey feathers quickly exceeded requests for macaw and parrot feathers. In April 1991, Larry Stone of the *Des Moines Register* published a brief notice requesting turkey feathers, and a second notice appeared in October 1991.

Between those two dates, Iowa hunters sent 75,000–80,000 wild turkey feathers. That same month, Gene Smith, then editor of *Turkey Call*, the magazine of the National Wild Turkey Federation, called me to say he wanted to publish an article in the magazine about the Project. It appeared in the January-February 1992 issue, and in the following year, the Project received 200,000 turkey feathers. By 1998, the total had swelled to about 2 million turkey feathers, and in the fall of 2013, we received the largest single donation of turkey feathers—approximately 235,000—from Mike Davis and his hunting partners in North Carolina. As of August 2014, we distributed more than 10 million wild turkey feathers and about 4.5 million macaw and parrot feathers free of charge to all thirty-two Pueblo villages.

It was noted earlier that the Project provided feathers to more than one thousand Pueblo people. For the sake of clarity, it must be noted that we did not send feathers *directly* to those thousand-plus people. We did send feathers to hundreds of individuals, but in many cases, we sent large quantities of feathers to a single person who then redistributed them to anywhere from a few individuals to dozens of individuals. In several villages, a person within a religious society sent a list of names and the feathers requested by each man. We took the list, packed the feathers in individual packages, and then sent a larger package containing all the individual requests to the person who had made and sent the list. This saved shipping costs and made the distribution work easier from our standpoint. Generally this worked well, although in one case, the man to whom we sent the package either sold or tried to sell the feathers. I was almost immediately notified by five men from the village;[19] the individual never received another feather from the Project, but I never learned what, if any, punishment he received within the village. In the past, depending on how such behavior was interpreted, for example as witchcraft, he might have been severely physically punished (see Cushing 1883:42–44).

PERKS

As noted on the request forms (figures 3.1 and 3.2), the feathers were a gift; nothing was asked in return. If asked what we would like in return, the answer was always prayers for good health. However, we occasionally received gifts from Pueblo or other Native American individuals, which were usually forwarded to those persons at zoos, bird clubs, and elsewhere who collected the feathers donated to the Project. We did receive other "gifts," for example, we were permitted to attend ceremonies, enjoy meals when visiting Pueblo homes, and were sometimes invited to spend the night or longer.

One memorable visit came several years ago at a Hopi village to which we had given feathers for more than fifteen years. As I sat watching the katsina dance, my host leaned over and asked what I thought of the dance, especially the feathers. I replied that I was impressed with the number and how they were being used. He said, "They're almost all yours." I was overwhelmed. On another occasion at the same village, I was invited to help men make objects, using wild turkey feathers, for distribution during a break in the dancing. I did as well as I could, learning to tie the feathers with a particular knot and other technical aspects of the work. The next day, it was gratifying to see the objects distributed among those Pueblo residents in attendance, especially when one of the objects I had made was publicly presented to me.

Another set of perks that have been extended on several occasions, though not directly to me, are meetings and tours at Pueblos for personnel from zoos that donated feathers. On occasions when the zoo personnel have attended professional meetings in Albuquerque and other Southwest venues, I have arranged for them to visit one or more Pueblos to meet Pueblo officials, tour the village, learn about environmental and conservation efforts in the village, and also about how the feathers they provided were used. This gave the zoo personnel greater insight into Pueblo life and a better understanding of the good they were doing by collecting feathers for distribution. The feedback was positive from both zoo personnel and Pueblo officials.

The greatest perk was the satisfaction that came with doing what we perceived to be the right thing. The Pueblos (and other Native Americans) were not well treated by the invading Spanish and the Euro-American cultures that followed. Anthropologists, too, have not always treated them well, imposing on their time and space, recording secret information, and then publishing it (e.g., Cushing 1882, 1883; Stevenson 1904; Bunzel 1932a, 1932b, 1932c; White 1932; Parsons 1932, 1939). One reaction to anthropologists, specifically to Cushing, is found in the 1994 volume of cartoons by the late Zuni artist Phil Hughte, and the Zuni with whom I've spoken over the years about Cushing are of decidedly mixed minds about him; Cushing remains a controversial figure, and the same can be said for other anthropologists. By contrast, the Project deliberately asked nothing in return for feathers, I never published sacred information acquired during the course of the Project, and I never will.

Another perk was an unintended consequence. The Illinois State Museum (ISM) has a moderately large collection of ethnographic objects from the Southwest. Some of these are almost certainly subject to repatriation under Native American Graves Protection and Repatriation Act (NAGPRA). Yet the ISM was never asked to repatriate a single Pueblo object, largely, I think, because of the Feather Distribution Project and the benefit it provided for Pueblo peoples, some of whom sat on their tribal cultural conservation boards or committees.

A final perk was the willingness of Pueblo people to participate in programs at the ISM and at conferences where the Museum organized seminars and symposia.

Pueblo artists came to the main Museum facility in Springfield, to its satellite museum at Dickson Mounds, Illinois, and to our Lockport Gallery, Illinois, to give presentations and conduct workshops for the public. Pueblo men participated in conference symposia such as the one in 2006, titled "Building Bridges: The Illinois State Museum and Four Communities," at the Joint Conference of the Association of Midwest Museums, the Illinois Association of Museums, and the Iowa Museum Association in Davenport, Iowa; a second symposium occurred in 2007, "Native American and Museum Collaborations: The Feather Distribution Project," at the Annual Meeting of the American Association of Museums (now the American Alliance of Museums) held in Chicago.

I want to recount a funny, almost embarrassing incident that happened at one village where we distributed many thousands of feathers. This occurred before Laura began to accompany me on my trips.

I was in the home of a host family with whom I had stayed on several occasions. One afternoon, the family of the man to whom I had been giving feathers and who lived in his wife's mother's house came for a visit to also receive feathers. With them was a young woman, one of their daughters, sister of the man I was giving feathers to, who was quite lovely and, as I learned, unmarried. As we talked around the dining table, her mother not so subtly asked if I had a wife. I said, "Yes," and asked why? She said it had been the practice in past times for men to have more than one wife. I replied, "Not in my family."

After dinner, they left, and my friend said the *real* purpose in their coming was their hope that I would be attracted to their daughter, his sister, so we could be married, and I would be obligated to give them *all* the feathers. To think of exchanging their daughter for feathers gives a strong indication of the importance of feathers within this Pueblo family, which was high-ranking ceremonially.

FEATHER CARE

As discussed, some feathers were used only once, especially wild turkey body feathers on prayer sticks and prayer plumes, which were placed at shrines and other locations with prayers for blessings and then allowed to deteriorate naturally. Other feathers, however, especially macaw and parrot tails and whole turkey fans, were used time and again. With care, and a little luck, they could last for decades. However, they could and did suffer damage from use; for example, long Scarlet Macaw and other macaw center tails on katsina masks could break when subjected to strong winds during the outdoor portions of the dance.

Probably the greatest threat to feathers was damage from insects such as mites and dermestids, both small arthropods, which eat feathers. To preserve feathers, at least on a short-terms basis, some Pueblo men use feather holders made of willow sticks tied together with leather strips and cotton string. This keeps feathers flat but offers no real protection from insects. A more common method, one frequently reported in the literature (e.g., Parsons 1939; C. Lange 1959), is the manufacture and use of wooden boxes with tightly fitted lids to hold the feathers. These are made from various woods but most often from Alligator Juniper (*Juniperus deppeana*). It's believed that the odor from the oil in the wood repels insects and keeps feathers safe. When asked how best to preserve feathers, my answer was to put them in sealable plastic bags and place them in a freezer. Since masks and other paraphernalia are often disassembled after use, this is a workable solution in most Pueblo villages that have refrigerators with freezers and freestanding freezers.

Feathers received from donors were sometimes damaged. The most common damage was frayed ends on tail feathers and cracked or broken quills. Frayed ends were treated by carefully cutting away the damaged portion and trimming the end so it resumed its naturally rounded shape, albeit a bit shorter than it was originally. One Pueblo didn't use feathers with broken quills because they believed the power of the feathers had been lost. The other Pueblos mended the broken end, usually by inserting a straw or a small twig in the end and binding the quill to reinforce it.

Feathers that aren't exactly straight can be straightened by steaming them directly or by placing them on a flat surface with a pressing cloth over them to prevent scorching, then using a steam iron set on "low" to straighten them. Another, older technique, was to place the feathers on a bed of warm sand and cover it with more warm sand, then leave it for a few minutes, or longer; this usually straightened the feathers. Feathers were precious, and no one wanted to waste them. These techniques were used by both Pueblo peoples and members of the Native American Church, and probably by others as well.

RESPONSES

One of the more troubling and frustrating aspects of the Feather Distribution Project was the lack of response by feather recipients—Pueblo, Native American Church (NAC) members, and other nations and tribes. It was troubling because when we didn't hear from recipients, we didn't know if the feathers had been received. In a number of instances over the years, we followed up with the question of whether the feathers had arrived, and sometimes were told they didn't. In one village, we learned that boxes with our shipping label were being stolen by one or more individuals who knew they contained feathers. In another instance, a NAC member rented a post office box because feathers sent to his home were apparently stolen by the proverbial "porch pirates" when left at the front door before he came home from work. The most frustrating aspect, however, was that in more than 90 percent of the cases, we heard nothing from recipients until they asked for more feathers. I understood that some people did not feel the need to say "thank you," but it was frustrating nonetheless not to know whether the feathers arrived. In the most extreme example, we shipped more than forty boxes of wild turkey feathers over an eight-year period and only heard twice from the person to whom they were sent on behalf of the group, both times when he asked for another large donation of specific feathers. Even the last shipment, of almost 25,000 wild turkey feathers in 2015, which contained an enclosed letter stating that it would be the last shipment and explaining why, brought no response. I found it difficult not to interpret the situation as indicating a sense of entitlement on the part of the recipient such that even a brief "thank you" was unnecessary.

The same sense of entitlement permeated behavior by other Native Americans, Pueblo Indians and non–Pueblo Indians alike: phone calls and emails were received stating that feathers were needed, with the apparent expectation that they would be sent immediately. Such entitlement behavior increased as the years went by, during which individuals received packages of feathers somewhat regularly.

This is not to say we never received thanks, and as I wrote earlier in this volume, we did sometimes receive jewelry, pottery, and other gifts as thanks for the feathers, gifts which were usually (if not personalized to either me or my wife) passed on to those who collected and provided feathers to the Project. But such gifts were the exception and not a general practice.

4

The Peoples Served

In an ideal world, the Project provided feathers to any and all Native Americans who requested them. But this wasn't an ideal world, and some Native peoples were specifically excluded. We did not provide feathers to those who would use them for commercial gain: for example, those who used feathers to make craft objects such as dream catchers, katsina dolls, jewelry, decorative objects, and the like. We also did not provide feathers to powwow dancers who perform for prize money,[20] nor did we provide feathers to Native American Church members who made fans and other paraphernalia for sale to other members or to the public. However, in 2001 we provided a variety of feathers not normally used by the Pueblos or other Native Americans to "Kows for Kids," a public art project in Portland, Oregon.[21] The Project was to raise funds for a nonprofit program to provide shelter and services for homeless children in the city. Katherine Ace, a local artist, requested feathers to decorate a life-size cow to display in the city, the cow to be eventually sold to raise funds for the program. We provided a number of feathers from commercial white turkeys and from non-American birds such as the Tawny Frogmouth (*Podargus strigoides*), an Australian and Tasmanian species. Her cow was named "Cow-mingled—A Cow-calf-ony of Cow-mingled Creatures."[22]

In some cases, people requested feathers in such large numbers that the request exceeded our capacity to provide them at the moment, or even in the near future, though we provided large numbers of wild turkey feathers to Pueblos when the request came at the height of, or just after, the fall and spring hunting seasons: for

https://doi.org/10.5876/9781646427543.c004

example, 25 pairs of whole wild turkey wings, and 1,500 individual wing feathers. About twenty years ago, an elderly Iowa hunter gave up turkey hunting, and donated his collection of 108 tail fans and 108 pairs of wings to the Project. We accepted these with gratitude and gave them all to a Second Mesa Hopi village to make all new ceremonial masks and other ritual paraphernalia. No one in the village could remember receiving such a singular bounty.

In one unusual instance, we received a call from a woman in Red Bud, Illinois, who was retiring from her craft business and wanted to know whether we could use her thousands of remaining feathers. I said we could, and made the roughly two-hour drive to her home. There were thousands of feathers, all commercial white turkey feathers that were dyed acid green and various neon fluorescent colors. We took them though they wouldn't be of use to Pueblo and NAC members; we donated them, instead, to the Native American Dance Theater, which accepted them and used them for "flash" in their costumes.

THE SOUTHWESTERN PUEBLOS

The Feather Distribution Project was created in 1982 in response to Fred Cordero's request to provide macaw feathers to Cochití Pueblo. In the time that followed, we provided feathers to Zia, Acoma, and most Hopi villages. The Project expanded its coverage until, by 2012, all thirty-two Pueblo villages had received feathers (see table 0.1).

The growth of the Project first developed informally. I had friends at Zia and Acoma and offered feathers to them. A colleague who attended a NAGPRA conference at the University of Colorado mentioned the Project to several Hopi officials in attendance, and requests for feathers soon followed; these same officials passed the word to other Hopi. Charles H. Lange, who initially introduced me to Fred Cordero, also had several friends at Zuni to whom he mentioned the Project, and these Zuni soon requested feathers. Pojoaque and Santa Ana became feather recipients through men I had met from those villages. Fred and Helen Cordero's daughter married a man at San Felipe, and feather distribution spread to that Pueblo. I wrote earlier that we arranged to distribute some 200,000 wild turkey feathers at one village, and approximately three hundred people showed up to receive them. Before this distribution in 1999, I gave a short slide presentation about the Project. After the distribution, I had collected well over a hundred names and addresses of people who wanted request forms (see figures 3.1 and 3.2) and to be put on the list to receive macaw and parrot feathers, as well as wild turkey. That same year, at Sandia, someone obtained a copy of the request forms, and within a matter of days, seventy men had mailed or faxed their requests for feathers to us. In two to three months, the number of individual requests swelled the roll of feather recipients. A year or so later, my friend Kathleen Grayson Smith developed a website for the Feather Distribution Project, which resulted in an enormous increase in new requests both from pueblos that had not previously received feathers and from pueblos where feathers had been distributed for years. The website also helped generate hundreds of new feather donors: zoos, bird clubs, veterinary clinics, and individual bird owners. By 2012, all thirty-two pueblos were receiving feathers.

Although the peoples are grouped together by the term "pueblo," the pueblos are diverse cultures. Six distinct languages are spoken among the thirty-two villages: Tiwa, Tewa, Towa, Keres, Zuni, and Hopi, and Keres is further divided into eastern (Cochití, Santo Domingo, San Felipe, Santa Ana, and Zia) and western variations (Laguna and Acoma). Kinship systems run the gamut from matrilineal to bilateral to patrilineal; some Pueblos have moieties, others don't; some have strong clans, others have weak ones or claim not to have clans; some have strong centralized village political structures, others are less centralized. These and other variations have long been noted and discussed in the literature (see, e.g., Kroeber 1917; Eggan 1950; Fox 1967; and Dozier 1970). I knew of this cultural diversity from my educational experience beginning in graduate school and continuing through my professional career. From the outset of the Project in 1982, Puebloan cultural diversity was immediately reinforced in my interactions with people and has continued to be reinforced throughout the thirty-four years of operation. Therefore, it was no surprise that feather requirements differ markedly from one Pueblo to another.

It's useful to take a moment to discuss the differences between the Eastern and Western Pueblos and how these differences affected the distribution of feathers and my own relationships with Pueblo people. As noted earlier, the first Spanish entrada (perhaps better termed an invasion) was in 1539 at the Zuni ancestral village of Hawikku. Led by Fray Marcos di Niza, the event ended badly for the Spanish when their demands were rejected and they were driven back to Mexico. Although the Spanish later established missions at Zuni, at the Hopi village of Awatovi, and the other two Western Pueblos of Acoma and its satellite village of Laguna, the Spanish presence was heavier among the Eastern Pueblo situated along the Rio Grande River and its tributaries. The Spanish presence in the East was so oppressive that the Pueblo Revolt of 1680, which began among the Eastern Pueblos and eventually spread to the Western Pueblos, drove the Spaniards back to Mexico City. They did not return to the Pueblo area until the Reconquest of 1692–1694. Again, their presence was much more pronounced in the east than in the west. And as Robin Fox demonstrates in his seminal book, *The Keresan Bridge* (1967), the Keres-speaking Pueblos provide the link between the eastern and western villages.

One consequence of this culture history is that the Eastern Pueblos are more closed to outsiders than the Western Pueblos, which meant that for the Feather Distribution Project, I was only permitted to stay overnight in two eastern villages, but I was able to stay overnight in almost every western village, and stay longer and more often. I was also permitted in society houses and kivas in some western villages, but never among the eastern villages. In the west, I participated in making ceremonial items for katsina ceremonies, but not in the east. I was given a special place at ceremonies in some western villages, for example, at Zuni Sha'lako, but was just one among hundreds of onlookers in the eastern villages. And I was never permitted to observe a katsina ceremony in the Eastern Pueblos, even when they were using feathers from the Project, but I saw dozens of katsina ceremonies at Zuni and Hopi.

When we distributed feathers among the Eastern Pueblos, women left the houses because such distribution was "men's work." By contrast, at Zuni and Hopi, women were often present as onlookers though they did not participate in the actual distribution other than providing their homes (Zuni and Hopi are matrilineal and matrilocal). When the distribution at Cochití shifted from Fred Cordero to J. D. Pecos, J. D.'s wife Caroline would leave the house after the meal, just as Helen, Fred Cordero's wife, did in their house. The same was true when I distributed feathers to Turquoise Kiva (moiety) members at Cochití. During one visit to Santo Domingo, I was invited for a meal, but when I went to my vehicle to bring in the feathers, all the women in the house left. All Pueblos, east and west, were hospitable, but the Western Pueblos were more ceremonially open once I had earned their trust that sacred information would not be divulged by me. Again, the Keresan bridge was at work in the east-west divide in that I stayed with families at Acoma, I was shown the embedded kivas when I visited the mesa-top pueblo, but I was never allowed inside a kiva. At Hotevilla, I briefly worked on construction of a new kiva. This should suffice to illustrate some of the important east-west differences, and while these differences affected how the Project functioned in the two areas, they never affected the depth of my friendships with Eastern Pueblo and Western Pueblo individuals.

As noted earlier, wild turkey feathers were the most important feathers, but the specific feathers requested (body, back, pre-fan, breast, fluff, tail, etc.; see figure 3.2), and even the colors of the specific feathers, varied among Pueblos, for example, some preferred only black turkey feathers, some wanted "red" (bronze-colored), and still others wanted the white-tipped Merriam's turkey feathers. Among some Pueblos, the color mattered not at all to the individuals; they simply required wild turkey feathers, and any color or body part would do. Nevertheless, sometimes preferences—differences—did matter, and not only did preferences differ from village to village, but they also differed within villages and within religious groups in a

given village. These differences, in turn, seemingly reflected the role of the individual in the village and society so that one man might request a turkey "beard" because
he needed it as a decorative element for ritual paraphernalia or to put inside a drum,
while another man in the same village but in a different society had no use whatso-
ever for a beard. There were also individual preferences that seem to be nothing more
than the individual preferences—a man liked this feather or that feather. Some men
requested red (or orange—the linguistic term varied for the feather) Scarlet Macaw
center tails that are all red, and some requested red ones with blue tips, not because
of any ceremonial or directional requirement, but because they preferred all red or
red with a blue tip. For other men, the color made no difference—red, blue, red
and blue, or red, blue, and yellow—but what mattered is length: the longer the
better, because on the back of a katsina mask, the longer feather displayed greater
movement in the breeze while dancing. The range of preferences was not endless,
but the information was kept and remembered (or at least was quickly accessible)
so that each man received his request, if possible. However, preferences are often
just that—preferences and not absolutes. On countless occasions, a man requested
a specific type and color of feather, for example, Scarlet Macaw center tails, only to
be told we didn't have any at that time. He then often asked, "What do you have?"
The answer might be "Greenwing Macaw (*Ara chloroptera*) center tails" (darker red
than the Scarlet Macaw tail, and turquoise rather than the almost lapis lazuli of
the Scarlet Macaw tip), to which he usually responded, "OK, send me those." He'd
receive three or four. Wing feathers were less problematic because our supplies were
greater, but macaw body contour feathers, especially red, yellow, and multicolor,
were often in short supply. The same is true for Amazon parrot tail feathers in all
color variations and, to a lesser extent, Amazon parrot wing feathers.

There are rules, but the rules apparently are not absolute. As Ladd (1963:31–32)
notes for the Zuni:

> The number and kinds of feathers used, following the erect duck feather, on the stick
> and on the pendant series, in all types of prayersticks, is entirely governed by what
> kinds of feathers are available. Not all prayersticks, even from the same household,
> will have the same series; but each individual stick within the pendant series should
> have the same number and same kinds of feathers.

One thing Ladd's statement means is that, at Zuni, there is a typology for prayer
sticks in which the series constitute the units of this typology. This subject has not
been well studied for the Pueblos and is open for research, which, in my opinion,
ought to be undertaken.

Requests for feathers were constant throughout the year. Even if no ceremony was
imminent, most men anticipated their needs months ahead of time and made their

requests accordingly. We received requests for feathers as far as a year in advance of the ceremony because the individual knew supplies were limited and wanted to make certain he received what he needed. This doesn't always happen; as I often told Pueblo men, there is no guarantee that we can provide the specific feathers you need, when you need them. We were wholly dependent on the feathers we received from donors. We had no feather factory. Furthermore, the greater the number of different feathers requested, the less likely it was that one would receive all of them when needed. When we had a large backlog of requests, the wait could be a year or more. In August 2011, the backlog was so large (many dozens of requests) and the wait had become so long (up to two years, in some instances), that we stopped accepting both first-time requests and repeat requests and posted this information on our website. This did not, however, stop the receipt of requests; they kept coming by the dozens. We wrote back that, because of the backlog, we were not taking requests but would put them in a file to be filled if and when we provided feathers to those on the original backlog list. In early June 2015, we finally filled the last requests in that file, after a wait of three to four years. Shortly thereafter, still in early June, we received five first-time requests from one family at San Felipe Pueblo and wrote back that they wouldn't be filled because the Feather Distribution Project would cease operation with my upcoming retirement at the end of June (see chapter 6).

In some cases, through repeated requests, we learned who needed feathers and when they were needed, and we sent feathers in advance of specific ceremonies such as winter solstice rites. In other instances, however, even when we knew which feathers would be needed, the specific requests changed from year to year, and we could not put aside feathers ahead of time in anticipation of sending them. Partly this happened because the same feathers could be used from one year to the next, if they were not damaged. Conversely, I was told by Pueblo officials, when they requested new feathers to replace old ones, that the old feathers had been used for many years, sometimes as long as twenty-five to thirty years, and had become "ratty." Requests also changed from one year to the next because, while the ceremony is the same, such as the one at the winter solstice or a specific rain dance, the group in charge of organizing the rituals was different that year and had different "feather protocols."

Our feather request forms (figures 3.1 and 3.2) made it clear that there are certain feathers we could not and would not provide due to federal and state laws—"It is illegal for us to send feathers from eagles, hawks, other raptors, passerine ['perching birds' such as jays, cardinals, woodpeckers and flickers, and so forth], and migratory birds. We never distribute feathers from these birds." The Pueblos clearly used the feathers from these birds (figure 4.1), but we never provided them. Several of the more commonly requested feathers—Black-billed Magpie (*Pica pica*), Yellow-billed

Figure 4.1. Hopi prayer plumes with eagle, flicker, macaw, and bluebird feathers.

Magpie (*Pica nuttalli*), and Greater Roadrunner (*Geococcyx californianus*)—were from birds not native to the Illinois area; only the Black-billed Magpie occurred here, but rarely. Regardless, we did not have feathers from these birds and would not provide them if we did, because to do so is prohibited by federal law. It is worth noting, there have been and are efforts to change these laws (so far unsuccessful) to permit Native Americans greater access to feathers. We supported the proposed changes.

LANGUAGE

Many Pueblos have native linguistic terms for "parrot" or "macaw" but do not distinguish between parrots and macaws; all macaws are parrots (*psittacines*), but not all parrots are macaws. For example, according to Hodge (1896:47), Zuni may have distinguished between parrot (*píchi*) and macaw (*mu la*), but Stevenson (1904:40) notes only the term *mu la* for "macaw," and no separate term for "parrot." Ladd

(1963:93) lists only *mu la* for "macaw" and does not have a distinguishing term for "parrot." My experience at Zuni is they used *mu la* for "macaw," but I never heard a separate term for "parrot," even though parrot feathers were often requested.

This lack of distinguishing terms—most Pueblo individuals use only the term "parrot" when requesting feathers—led to problems over the years. Fortunately, I quickly learned to ask which feathers a person meant—the long tail feathers of the macaw (all species) or the much shorter tail feathers of the Amazon parrot or even the African Grey Parrot. This distinction was made on our feather request form (figure 3.1) but still required clarification or explanation from time to time. The form also had information on the macaw species and the color(s) of the feathers to clarify further and reduce confusion.

The need for this became clear more than two decades ago when I was in the restored Our Lady of Guadalupe Mission Church at Zuni Pueblo with the late Alex Seowtewa, the artist who, along with his sons, painted the wonderful murals of the *katsinam*, birds, and other figures and ritual objects on the walls. Looking at the macaw tail feathers depicted on the wall above and to the left of the altar, Alex asked whether I could provide feathers like those he had painted. The feathers were basically red and blue, and I *assumed* they were from the Greenwing Macaw (*Ara chloroptera*). I assured Alex that the Project could provide them, and when I returned home, we sent a package of Greenwing Macaw center tails to him. They were the wrong feathers! Superficially, Greenwing Macaw and Military Macaw (*Ara militaris*) tail feathers are visually similar; both are red and blue, but the undersides of the Greenwing tail feathers are red, whereas the undersides of the Military tail feathers are yellow or yellow-orange. There can also be tinges of yellow on the top surface of a Military Macaw tail feather. My oversight was my failure to ask Alex the color of the underside of the feathers in his mural. Had I done so, and had he said yellow, he would have received Military Macaw tail feathers—the correct feathers—the first time. However, he was able to use the Greenwing Macaw feathers as well. Furthermore, I learned in a later visit with him, certain details in the murals are not precisely correct, in order to avoid disclosing sacred information. The same is true of much of the work by other Pueblo artists and katsina makers.

There is an interesting note to all this. I note earlier that Octavius Seowtewa (2022) stated that the Macaw Clan is the largest Zuni clan. Octavius Seowtewa provides several sources from which the Zuni obtain macaw feathers. Curiously, he makes no mention of the Feather Distribution Project. This is curious for two reasons: first, in 1998, Octavius and another Zuni man met me and my wife Laura at the 22nd Annual Convention of the National Wild Turkey Federation in Indianapolis to help recruit new donors to the Project, in this case specifically for wild turkey feathers the Zuni use in great numbers, as noted earlier, and including for the making of the Mother Corn (Seowtewa 2022); and second, Octavius's father, the late Alex Seowtewa, who I called "Older Brother" and who called me "Younger Brother" or "Little Brother," was regularly sent macaw and turkey feathers, some of which he told me were given to Octavius.

I noted above that a request for "red" turkey feathers actually referred to the bronze-colored ones. When the request was originally made, I thought we had been asked for feathers from a so-called heritage turkey such as the Bourbon Red. But no, "red" equaled "bronze" in the mind of the individual, as expressed linguistically, just as "orange" often means to Pueblo men what I call "red" or "red-orange" when they refer to Scarlet Macaw center tail feathers. And to be honest, sometimes Scarlet Macaw center tail are more red-orange than red.

Finally, one should never underestimate the importance of feathers or a Pueblo individual's focus on them, as the following account illustrates. One afternoon the phone rang in my office, I answered it, and a Zuni man said, "It's Bernard," who I recognized as one who had received feathers on several occasions. I had some difficulty hearing him as there was a great deal of background noise. I asked where he was calling from and what I could do for him. He replied that he, his cousin Larry, the other Zuni "hotshots," and more firefighting teams were fighting a major wildfire in Arizona, which was the source of the background noise I heard. He said he and Larry watched the flames as they shot upwards, and the color reminded them of the orange-red of Scarlet Macaw tail feathers, and so he called to request some center tails. In the middle of fighting a fire, with his life possibly in danger, he was thinking about Scarlet Macaw center tail feathers.

I told Bernard that I would send the feathers but asked him to please pay attention to the fire and his work because of the inherent danger. Bernard replied, "Larry has it under control"; in fact, the fire was officially listed as out of control at the time, although it was eventually extinguished several days later. Larry did *not* have it under control.

This incident illustrates the importance of macaw feathers and just how focused individuals are on them. It is also interesting that Bernard had my office telephone number in his cell phone call file.

Occasionally we received a letter, email, or telephone call that was emotionally moving, such as the following from a Cochití Pueblo mother of a teenage son:

Dear Sir,

I wanted to send you a Thank You. You sent my son [S. S.] here in Cochiti a box of feathers. I have never seen that boy smile so big. He has used them and is using them quite often. [S] has made some headdresses [small head bundles] for some of the boys to use for feast and for the holidays. So please know that your feathers are in the community and are being put to good use. I feel that it has made my son stronger and he understands the importance of giving. So thank you again and may you be blessed for the help you have sent to Cochiti.

[Signed N.P.]

P.S. Thank you for always remembering the man [Fred Cordero] you saw for Feast Day the first time you came and he asked you if you could get feathers. I have heard about your time in Cochiti. ☺

In short, the Project was a learning experience for both the Pueblos and me. Another example of the Pueblo learning experience was a result of my archaeological training, which provided information and time depth that most Pueblo people don't have. This was noted earlier with regard to the present-day Pueblos' lack of knowledge about the practice of burying turkeys with the dead at Basketmaker III and Pueblo II–III sites. Furthermore, on the few occasions when I gave presentations at Pueblo villages on the Feather Distribution Project, at which I discussed the thousand-year-plus history of Pueblo use of macaw feathers, the information was clearly new to many or most in the audience and provoked numerous questions and comments. Again, such events were learning experiences for all of us.

THE SIGNIFICANCE OF FEATHER SIZE

Another important factor is the length of tail feathers. Scarlet Macaw center tails are the longest tail feathers, both absolutely and relative to the size of the bird. The Hyacinth Macaw (*Anodorhynchus hyacinthinus*) is substantially larger than the Scarlet Macaw, and the Greenwing Macaw (*Ara chloroptera*) is also larger than the Scarlet Macaw, but their center tail feathers are on average just slightly shorter than Scarlet Macaw center tails. The extremely long length of the Scarlet Macaw center tails was probably a factor in the general Pueblo preference for them over the feathers of other macaws;[23] we received far more requests for Scarlet Macaw center tails than we did for the center tails of any other species. Color was also a factor, as noted earlier; Scarlet Macaw feathers symbolize the sun's rays. Blue-and-Yellow Macaw (*Ara ararauna*) center tails (sometimes called Blue-and-Gold) and Greenwing Macaw (*Ara chloroptera*) center tails were the second most commonly requested tails. Military Macaw (*Ara militaris*) feathers, although available since Ancestral Pueblo times, were less commonly requested than Scarlet Macaw, Blue-and-Yellow Macaw, and Greenwing Macaw center tails, which possibly reflected the fact that the Military Macaw has the shortest center tails among the large macaws. Military Macaws are also the least colorful and the least dramatically marked of the large macaws; the Hyacinth Macaw, with its large head and body, is

Figure 4.2. The five large macaws whose feathers are used by the Pueblos: (*clockwise from top left*) Scarlet, Blue-and-Yellow, Military, Hyacinth, and Greenwing.

a rich violet-blue color, with bright yellow facial markings that give it a striking and distinctive appearance. Figure 4.2 depicts the five large macaws whose feathers are used by the Pueblos today.

The Hyacinth Macaw is native to central South America, found mostly in Brazil, and the Greenwing Macaw is native to eastern Panama and from Colombia and

Venezuela south to northern Argentina. Neither species has ever been found at archaeological sites in the Southwest; trade routes, although they extended south into Mesoamerica, do not seem to have reached that far south into Central America or into South America. The current-day Pueblo use of Hyacinth Macaw and Greenwing Macaw feathers by the Pueblos is certainly a post-contact development and almost assuredly post–World War II. The Project included Hyacinth Macaw and Greenwing Macaw feathers on our feather request form (figure 3.1) *only* because Pueblo men asked for them. In accordance with professional anthropological ethics, our policy was not to introduce new elements into the Pueblos—in this case, feathers not traditionally used and especially feathers from non-American bird species—unless specifically requested. Over the years, a few men requested feathers from hybrid macaws such as the Harlequin and Catalina, and we provided them. As hybrids, these macaws have no true scientific names: the Harlequin is a cross between the Greenwing Macaw and the Blue-and-Yellow Macaw and so is represented as *Ara chloroptera* × *Ara ararauna*; the Catalina is a cross between a Scarlet Macaw and a Blue-and-Yellow Macaw and so is represented as *Ara macao* × *Ara ararauna*. Occasionally Pueblo men requested the red tail feathers from the African Grey Parrot (*Psittacus erithacus*); from various small macaws, for example, Illiger's Macaw (*Primolius maracana*) and the Red-shouldered Macaw, also called Hahn's Macaw and Noble Macaw (*Diopsittaca nobilis*); cockatoos (*Cacatua* sp.), especially the crest feathers; and a host of other parrots and exotics that have caught their eye such as the Blue-bellied Roller (*Coracias cyanogaster*), an African bird with iridescent blue feathers. If we could legally do so, we filled these requests, but for the Blue-bellied Roller and some other exotics, we were wholly dependent on zoos, and supplies were small: for example, fewer than one hundred Blue-bellied Roller feathers per year in the best years.

The late Charles H. Lange (personal communication) once told me Cochití Pueblo briefly used Ring-necked Pheasant (*Phasianus colchicus*) tail feathers in the 1950s as substitutes for macaw center tail feathers when macaw long center tail feathers were in short supply. I occasionally saw pheasant tail feathers used on masks at Western Pueblos and atop Corn Dance poles at Rio Grande pueblos as apparent substitutes for macaw center tail feathers. This practice was short-lived.

In one instance several years ago, I had Scarlet Macaw and other macaw center tails with me in my car during a trip to distribute feathers. I stopped at a Hopi Pueblo to attend a dance and noticed that one mask had pheasant feathers instead of macaw center tail feathers. I asked why and was told by my host family that the man who made the mask had no macaw tail feathers. I asked what color was needed, went to my car, extracted a half dozen Blue-and-Yellow Macaw center tail feathers, and immediately offered them to my host family, who accepted them. After a break in the dancing, when the katsinam returned to the plaza, the pheasant tail feathers were gone, and the macaw center tails were in their place. Pheasants are native to Asia, were introduced into Europe, and then were brought to North America for sport hunting. As such, they are not part of traditional Pueblo lore, and their brief use in Pueblo ceremonies, especially masked ceremonies, seemed to occur *only* when macaw center tails were unavailable.

NUMBERS

The Feather Distribution Project provided feathers to about a thousand individuals in the thirty-two Pueblos. According to the 2010 United States Census, there are approximately 73,000 Pueblo people, so the Project provided feathers to approximately one in seventy-three Pueblo individuals. This ratio increases if young children and others who do not participate in the ceremonial systems are excluded. There were about 332 million people living in the United States in 2010. To put the percentage of Pueblo people receiving feathers (ignoring exclusions) in relation to the total US population, if the Project provided feathers to the American population in general, it would distribute feathers to more than 4,548,000 people. Thus, the Project serves a significant portion of the relevant Pueblo population. Over the years, the specific people served changed: some recipients died, others moved and dropped out of the ceremonial system, and new recipients were added to the Project roster. More than 99 percent of the recipients were male, but women were often the ones who actually requested the feathers for male relatives. One Hopi woman, for instance, called or wrote to request feathers for her grandfather and father because her English, both spoken and written, was much better than theirs. Having met her male relatives, I knew this to be true.

From its inception in 1982 through its cessation in 2015, the Feather Distribution Project provided almost 15 million wild turkey, macaw, parrot, and duck feathers free of charge to Pueblo peoples in all thirty-two villages in New Mexico and Arizona. It generally met its goals, outlined earlier, though there was still commercial trade in feathers, some legal, some illegal, and we did not completely eradicate the destruction of bird populations and habitat in Latin America and other parts of the world. Nevertheless, the Project was a positive force for change in the composition and economics of the feather trade, as well as a benefit to the Pueblos. It demonstrated that Sol Tax's concept of "action anthropology" was a workable idea and that anthropology could make a difference—a positive contribution to Native American and American societies.

THE NATIVE AMERICAN CHURCH

Although the very top of the Feather Distribution Project Website stated that the purpose of the program was to provide feathers to Pueblo Indians, not long after it went online, requests for feathers started to arrive from Native American Church (NAC) members. The Native American Church is also known as the Peyote Religion or Peyote Cult (La Barre 2012). Although the use of peyote (*Lophophora williamsii*) as a means to personal enlightenment and growth extends back to pre-Columbian times, the modern NAC began in the 1890s. The general goal is to find harmony between oneself, one's community, one's environment, and life in general through visions resulting from ingesting peyote under the guidance of a spiritual leader (the "Road Man"). The NAC probably has about 250,000 members nationwide from some fifty tribes. Some chapters accept non–Native Americans, others do not, and this has been a long-standing controversy and point of contention.

The 1990 US Supreme Court decision in *Employment Division, Department of Human Resources of Oregon v. Smith* put into question the legal use of peyote by Native Americans and put members of the NAC in legal jeopardy.[24] Congress attempted to rectify the situation with passage of the American Indian Religious Freedom Act of 1978 (42 U.S.C. § 1996), that is, the American Indian Religious Freedom Act Amendments of 1994 (42 U.S.C. § 1996a). In terms of the Feather Distribution Project, requests for feathers rose substantially in subsequent years and resulted in a proportionate increase in the distribution of feathers to NAC members, because, aside from macaw and Amazon parrots, the majority of feathers requested are from species whose feathers we did not receive donations of or received in small numbers, such as tail feathers from the Laughing Kookaburra (*Dacelo novaeguineae*) of Australia.

At first, NAC requests often came by telephone, mail, or email in the form of "I'm not a Pueblo Indian, but I still need feathers for Native American Church rituals. Do you supply them to us?" Initially our response was not to provide them, because our focus was on the Pueblos, and except for wild turkey feathers, we didn't receive sufficient numbers of feathers to supply even all the Pueblo requests. However, NAC members made it clear that although they wanted macaw tail feathers, they also would accept a wide variety of tail feathers such as those from the Rhino Hornbill (*Buceros rhinoceros*) of Malaysia and other hornbill species to make fans, feathers from birds of no interest to the Pueblos.[25] The same applied to the tail feathers of the Eclectus Parrot (*Eclectus roratus*), which is native to New Guinea, the Solomon Islands, and other nearby areas of the Pacific (figure 4.3) and to relatively exotic species such as the Laughing Kookaburra (*Dacelo novaeguineae*) from Australia, as noted above. Native American Church members also used a variety

Figure 4.3. Native American Church Eclectus Parrot feather peyote fan.

of different tail feathers to create a fan. While occasionally a Pueblo man used a macaw tail feather with a damaged tip, trimming it into a uniformly rounded shape, NAC members routinely trimmed the tips of macaw tail feathers, both damaged and undamaged, to make them uniform for use in fans (figure 4.4). Like the Sandia Pueblo use of damaged macaw and parrot feathers to make a man's head bundle

Figure 4.4. Native American Church peyote fan made from damaged and trimmed Greenwing Macaw feathers.

(figure 4.1), the trimming of tail feathers is an excellent example of the conservation of a precious resource. Almost all feathers were precious, and the practice of trimming and using them demonstrated this.

Like the Sandia Pueblo use of damaged macaw and parrot feathers to make a man's head bundle (figure 0.2), the trimming of tail feathers is an excellent example of the conservation of a precious resource. Almost all feathers were precious, and the practice of trimming and using them demonstrated this.

Native American Church members liked the bright colors of the Scarlet Macaw and other macaws and parrots. But they also liked bold patterning on feathers such as the wide black and white horizontal bands of the Rhino Hornbill and other hornbill species. The Laughing Kookaburra (*Dacelo novaeguineae*) of Australia has tail feathers with bold brown, black, and white patterning that appealed to some NAC members, especially the Navajo; requests for Laughing Kookaburra tail feathers far exceeded the supply on hand, which came exclusively from two or three zoos. Other favorites, more colorful than the Laughing Kookaburra tail feathers and also boldly patterned, were the tail feathers from the Glossy Black Cockatoo (*Calyptorhynchus lathami*) and the Red-tailed Black Cockatoo (*Calyptorhynchus banksii*), both of which have striking red and black tail feathers. These, too, were always in short supply; only one zoo and one private donor provided them to the Project, and only about once per year. Feathers from the Kori Bustard (*Ardeotis kori*), also frequently requested, were rarely provided, because we seldom received them from zoos, and they were not a species kept by pet bird owners.

The Feather Distribution Project provided about 200,000 feathers to NAC members throughout the United States. Unlike the Pueblos, we distributed feathers to both men and women within the NAC, though the number of men was much greater. The artistry displayed in making fans and other ceremonial paraphernalia, however, did not seem to favor men over women; both were equally adept at the work, as the fans shown indicate.

The great majority of NAC members to whom we distributed feathers were west of the Mississippi River, and the largest numbers were in the Four Corners area of the Southwest, followed by the Dakotas and Oklahoma (where the modern NAC originated in the 1890s). Most members who we supplied were probably Navajo, but Cherokee, Kiowa, Lakota, Ogallala, Paiute, Ute, Cheyenne, Blackfeet, and Crow, among others, were also represented. In most instances, we sent feathers to individuals, but in two instances, they were sent to NAC chapter houses for distribution among members. Furthermore, in contrast to the Pueblos where feathers were rarely sent to women, the Project sent a significant number of feathers in response to requests from NAC women members who made fans. These women were often as accomplished in their artistry as were the men; figure 4.3 depicts a fan made by Michelle Yazzie, a Navajo woman member of the NAC.

It's worth noting that two problems arose with NAC members. Some years ago, a Navajo NAC member requested feathers, which we sent. A few weeks later, he requested more feathers; again, they were sent. As time passed, the requests became more frequent until he called at least once a week, and sometimes more often. He always requested feathers to make a fan.

At some point, I asked him why he made so many different fans? I knew that some NAC members had more than one fan for personal use, but no one of whom I was aware had dozens. He told me he made them for others; this was primarily how he made his living. I told him we wouldn't send more feathers, because they were not intended for commercial use. He then commenced into an angry tirade about how the White man always put down Indians, that it had been this way for centuries, and that I was just another White man who didn't want Indians to prosper. I tried to explain: I had told him from the outset that the Project was opposed to the commercial use of the feathers it provided, and if we learned that recipients sold the feathers they had received for free, whether directly or as part of crafts such as fans, no more feathers would be sent. He continued his tirade until I finally hung up the phone. We never again sent feathers.

The second example also occurred years ago and involved a Minnesota NAC member. He requested feathers for a fan, preferably hornbill tails. At that time, we rarely received hornbill tails from zoos, but when we did, I put them aside for him. Months after his initial request, about a dozen hornbill tails were sent. In time, he responded that most of the tails weren't usable, because they didn't match each other very well. We sent more; again they were not suitable for one reason or another. This pattern continued for two or three years, by which point it was clear that nothing we sent would satisfy him, even when, at his request, we switched to macaw side tails. We finally stopped sending feathers, and I sent a letter explaining why: We clearly could not meet his requests or standards no matter the types of feathers we sent. He never responded to my letter and never again requested feathers.

THE OTHER NATIVE AMERICAN TRIBES AND ORGANIZATIONS

As the Project grew through its thirty-four years of existence, word spread that feathers might be available to non-Pueblo groups. Native American Church members were the first to make inquiries and later receive feathers, but in the last decade or so of the Project's existence, other groups contacted us and received feathers.

The first of these was the Cherokee Nation of Tahlequah, Oklahoma. For some years, the Cherokee had received wild turkey wing and tail feathers from the National Wild Turkey Federation. However, the Federation decided to stop distributing feathers to Native American groups and to others—to get out of feather distribution to reduce expenses—and directed all further inquiries to the Feather Distribution Project.

The Cherokee Department of Natural Resources got in touch with us in 2008 to request the same feathers they had received previously from the National Wild

Turkey Federation (NWTF). They most especially wanted primary and secondary wing feathers for fletching on traditional hunting arrows (figure 0.3), and tail feathers were also needed. We began to provide wild turkey feathers in 2008 and sent dozens of packages over time, notably thousands of wild turkey feathers for young Cherokee women to make traditional turkey feather capes or robes. We did not lack for wild turkey feathers and provided all the Pueblos with what they required at any given time and then provided them to other Native American groups.

Also in 2008, the Wyandotte Nation of Oklahoma, only about eighty miles north of Tahlequah, requested wild turkey tail and wing feathers to make traditional headdresses (*gus-to-weh* or *kus-to-wa*) for the installation of new chiefs (figure 0.1). The Wyandotte had heard about the Project from the Cherokee, and like the Cherokee, had previously received some feathers from the NWTF. We periodically sent the Wyandotte the needed wild turkey feathers for making headdresses. The curious thing is that in both cases, apparently there are few turkey hunters in either nation and certainly not enough to provide the number of feathers needed by the two nations.

The following year (2009), two Pomo rancherias in California called to request wild turkey wing feathers, preferably secondary, to make feather screens (figure 0.4). It's not clear how they heard about the Feather Distribution Project, but most likely, given the feathers they wanted, it was through the NWTF. We provided both Pomo rancherias with the feathers, and because these have been used from one occasion to the next and carefully handled, we were never asked to provide replacement feathers.

The Seneca in upstate New York contacted us in 2009 to request wild turkey feathers—wings, tails, and larger body feathers—for a traditional headdress or cap (*gus-to-weh*, the same term as among the Wyandotte, who are also Iroquoian speakers [figure 0.2]). Word of mouth between the Seneca and Cherokee led the Seneca to us, and we provided feathers to them on four occasions. They had only a few headdresses and their use was limited, so they should have lasted for years if handled carefully. We received a fair number of wild turkey feathers from upstate hunters in New York, so that the Seneca apparently didn't engage much in turkey hunting was curious. Or maybe it was simpler to obtain them from us. Again, there was no shortage of wild turkey feathers, so these were easy requests to fill.

Still later in 2009, we received a request from the Cowlitz Tribe in southwestern Washington State for forty wild turkey body feathers for the manufacture of traditional talking sticks. The request originally went to the NWTF from a Cowlitz tribal member, the NWTF forwarded the request to us, and we sent the feathers. In 2010, a Coushatta Tribal Heritage Department official called the NWTF with a request for wild turkey tails to make a traditional fan. Again, the request was

Figure 4.5. Ocellated Turkey.

forwarded to us, and we filled it. After that, we received no requests for feathers other than from Pueblo and NAC individuals.

On an irregular basis, the Project also provided feathers from exotic species to a few California Aztec dance groups. We occasionally received feathers from people who raise Great Argus Pheasants (*Argusianus argus*), Lady Amherst's Pheasants (*Chrysolophus amherstiae*), Golden Pheasants (*Chrysolophus pictus*), and Palawan Peacock-Pheasants (*Polyplectron napoleonis*), all native to Asia, and also from zoos that have these birds. One zoo had Ocellated Turkeys (*Meleagris ocellata*) (figure 4.5) which are found primarily on the Yucatan Peninsula, and they sent the feathers to us. The long showy tail feathers of the first three species were especially prized for headdresses by Aztec dance groups, even though the Aztec and other Mesoamerican peoples never had access to these feathers before recent times. The same is true for the Palawan Peacock-Pheasant, which has short, beautiful tail feathers. The Ocellated Turkey was native to Yucatan—the species was domesticated by the Maya, among others—and elsewhere in Mesoamerica. Its feathers were available and used, and it is the most colorful of all the wild turkeys The Aztec dance groups did request macaw center tails, but we did not provide them because we did not have sufficient supplies to provide for all Pueblo requests.

The most spectacular bird in Mesoamerica is probably the Resplendent Quetzal (*Pharomachrus mocinno*), and the use of its feathers by the Aztecs and others is well documented in the literature and in artwork (Dibble and Anderson 1959, Diaz and Rogers 1983). We never received a single Resplendent Quetzal feather, and I did not know of any zoo in the United States that had the bird. Curiously, only one Aztec dance group ever requested Resplendent Quetzal feathers, historically the obvious choice for headdresses. However, many zoos have the Indian Peacock (*Pavo crista-tus*), and we did provide a few of the tail feathers to Aztec dance groups. Most zoos tended to sell these feathers in their gift shops or allowed visitors to pick up molted feathers. The few we received were usually in fair to poor condition, partly because their length makes it difficult to find boxes or tubes long enough, and because their relatively weak rachis (the center "stem" of each feather) meant they broke easily.

The final "others" are prisons and Native American inmates. The first requests came from inmates in Colorado and Washington State institutions, and all were for wild turkey feathers. Indeed, until spring 2014, no requests were received for feathers other than wild turkey feathers. We sent the requested feathers directly to the inmates, which was our mistake. It's unclear what happened to the feathers, but they apparently never reached the inmates who requested them. We later learned from prison chaplains that prison administrators consider turkey feathers—especially large primary and secondary wing and tail feathers—as potential weapons; the quill ends can be sharpened and used to stab people. (Who knew?) While most administrators did not ban feathers outright, for fear of violating inmates' freedom of religion rights, they did insist they be sent to the chaplains and not to the inmates; the chaplains then snipped off the quill tip to lessen the potential use of the feathers as weapons. All feathers were then mailed to prison chaplains with the names of those inmates requesting them inside the package. In the last couple of years of the Project, feathers were sent to chaplains in California, New Mexico, North Carolina, and Texas prisons. Starting in October 2013, we sent large numbers of feathers, mostly wild turkey but also some other species, to Chaplain Raymond A. Clark, the American Indian Coordinator for all North Carolina prisons, for distribution throughout the state's prison system to the Native American inmates who requested feathers.

A request came from a Native American in a North Carolina maximum security facility who wanted Hyacinth Macaw (*Anodorhynchus hyacinthinus*) tail, wing, and body feathers. This was an unusual request because Hyacinth Macaw feathers were not commonly used by the Navajo; nevertheless, we sent them to the prison chaplain and received a note back from the inmate thanking us for them.

It was unclear how prison inmates used the feathers we sent. Obviously, they couldn't practice the rites of the Native American Church, because peyote and other hallucinogens were banned. We know some feathers were made into fans and used in outdoor "smoking" ceremonies with the burning of sage and sweetgrass; the fans were used to waft the smoke over the person's head and body for purification. Chanting and singing (and drumming?) accompanied some of these rituals, which were probably limited in scope by prison restrictions on behavior. A few prisons in the United States did have sweat lodges, and sweat lodges were permitted in prisons by the Religious Land Use and Institutionalized Persons Act of 2000, although most requests by prisoners to build sweat lodges for religious use were not routinely agreed to and seemingly were adjudicated individually through the court system. In short, we did not know how feathers we send to prisons were used by inmates, only that they were.

Finally, one of the stranger requests we have received for feathers came in 2012 from an archaeologist who had arranged a meeting with the Hopi Pueblo Cultural Office to present a research proposal for which he wanted tribal approval and assistance. He thought the meeting would proceed better and that his proposal might be looked upon more favorably if he presented the group with a gift, specifically, tobacco and Scarlet Macaw center tail feathers. He wrote to request the feathers.

I replied that we didn't have sufficient Scarlet Macaw center tails to give him three (our usual number) for each group member, and that wild turkey feathers were more important on a daily basis in Hopi life; we could provide wild turkey feathers. After an exchange of emails, he agreed to the turkey feathers, and we sent them. We never received any response, not even an indication the feathers had been received. To be fair, only a small percentage of recipients thanked us, and then usually when they called or wrote asking for more feathers.

5

The Operation of the Feather Distribution Project

Almost from the outset, I was concerned with the long-term viability of the Project and what would happen to it when I was no longer able to operate it. Not to put too fine a point on it, no one lives forever, and after thirty-four years, I had less energy and fewer resources to continue the work. Fred Cordero, the Cochití man who first requested feathers in 1970, had died in 1994 at age eighty-nine. His successor, Joe D. Pecos, had died in 2010, also at age eighty-nine.[26]

To prepare for the time when I would no longer able to operate the Project, perhaps influenced by the transition from Fred to J. D.,[27] I attempted to find a person or, preferably, a Pueblo group such as the All Pueblo Council of Governors in Albuquerque to assume responsibility for its continuation. Starting in 1990, several attempts were made but none succeeded. In conjunction with the eventual transfer of operations, I developed plans for a macaw and parrot sanctuary and one for a turkey facility, both to be operated by Pueblo personnel and to serve all the Pueblos, including the Hopi (see appendixes A and B). Three of my efforts involved a state office in New Mexico; the first two attempts failed when the state officials with whom I was negotiating were forced to resign. In the third attempt, the new official was not a Pueblo member and was not interested in a program that benefited mainly the Pueblo Indians in the state.

Next I tried to work with a Pueblo that had a successful casino, based on the interest of a Pueblo member and friend who had received feathers for several years, and because I thought some casino revenues could be used to fund the costs of the Project, once the Pueblo had agreed to take it over. However, after about two and a half years of negotiations, working with and through this friend from the village, I was not given the opportunity to present my ideas to the village council and was further told the council would not consider hiring the necessary personnel. Nevertheless, twice I was asked to provide dates when I could travel to New Mexico to meet with the council. I provided the council with a number of possible dates over several months, but the council could not or would not agree to any of them. About a year later, I was asked by another friend in the village to call a Pueblo official at his office. I called four times on different days, but each time, I left a voicemail message because no one answered the phone during the listed office hours. My calls were never returned, and my effort to transfer the Project to the Pueblo finally ended in 2012.

In 2007 a phone call requesting feathers was received from a Navy medical corpsman stationed in Arizona. He claimed to be of Santo Domingo and Hopi descent. From then until 2011, he called with some regularity, and we sent feathers as requested, sometimes to his home and other times (wild turkey feathers) to where he was posted, for example, aboard ship in the Mediterranean, so he could make prayer sticks. During the course of this relationship, I mentioned the time was approaching when I must turn the Project over to a Pueblo organization or village, or close it down. In 2011, he expressed an interest in taking it over, and I sent him the materials in appendixes A and B along with other materials pertaining to the operations of the Project, including the costs involved. The costs did not deter him, or so he said.

We then discussed the possibility that he and his wife would come to Springfield to see how the Project operates, and looked at various dates. However, by this point, some things he said did not seem quite right, such as his claim that as a member of Santo Domingo (which he did not know had worked to rename itself as Kewa Pueblo—eventually an unsuccessful effort), he claimed to speak both Tewa and Tiwa, but Santo Domingo is Keres-speaking. He also used what he said were Hopi words on occasion when speaking with me. I do not speak Hopi, but the words and his pronunciation both seemed incorrect. And so I decided to do research on him—what lawyers call "due diligence." The results were interesting and disheartening.

There is a great deal of junk and misinformation on the internet, but with care, the technology can yield major benefits. The first thing I learned from the *Desert Warrior* online publication for the Yuma, Arizona, military base where he had been stationed was that he is San Carlos Apache. To double-check, I called first friends and then officials at Santo Domingo Pueblo to inquire whether this man was known to them or on their tribal roll. He wasn't. I did the same at Hopi, most specifically for Kykotsmovi, where he claimed to live at his grandfather's house when at the village. This was another apparent error by him; the Hopi are matrilineal, and I thought he would mention his home as his grandmother's. No one at Kykotsmovi knew him or his supposed grandfather. He was not on the Hopi tribal roll, nor was anyone by his grandfather's name on the tribal roll. I had written down the supposed Hopi words he used and asked good friends at Hotevilla and Mishongnovi whether these were Hopi words and, if so, what they meant. They replied that they weren't Hopi words, and my Hotevilla friend said they were "gibberish."

The final "nail in the coffin" was when I found a Facebook listing for a Navajo group, "Dikon Azee Bee Nahagta of Dine Nation." The posts by this man for 8 June 2011 and 5 July 2011 listed various feathers for sale, and he referred to his own Facebook page for the prices. The types of feathers (macaw, Alexandrine Parrot, and others) were those we had recently sent to him, and the dates of the two posts were shortly after we had sent them. I was dismayed because his scam had gone on so long, but glad I found out before turning the Project over to him. I wrote a letter to him in December 2012 informing him of our findings but never received a reply. However, Hopi, Santa Ana, and Zuni friends of mine have told me (personal communication, May, June, and July 2014) he contacted them with offers to sell feathers. I don't know where he now obtains feathers—perhaps he is scamming a zoo or bird club—but I have warned those I know about dealing with him, told them of my experience with him, and furnished them with documentation.

Most recently I shifted my efforts to the All Pueblo Council of Governors in Albuquerque, New Mexico. Despite the support and urging of a Pueblo official, twice submitting cover letters with copies of publications about the Project and the materials in appendixes A and B, and making several follow-up telephone calls to the chair of the Council (I did not get past his secretary), I never received a written response or even an acknowledgment of receipt of the materials, nor were my calls returned. All I've heard by way of a third-party Pueblo individual is that these men are interested in political matters, are little involved in Pueblo ceremonial life, and have no interest in things such as the Feather Distribution Project. I had not given up on the plan that a Pueblo person, village, or inter-Pueblo organization would eventually take over the Project, but was unsure what next to try. This is further discussed in chapter 6.

There were additional issues that complicated the situation and affected who might have taken over the Project. One was the accumulation within the Project paperwork of a great deal of sacred information. Pueblo secrecy about their ceremonial activities is well known and well documented. Project correspondence contains names of religious officers, religious society members, the feathers they require and the uses to which they are put, and more. Some of the information is not even shared within the village, or between the sexes, or between adults and children. There are even drawings of katsinam and sacred objects never before published. What goes on at Zuni or a Hopi village is usually not to be shared with someone from Taos or Cochití. So, before the Project records could be turned over to someone or some group, all such restricted information must be purged. Yet this would reduce the efficiency of the Project operations. I know, for example, when certain feathers are needed in particular villages; I know much about the ceremonial calendars and send wild turkey or other required feathers ahead of time so they will be available *before* the ceremony occurs, when the preparations are underway. As noted in appendices A and B, any transfer of the Project records would occur only with permission of those involved, and a pan-Pueblo consensus was difficult to imagine and would probably have been even more difficult to obtain.

Then there was the issue of sex. Men in several villages have told me they do not want women handling the feathers—"it's men's work."[28] This is not true for all villages, for example, women may be present at Zuni and Hopi when I distribute feathers, but generally not among the Rio Grande Pueblos. It was mentioned earlier that a woman graduate student who wanted to accompany me on a feather distribution trip balked when she was told she could not be present at the actual distribution in the Rio Grande Pueblo villages. This exclusion of women has extended to the volunteers who sort feathers; most are male, and the women who sort feathers are usually postmenopausal, when they no longer pose a danger ceremonially. If they're not postmenopausal, the feathers they sort do not go to villages that would object to this. This restriction has prevented one or two women from the possibility of taking over operation of the Project.

The process by which individuals received feathers began with an inquiry via telephone, email, fax, or letter, then filling out the forms (figures 3.1 and 3.2). The person then received the requested feathers, though it may have taken weeks, months, or even a year or more, depending on what feathers were requested and the supplies on hand of those feathers. For those who requested every feather on the forms, there was usually a long wait.

Obtaining and processing feathers was more complex. Most often, zoos and other institutions, bird clubs, veterinary clinics, and individuals wrote or called offering feathers. In some cases, we made a "cold call" using the mail or email to a zoo, bird club, or breeding facility to request feathers. Occasionally this worked; most often it did not, but if a zoo birdkeeper asked for feathers on our behalf, zoos which did not respond to us before usually agreed to donate feathers. The American Association of Zoo Keepers (AAZK) network is strong and effective in this regard. So is the American Zoological Association (AZA) network. Once a zoo donated feathers, the keepers were usually amenable, upon request, to expanding the number of birds from which they collected feathers. For instance, the St. Louis Zoo responded to our request for Wood Duck (*Aix sponsa*) and Mallard Duck (*Anas platyrhynchos*)[29] feathers that some Pueblo men specifically requested.

Repeat donors were essential to whatever success the Project had, and this applied to zoos as well as to bird clubs and individuals. The Brookfield Zoo, for example, provided feathers starting in 1989, and it was the longest-contributing zoo donor. Bird clubs such as Kentuckiana Feathered Friends (1989)—the longest-contributing club—and the Peninsula Caged Bird Society (1999) donated tens of thousands of feathers over the years. Perhaps the most remarkable example of a bird club's efforts to provide feathers was the Hong Kong Parrot Club, which obtained the necessary CITES permits (see appendix D)—a difficult task—in order to send feathers to us. In exchange for feathers, I visited zoos and bird clubs throughout the United States to deliver presentations about the Project at no charge to the donor organization[30] and to acknowledge donors in publications about the Project. I also participated in podcasts, television videos (see the project website), gave interviews with print and electronic media journalists, and wrote for bird-related publications to increase awareness of the Project (e.g., Reyman 1999, 2009), and to thank donors publicly. In fact, among the problems a Pueblo or Pueblo group would have in taking over the Project would be in the area of public relations—finding a good public speaker with the time and ability to travel for public presentations.

There was an aspect to the Project which bears mention. While most Pueblo individuals are pleased with the Project and happy to receive feathers, especially free of charge, a few Pueblo men and women criticized it: "We should not accept feathers from an Anglo"; "It is wrong because it gives you control of our religion" and "What's the real reason you are doing this? What's the catch? What do you really want? No one gives feathers for free. Nothing is free."

The skepticism was understandable after centuries of oppression and exploitation by the Spanish and later Euro-Americans, and one cannot satisfy all the critics and naysayers. One response was "OK, you take over the Project." It was a serious offer, but no one ever accepted it. "Too much work for no pay" was a frequent response, followed by a lack of time as a reason for not doing it.

At times I replied that if the person objects to receiving free feathers from the Project, then we could stop providing them or the individual could refuse to accept them. But this didn't happen either.

At the most fundamental level, feathers were too precious and necessary not to be accepted. Nevertheless, because no Pueblo organization nor even a Pueblo individual agreed to take over the Project, the time came when the Feather Distribution Project ended and things returned somewhat to where they were prior to 1982. This is discussed further in chapter 6.

Figure 5.1. Feathers sorted and ready for shipping.

Once feathers were received, they were placed in a walk-in freezer in the Decontamination Room at the Illinois State Museum's Research and Collections Center (RCC), where they underwent a repeated freeze and thaw process to kill parasites, bacteria, and viruses. After this was completed, wild turkey feathers usually received no further treatment other than sorting by volunteers into constituent body parts (wings, tails, breast, back, etc.) and placed in plastic bags for shipment to those who requested them. Often the turkey feathers were not even sorted but were forwarded, as received, to Pueblo individuals. Macaw and parrot feathers (and duck and goose feathers) were washed, dried, and sorted by species (for example, Scarlet Macaw, Amazon parrot) and into tail, wing, and body contour feathers, then bagged for shipment (figure 5.1; the stuffed toy birds were often sent by donors and others and were donated to a local children's hospital unit). Volunteers did most of this work.

When the processing was complete and the feathers sent, which usually took about a week or two, the donor received an email or letter of thanks containing a statement about where the feathers were sent, and reimbursement of postage, if requested. For example, if the donor sent feathers from an Amazon parrot (*Amazona* sp.), the letter might read in part, "The Amazon parrot feathers you donated were sent to a Navajo member of the Native American Church in eastern Arizona to make a ceremonial fan." An image of such a fan (figure 4.3) might be included if the donor had not received one previously. Correspondence with donors was critical: they wanted to know that their feathers arrived safely, to whom they were distributed, and how they might be used. We tried to provide information within the limits of keeping sacred matters confidential. For instance, we might tell a donor that the feathers were used in an initiation or rain ceremony, without giving specific details. Not divulging sacred information was essential in order to maintain the trust of the Pueblos, and such trust was one of the foundation blocks upon which the Project was built.

Another ongoing task was the constant scramble or scrounging to find suitable boxes to ship feathers. They had to be large enough to hold a wild turkey fan, an entire cape, or the long macaw center tail feathers (mailing tubes worked best for tail feathers) without damaging them in transit. Letters to donors and recipients also took time to write, and over the duration of the Project, we generated some 45,000 documents. The expenses to operate the Feather Distribution Project included plastic bags for packing feathers, postage, boxes, wrapping paper, and other supplies, travel to the Southwest to distribute feathers, and travel elsewhere to give presentations. Expenses were largely out of pocket. We occasionally received an honorarium, and bird clubs occasionally provided financial support; most notably the Kentuckiana Feathered Friends were extremely generous. When the Project began, the operating costs were a few hundred dollars per year. However, over the thirty-four years, all costs rose significantly—travel, postage, and commodities—so the yearly cost was usually in excess of $12,000, and in some years was more than $15,000.[31] Furthermore, the Feather Distribution Project was not my primary job—Curator of Anthropology at the Illinois State Museum was—and I could not work on it during my regular workday hours because of the constitutional separation of church and state: the Project directly supported traditional Pueblo religion as well as the religious practices of the Native American Church.

Although the Project was then housed in my office laboratory at the Illinois State Museum, neither my time nor the Project's expenses such as postage and travel were paid by the Museum. The time spent to wash, dry, sort, and pack feathers was my own time and was in addition to my regular working hours at the museum. Washing and drying were mostly done at home; sorting was done in my laboratory with the help of volunteers. During its thirty-four years of operation, approximately four hundred people, from elementary school children to scouts to church groups to senior citizens, helped with the sorting, and a dozen or so regularly helped.

Macaw and parrot feathers were washed, but turkey feathers were not (too many feathers and too difficult to wash and dry because of all the down and fluff). Washing consists of placing the feathers in a large sink filled with warm water and a mild, sudsy detergent. The feathers are agitated gently by hand for a few minutes and then allowed to soak to remove dust, dirt, droppings, and other debris. After the water cooled, the feathers were removed and the water squeezed out. Smaller feathers were placed in double bags, which were then placed in a clothes dryer with fabric softener sheets to dry and "fluff" them thoroughly. Tail feathers and primary wing feathers were laid flat on nylon mesh racks to dry; putting them in the dryer would bend or break them. Once dry, feathers were moved to my laboratory for sorting, bagging, and preparation for shipping (figure 5.1).

Except in rare circumstances, feathers sent to the Pueblos were shipped via the United States mail, generally parcel post. Occasionally, if feathers were needed quickly and the package or tube was light, they were sent via first-class priority mail. Only once was a package shipped by UPS, and then, the Pueblo voluntarily paid the cost for the requested 1,500 wild turkey tail feathers. In most cases, feathers were sent to PO boxes. Many Pueblos lacked street names for delivery, and even where there were street names, most people preferred to pick up the packages at the post office. Theft from curbside mailboxes was an occasional problem. A few people, both Pueblo men and Navajo men, and women or other members of the Native American Church, lacked even PO boxes and received their feathers at general delivery in the local post office.

For whatever reason(s), mail *to* the Southwest was oftentimes inordinately slow. It sometimes took a week or two (or more in a few instances) for a package of feathers to travel from Springfield, Illinois, to New Mexico and Arizona. One reason was the postal service's sometimes seemingly byzantine routing system. Several years ago, when in Gallup, New Mexico, I remembered that I'd neglected to give a Zuni man something I had brought for him. I didn't want to drive back to Zuni, so I decided to send it in an envelope via first-class mail to Zuni Pueblo, a distance of about thirty-five miles. The postal clerk at the Gallup post office told me it would take four days—first, to be sent to Albuquerque to the postal routing center, and then back to Gallup for delivery to Zuni. I asked whether he could simply stamp the postmark on the envelope and put it in the box of the carrier who serviced Zuni, but he told me that regulations did not allow this. I drove back to Zuni, dropped the letter at the man's house, and continued my trip to the Hopi mesas.

ALTERNATE INCOME

One final aspect of the Feather Distribution Project operation merits a few words: alternate income for feather procurers in Latin America and elsewhere. If we intended to stop those in the rainforests and other environments from capturing macaws and parrots for sale or killing them for their feathers, we needed to provide alternate sources of income that were at least as profitable. This should not be difficult. The real money is made by those who sell live birds in markets and who smuggle the birds and feathers across national borders, such as from Mexico into the United States. Those who capture the birds or kill them and pluck their feathers—processes that often destroy habitat as well—make very little for their efforts. The task, then, was to provide them with alternate sources of income more profitable than what they earned from their (generally illegal) activities. What follows were four of many possibilities that then existed (and still do). But first, full disclosure: I had no economic interest in any of these suggested alternatives.

Yachana Jungle Chocolate, a wonderful Ecuadorian product for chocolate lovers, is available in several varieties from online sources (for example, https://thehungersite.greatergood.com/store/ths/item/1381/yachana-jungle-chocolate) and from fair trade stores in the US. It's made from renewable resources such as the cacao bean and sugarcane, provides Ecuadorian farmers with a higher income for their cacao, and does not involve destruction of rainforest habitat.

Lacuma Designs (https://www.lucuma.com) in Peru manufactures a wide range of quality fair trade goods that appeal to bird lovers, such as the Amazon parrot card in figure 5.2 made from recycled paper. Peruvian people learned the skills necessary to produce these items and could earn a higher income than that obtained from exploiting macaws and parrots in the rainforest and mountain areas.

Another Ecuadorian product is the carving in figure 5.3, made from wood of the balsa tree (*Ochroma pyramidale*), a sustainable resource. Like the other products, these carvings are available in fair trade stores, come in a wide variety of motifs that appeal to macaw and parrot owners, and are reasonably priced yet provide carvers with substantially more income. Balsa trees are found in Brazil as well as Ecuador, and if enough men (it's men who capture and kill macaws and parrots) learn to carve these figures, and if the figures catch on in the American market as have the Oaxacan wood carvings (*alebrijes*), this would greatly relieve the pressure on birds and habitat in Ecuador and Brazil.

Prior to World War II, the tagua palm (*Phytelephas* sp.)—also known as the ivory palm, for the resemblance of its nut to elephant ivory in color and texture, a resemblance reflected in its scientific name—was a major source of material for buttons on shirts and blouses (as shell had been until the early 1930s). The trees are found mainly in Ecuador, Bolivia, Colombia, Peru, and northwestern Brazil and are a sustainable resource. With the ban on elephant ivory, the tagua palm nut became widely utilized for jewelry (figure 5.4), carvings, and other accessories. Again, training carvers in Latin America would provide an alternate economic activity to the capture and killing of birds, and without the accompanying harm to the habitat.

The Feather Distribution Project promoted these economic alternatives for two decades as ways to lessen the destruction of bird populations and their habitats,

Figure 5.2. Lacuma Designs Amazon parrot note card, Peru.

Figure 5.3. Macaw carving made from balsa wood, Ecuador.

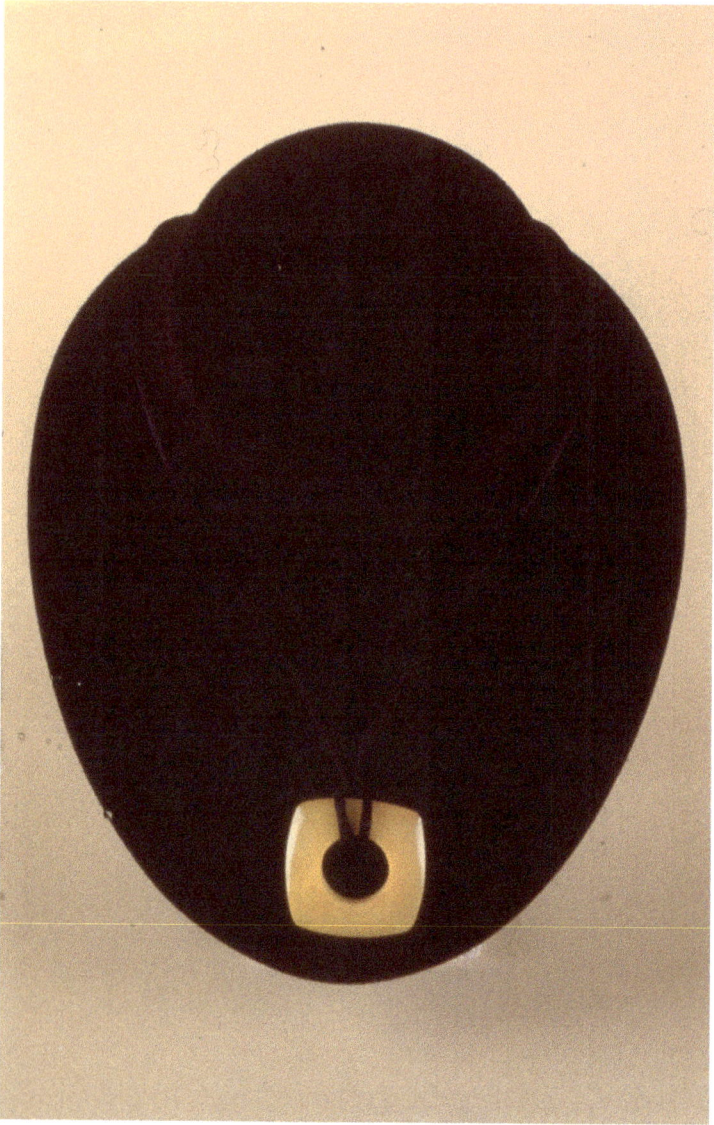

Figure 5.4. Tagua palm nut pendant necklace, Ecuador.

as well as to reduce the smuggling of birds and feathers. These were important in the overall plan to eliminate eventually the commercial market for feathers, which began when the Project provided feathers free of charge to the Pueblos, Native American Church members, and others.

6

The End of the Feather Distribution Project

Until I began writing and revising this manuscript, I retained hope that there would be a continuation of the Feather Distribution Project, that a Pueblo organization would step up at the eleventh hour to assume responsibility for the ongoing operation of the Project. As discussed earlier, various attempts over the years to have a Pueblo organization—preferably a pan-Pueblo organization such as the All Pueblo Council of Governors in Albuquerque—or even an individual village take over the Project were unsuccessful. At the time I began writing, we had finally filled the last four first-time requests and were in the process of distributing the remaining few thousand feathers; when done, the Project ceased operation, on 30 June 2015. We had not accepted any new requests for feathers since August 2011 and had limited the acceptance of repeated requests. Because the few remaining requests in our then-current backlog were for almost all the feathers we offered on our forms (figures 3.1 and 3.2), it took longer than anticipated to fill them. However, they were filled in early June 2015, and at that point, after thirty-four years and around 15 million feathers provided free of charge, the Feather Distribution Project effectively ceased to operate.

During a July 2014 trip to the Southwest to distribute feathers, attend ceremonies, and visit Pueblo and Navajo friends, there were opportunities to discuss the closure of the Project with people from Acoma, Santa Ana, Sandia, Zuni, and Hopi. Several of these friends were told months before that the Project was nearing the end of its existence. All were people with a direct stake in the Project because they

https://doi.org/10.5876/9781646427543.c006

distributed feathers on our behalf to others in their respective villages. Once told the Project would cease by the end of June 2015, there was great disappointment about the Project's cessation and distress about how and where they would obtain feathers once this happened. All said they could not personally take over the Project as individuals; they did not have the resources and expertise. But all also said they hoped there would be some way the Project could continue.

One suggestion made by three or four people was that, perhaps, zoos, bird clubs, and individual donors could send feathers directly to them for distribution within their villages. This suggestion was possible, and I discussed it with a few donors as the Project approached the end of its operation. Several donors said they would continue to send feathers to individuals who have given permission for me to provide their names and addresses to the donors. It's also possible this small effort would eventually regenerate the Project, though not to the extent of its previous status; the problems of sufficient resources and expertise remain serious obstacles.

The people with whom I spoke were not likely to be able to do all the various things that made the Project successful: most notably, presentations to zoos, bird clubs, and other donor organizations. Another factor was age: one man with whom I discussed this was seventy-eight, and another Pueblo member, who headed a resource department in her village, was in her early sixties (she has since died). The youngest was a thirty-year-old Zuni man, young enough to take over the Project if he had the necessary resources, and he was hopeful of keeping it going, at least within his village. Unfortunately, this did not happen.

A further suggestion, made some years ago, was to incorporate the Project as a not-for-profit organization, develop a board of directors, and seek grants and other financial support. I never pursued this, because the Project had an account through the Illinois State Museum Society Foundation to which tax deductible donations in support of the Project could be made. Over the years, we received several thousands of dollars from bird clubs, and honoraria for presentations were also deposited in the account to pay for Project expenses. These were sufficient to the extent that it then seemed too much bother and expense to develop a formal structure for the Project. Past experience also made it clear to me that I did not work well with boards. In hindsight, I have some regret that I did not pursue this at the time.

Several years after my June 2015 retirement from the Museum, I reconsidered the possibility of creating such an organization to keep the Project operating in the future, but my efforts were unsuccessful. Finding board members and especially the right person to run the Project were the challenges. Again, I had no success in finding the right people (I'm not good at networking), and time ran out. The Feather Distribution Project is no longer extant except for a very few direct donor-to-recipient gifts of feathers. A friend who is a Zen practitioner told me that all things have a natural life path, and perhaps the Feather Distribution Project came to the end of its path.

The forty-one volumes of correspondence containing some 45,000 pages—letters, emails, photographs, and other documents—have been deposited in the archive of the Glenn Black Laboratory of Archaeology in Bloomington, Indiana, my under-graduate university.

Acknowledgments

Whatever success the Feather Distribution Project achieved during its thirty-four years of existence was due, at the most fundamental level, to those who provided the feathers. Bob and Diane Streul, then owners of the Hillside Pet Shop in Ottawa, Illinois, who provided the first feathers for the Project, deserve special mention and thanks for their understanding and generosity. It is not possible to list the thousand-plus individual donors, or the hundreds of volunteers over the years who sorted feathers, but I must mention Barbara Anderson and her son, Tom, who have sorted several hundred thousand feathers over the five-plus years they volunteered for this work. We do, however, list the names of the zoos, animal parks, bird clubs, businesses, and organizations that sent feathers both occasionally and on a regular basis. Without a steady supply of donated feathers, the Project could not have operated for as long as it did and would not have had such a positive effect on the lives of Native American peoples in the Southwest and elsewhere in the United States.

Zoos and Wildlife Parks: Adventure Aquarium, Animal Adventures, Animal World & Snake Farm, Audubon Nature Institute, Beardsley Zoo, Bergen County Zoological Park, Birmingham Zoo, Central Florida Zoo & Botanical Gardens, Discovery Cove, Downtown Aquarium Denver, Downtown Aquarium Houston, Elmwood Park Zoo, Erie Zoo, Great Plains Zoo and Delbridge Museum, Gulf World Marine Park, Henry Vilas Zoo, Jenkinson's Aquarium, Kansas City Zoo, Knoxville Zoo, Mesker Park Zoo, Milwaukee County Zoo, Moody Gardens, National Aquarium at Baltimore, Natural Encounters, Newport Aquarium,

https://doi.org/10.5876/9781646427543.c007

Oakland Zoo, Philadelphia Zoo, Phoenix Zoo, Rolling Hills Wildlife Adventure, Sacramento Zoo, Safari West, San Diego Zoo, Scovill Zoo, St. Augustine Alligator Farm Zoological Garden, St. Louis Zoo, Six Flags Discovery Kingdom, Turtleback Zoo, Utica Zoo, Wild Florida, Woodland Park Zoo, Zoo Atlanta, and Zoo Miami.

Bird Clubs, Businesses, and Organizations: Always Birds First, Baltimore Bird Fanciers, Bird Clubs of Virginia, Bird Love, Birds of a Feather, Carvalho's Friends of a Feather, The Crab Shack, Fallston Veterinary Clinic, Feathered Follies, Gainesville Bird Fanciers Club, Gateway Parrot Club, Georgia Cage Bird Society, Good Bird, Inc., Hong Kong Parrot Club, Illinois Bird Fanciers, Jesse's Hunting Page, Kentuckiana Feathered Friends, Kersting Bird Medicine and Surgery, The Landing Zone Parrot Sanctuary, Midnight Iguana Tattoo, Montreal Bird & Exotic Animal Hospital, National Wild Turkey Federation, Nightwing Studio, Peninsula Caged Bird Society, Phoenix Landing, Rainforest Café, Simmons Animal Hospital, Southern Nevada Parrot Education, Rescue & Re-homing Society, Saint Louis Avian Rescue, South Jersey Bird Club, Todd Marcus Birds Exotic, Tropics Exotic Bird Refuge, Wings of Hope, and York Area Pet Bird Club.

Several individuals merit special mention. First and foremost is my wife, Laura, who has worked in all aspects of the Project, traveled with me to distribute feathers, and supported my expenditure of our money to operate the Project. Kathleen Grayson Smith created and, as necessary, updated and improved the Feather Distribution Project website; Catherine Vine, a former bird keeper at the Philadelphia Zoo, created a beautiful poster for the Project that was distributed to zoos, clubs, and veterinary clinics around the country to promote the Project and to recruit new feather donors. She was also instrumental in directly recruiting other zoos and organizations to donate feathers; Eric Jeltes, a bird keeper at the St. Louis Zoo, helped promote the Project through a local television program (see the Feather Distribution Project website) and also recruited other zoos as donors; Tiffany Palumbo Chapman, a bird keeper at several zoos and organizations, did the same as she moved from one position to another. Among the individual feather donors, Mike Davis, a turkey hunter from North Carolina, deserves a special "thank you" for the hundreds of thousands of wild turkey feathers he shipped and hand-delivered to the Project. I am so grateful to him.

First Gary Andrashko and then his successor, Doug Carr, the two Illinois State Museum staff photographers, took several of the photographs used in this volume. Doug also designed and produced the three maps of the distributions of the Scarlet Macaw, the Military Macaw, and the Blue-and-Yellow Macaw and the trade routes into the American Southwest.

The Feather Distribution Project would never have come into existence if it had not been for that question asked by the late Fernando (Fred) Cordero of Cochiti

Pueblo at the 14 July 1970 Feast Day: "Can you get us macaw feathers?" All Pueblo people and other Native Americans ultimately owe Fred a "thank you" and their gratitude.

Although confidentiality prevents disclosing their names, I am indebted to several dozen Pueblo men and three women, who distributed feathers to others in their villages on behalf of the Project. Without their assistance, we would not have reached as many Pueblo recipients as we did. Thank you all. And to my Pueblo and Navajo friends and colleagues, who welcomed me into their homes, fed me, and provided much of the information in this book, my thanks and gratitude for your help, friendship, and trust.

Dr. Tessie Naranjo of Santa Clara Pueblo, a friend of almost thirty years, and Dr. Joseph Suina of Cochití Pueblo read an earlier version of this manuscript. I am grateful for their reviews and helpful comments which improved this version.

My wife, Laura, helped with all phases of the Project, from washing and sorting feathers to traveling with me on numerous occasions to deliver them. I am so grateful to her for her efforts and support.

Finally, my thanks and appreciation are extended to Darrin Pratt, editor for the University Press of Colorado, and Skylar Cooper, editorial assistant, who shepherded the manuscript through to its publication.

Appendix A

Proposal for an All-Pueblo Macaw and Parrot Sanctuary

It is proposed that the New Mexico Pueblos and the Hopi, collectively, construct, staff, and maintain a not-for-profit sanctuary and aviary for macaws and parrots. The functions of the proposed facility are to:

1. Provide aviculturally proper and humane long-term housing and care for unwanted macaws and parrots (see below);
2. Distribute molted feathers from these birds to enrolled Pueblo members for use in and to preserve traditional cultural activities (assumption and expansion of the Feather Distribution Project);
3. Provide avian veterinary care for birds owned by enrolled Pueblo members;
4. Provide jobs and additional economic opportunities to enrolled Pueblo members;
5. Further Pueblo community economic development; and
6. Operate as a tourist facility and educational center within the State of New Mexico.

This proposal is made because of the continuing need by the Pueblos for macaw and parrot feathers, the difficulty in obtaining these at little or no cost, and because the Feather Distribution Project cannot be operated indefinitely by Dr. Jonathan E. Reyman.

Location: Within the State of New Mexico or on a specific Pueblo's land on or near the Albuquerque–Santa Fe corridor (preferred).

https://doi.org/10.5876/9781646427543.c008

Description: The proposed facility (to be expanded as necessary) would consist of a large, semi free-flight aviary (e.g., 200′ long × 100′ wide × 30′ high) with an adjacent veterinary facility, a secure holding area for birds unable to fly, and a visitor's reception center and gift shop.

The gift shop would carry bird-related items such as T-shirts, postcards, stationery, mugs, key chains, etc. It could also be an outlet for traditional Pueblo arts and crafts that are bird related, for example, pottery with macaw, parrot, and feather motifs, ceramic bird figurines, jewelry with bird and feathers designs, etc. A small museum featuring the 1,000–1,500-year history of Pueblo use of macaws and parrots from the Ancestral Pueblo period to the present would be a further addition to the facility. However, no sacred or other culturally sensitive material would be displayed.

Personnel: Initially, the facility would require an avian veterinarian, two assistants, a facility manager, two to three maintenance personnel, a secretary-receptionist, a bookkeeper, security personnel (contract), and two to three gift shop personnel. Ideally, all personnel would eventually be Pueblo people, but initially this would probably not be the case. It is anticipated that, if successful, the facility would eventually employ upwards of several dozen people.

At present, there are at least three enrolled Pueblo members who are veterinarians, but I do not know whether any are certified avian veterinarians. Although certification is not required, it would increase the level of professionalism, especially in the public's perception. Funds might be provided for one or more of these veterinarians to obtain avian certification.

Funding: Initial construction costs and operating expenses could come from casino revenues and/or from federal, state, and private foundation funds that might be available for both start-up and subsequent costs. The Small Business Administration might also be a funding possibility. Those Pueblos without casinos could provide in-kind contributions such as construction labor, materials, and support once the facility is completed. Such support might include agricultural products (corn, fruit, etc.) to feed the birds. Once the facility is completed, additional revenues would come from visitor admission fees and gift shop sales.

Macaw and Parrot Stock: The initial population of the sanctuary/aviary would come from four sources:

  1. Macaws and parrots past breeding age, acquired from breeders who no longer want them;

2. Pet birds that owners no longer can care for or want;
3. Birds from rescue organizations which have too many birds or which seek homes for birds they acquire; and
4. "Rescues"—birds for which homes are needed because of domestic crises.

If a certified quarantine facility could be established and maintained, it is possible that additional birds might be obtained from the federal and state (?) governments, that is, birds which have been seized from smugglers, drug dealers under RICO prosecutions, etc.

Some birds probably would be of breeding age, so it's possible that a breeding program could be established (although this is not recommended, at least at the outset). This would provide additional feathers and could provide additional revenues, if the young birds are sold after weaning and hand raising. Such a program would require additional, trained personnel, including zoologists specializing in bird genetics.

External Assistance: With permission, I would turn over the records of the Feather Distribution Project to the proposed facility [note: This is no longer possible, because since, I deposited the records, as part of my professional library, to the Glenn Black Laboratory of Archaeology]. These records include sources for feathers, contacts for acquiring birds, and other information. I would also assist in obtaining technical and other support for the facility from the American Federation for Aviculture, the American Zoological Association, the American Association of Zookeepers, and related organizations. Zuni's Department of Natural Resources, Fish and Wildlife Division, constructed and maintains an eagle sanctuary, and their assistance could be sought for the establishment and maintenance of the proposed facility. Private, federal, and state funds might also be available to help support the facility.

Extensions: In addition to the above-mentioned job and economic opportunities, the proposed facility would encourage small-scale, local Pueblo farming activities to provide food for the birds. In time, this facility and the proposed turkey facility could help to revitalize Pueblo farming for those who wish to continue with this activity. It could also provide practical training in business and museum management, public relations, and other fields.

Appendix B

Proposal for an All-Pueblo Wild and Domestic Turkey Facility

It is proposed that the New Mexico Pueblos and the Hopi, collectively, construct, staff, and maintain a not-for-profit, organically raised, free-ranging turkey population and processing plant. The functions of the proposed facility are to:

1. Raise and to sell locally, regionally, and nationally, processed, free-ranging turkeys based on an initial wild turkey population;
2. Provide feathers from these turkeys to enrolled Pueblo members for use in and to preserve traditional cultural activities (assumption and expansion of the Feather Distribution Project);
3. Provide jobs and additional economic opportunities to enrolled Pueblo members;
4. Further Pueblo economic development; and
5. Operate as a business, tourist, and educational facility within the State of New Mexico.

This proposal is made because of the continuing need by the Pueblos for wild turkey feathers and because the Feather Distribution Project cannot be operated indefinitely by Dr. Jonathan E. Reyman. [note: By the 2025 publication of this book, the Project had ceased to exist.]

Location: On State of New Mexico land (preferred) or on a specific Pueblo's land.

https://doi.org/10.5876/9781646427543.c009

Note: **This facility must be separate from the proposed macaw/parrot facility [appendix A] to avoid disease and other health issues for the birds.**

Description: The proposed facility would consist of an area to "house" and support the turkey population, a research laboratory (and possible incubating facility), an office, a processing plant, a visitor's center, poultry shop, gift shop, and maintenance building. At a later date, a small museum featuring the 1,500-year history of Pueblo use and domestication of the wild turkey from the Ancestral Pueblo period to the present could be added.

The poultry shop would sell whole turkeys and turkey products, both fresh and frozen. The gift shop would sell turkey-related items such as T-shirts, mugs, etc., plus a selection of traditional Pueblo arts and crafts with turkey motifs such as pottery, turkey ceramic figurines, jewelry, and other items. Although some Pueblos such as Zuni offer turkey hunting on their lands, the facility could operate as a central contact point for other Pueblos, including making reservations for hunting and the employment of Pueblo guides.

Personnel: Initially, the facility would require an avian biologist / wildlife manager, perhaps a veterinarian, a facility manager, business manager, bookkeeper, butchers, meat packers, a secretary-receptionist, two to three gift shop personnel, poultry sales and shipping personnel, security personnel (contract), and three to four maintenance personnel. It is anticipated that, if successful, the facility would eventually employ directly some 50–75 Pueblo people.

Funding: Initial construction costs and operating expenses would come from a combination of loans from the Small Business Administration, loans or grants from other federal, state, and private foundation sources, and from casino revenues. Once the facility is completed, additional revenues would come from poultry and gift shop sales and museum admission, and, perhaps, visitor admission fees (for processing plant tours).

Turkey Stock: The National Wild Turkey Federation (NWTF) has re-stocked the Zuni and other tribal lands in the Southwest. Initially, it might be possible to have them stock the land at the facility in exchange for its use as a hunting area. It might also be possible to purchase eggs to be incubated and hatched at the facility. The relatively few turkeys in the Pueblos might also be utilized as a source for eggs and live birds for the facility. The acquisition of breeding stock for the population needs further study, including the possibility of raising so-called "Heritage" breeds, for example, Standard Bronze, Bourbon Red, Narragansett, Blue Slate, Jersey Buff,

Slate, Black Spanish, White Holland, Royal Palm, White Midget and Beltsville Small White, some of which such as the Bourbon Red and Royal Palm have feathers, the colors of which are especially appealing for some ceremonial uses.

Once acquired, however, the turkeys could be free-ranging over the area, though naturally available foods could be supplemented by planted crops (e.g., chufa) and direct feeding of organically grown corn and other feed.

External Assistance: With permission, I would turn over the records of the Feather Distribution Project that pertain to wild turkey feather use to the proposed facility. These records include sources for feathers, contacts for acquiring birds, and other information. [Again, note that this is no longer possible, because since, I deposited the records, as part of my professional library, to the Glenn Black Laboratory of Archaeology.] I could help to obtain assistance from the NWTF for the facility. Assistance from State of New Mexico wildlife managers and possibly USF&W personnel would also be sought.

Extensions: The turkeys, whole and in parts, could be marketed, at premium prices, both locally and especially in large cities as "genuine, free-ranging, organically fed Pueblo turkeys." *"Buy America's bird from America's First People"* should have strong market appeal. Product quality, of course, must be high to match the premium price.

In addition to the above-mentioned jobs and economic opportunities, the proposed facility would encourage small-scale, local Pueblo farming to provide feed for the turkeys. In time, this facility and the proposed macaw/parrot aviary could help to revitalize Pueblo farming for those who wish to continue with this activity. It would also provide training in business and wildlife management, processing plant operations, public relations and advertising, and other fields. ***Note, again, however, that the proposed turkey facility and the proposed macaw/parrot facility must be kept at a substantial distance from each other, to ensure the biological health of the respective bird populations.***

Appendix C

Birds Protected by the Migratory Bird Treaty Act (Updated 2018)

The Migratory Bird Treaty Act makes it illegal for anyone to take, possess, import, export, transport, sell, purchase, barter, or offer for sale, purchase, or barter, any migratory bird, or the parts, nests, or eggs of such a bird except under the terms of a valid permit issued pursuant to Federal regulations. The migratory bird species protected by the Act are listed in 50 CFR 10.13.

The US Fish and Wildlife Service has statutory authority and responsibility for enforcing the Migratory Bird Treaty Act (MBTA) (16 U.S.C. 703–712), the Fish and Wildlife Improvement Act of 1978 (16 U.S.C. 742l), and the Fish and Wildlife Act of 1956 (16 U.S.C. 742a–j). The MBTA implements Conventions between the United States and four countries (Canada, Mexico, Japan, and Russia) for the protection of migratory birds.

WHAT CRITERIA ARE USED TO IDENTIFY INDIVIDUAL SPECIES PROTECTED BY THE MBTA?

A species qualifies for protection under the MBTA by meeting one or more of the following four criteria:

1. It is covered by the Canadian Convention of 1916, as amended in 1996, by virtue of meeting the following three criteria: (a) It belongs to a family or group of species named in the Canadian Convention, as amended; (b) Specimens,

photographs, videotape recordings or audiotape recordings provide convincing evidence of natural occurrence in the United States or its territories; and (c) The documentation of such records has been recognized by the AOU or other competent scientific authorities.

2. It is covered by the Mexican Convention of 1936, as amended in 1972, by virtue of meeting the following three criteria: (a) It belongs to a family or group of species named in the Mexican Convention, as amended; (b) Specimens, photographs, videotape recordings or audiotape recordings provide convincing evidence of natural occurrence in the United States or its territories; and (c) The documentation of such records has been recognized by the AOU or other competent scientific authorities.

3. It is listed in the annex to the Japanese Convention of 1972, as amended.

4. It is listed in the appendix to the Russian Convention of 1976.

In accordance with the Migratory Bird Treaty Reform Act of 2004 (MBTRA) (Pub. L. No. 108–447, 118 Stat. 2809, 3071–72), we included all species native to the United States or its territories, which are those that occur as a result of natural biological or ecological processes (See 70 FR 12710, March 15, 2005). We did not include nonnative species whose occurrences in the United States are solely the result of intentional or unintentional human-assisted introduction(s).

LIST OF MIGRATORY BIRD SPECIES PROTECTED BY THE MIGRATORY BIRD TREATY ACT (UPDATED 2018)

Very few of these species were distributed by the Feather Distribution Project because they were protected as endangered and/or threatened species—for example, eagles and hawks—as well as protected by their migratory status. Macaws and most parrots are not migratory but many species, including all macaws, are endangered. They are protected by the CITES treaty, but the Project had the necessary permits to distribute them.

TABLE C.1. List of Protected Species 2018 (**X** = species used by the Pueblos). Species are listed by the scientific name of each species followed by the common name.

Dendrocygna autumnalis	Black-bellied Whistling-Duck
Dendrocygna arborea	West Indian Whistling-Duck
Dendrocygna bicolor	Fulvous Whistling-Duck
(2) SUBFAMILY ANSERINAE	
Anser canagicus	Emperor Goose
Anser caerulescens	Snow Goose
Anser rossii	Ross's Goose
Anser albifrons	Greater White-fronted Goose
Anser erythropus	Lesser White-fronted Goose
Anser fabalis	Taiga Bean-Goose
Anser serrirostris	Tundra Bean-Goose
Anser brachyrhynchus	Pink-footed Goose
Branta bernicla	Brant
Branta leucopsis	Barnacle Goose
X *Branta hutchinsii*	Cackling Goose
X *Branta canadensis*	Canada Goose
Branta sandvicensis	Hawaiian Goose
Cygnus buccinator	Trumpeter Swan
Cygnus columbianus	Tundra Swan
Cygnus cygnus	Whooper Swan
(3) SUBFAMILY ANATINAE	
Cairina moschata	Muscovy Duck
X *Aix sponsa*	Wood Duck
Sibirionetta formosa	Baikal Teal
Spatula querquedula	Garganey
Spatula discors	Blue-winged Teal
Spatula cyanoptera	Cinnamon Teal
Spatula clypeata	Northern Shoveler
Mareca strepera	Gadwall
Mareca falcata	Falcated Duck
Mareca penelope	Eurasian Wigeon
Mareca americana	American Wigeon
Anas laysanensis	Laysan Duck

continued on next page

TABLE C.1—*continued*

Anas wyvilliana	Hawaiian Duck
Anas zonorhyncha	Eastern Spot-billed Duck
X *Anas platyrhynchos*	Mallard
Anas diazi	Mexican Duck
Anas rubripes	American Black Duck
Anas fulvigula	Mottled Duck
Anas superciliosa	Pacific Black Duck
Anas bahamensis	White-cheeked Pintail
Anas acuta	Northern Pintail
Anas crecca	Green-winged Teal
Aythya valisineria	Canvasback
Aythya americana	Redhead
Aythya ferina	Common Pochard
Aythya baeri	Baer's Pochard
Aythya collaris	Ring-necked Duck
Aythya fuligula	Tufted Duck
Aythya marila	Greater Scaup
Aythya affinis	Lesser Scaup
Polysticta stelleri	Steller's Eider
Somateria fischeri	Spectacled Eider
Somateria spectabilis	King Eider
Somateria mollissima	Common Eider
Histrionicus histrionicus	Harlequin Duck
Melanitta perspicillata	Surf Scoter
Melanitta deglandi	White-winged Scoter
Melanitta stejneger	Stejneger's Scoter
Melanitta nigra	Common Scoter
Melanitta americana	Black Scoter
Clangula hyemalis	Long-tailed Duck
Bucephala albeola	Bufflehead
Bucephala clangula	Common Goldeneye
Bucephala islandica	Barrow's Goldeneye
Mergellus albellus	Smew
Lophodytes cucullatus	Hooded Merganser

continued on next page

TABLE C.1—*continued*

X *Mergus merganser*	Common Merganser
Mergus serrator	Red-breasted Merganser
Nomonyx dominicus	Masked Duck
Oxyura jamaicensis	Ruddy Duck
(ii) Order Phoenicopteriformes	
FAMILY PHOENICOPTERIDAE	
Phoenicopterus ruber	American Flamingo
(iii) Order Podicipediformes	
FAMILY PODICIPEDIDAE	
Tachybaptus dominicus	Least Grebe
Podilymbus podiceps	Pied-billed Grebe
Podiceps auritus	Horned Grebe
Podiceps grisegena	Red-necked Grebe
Podiceps nigricollis	Eared Grebe
Aechmophorus occidentalis	Western Grebe
Aechmophorus clarkii	Clark's Grebe
(iv) Order Columbiformes	
FAMILY COLUMBIDAE	
Patagioenas squamosa	Scaly-naped Pigeon
Patagioenas leucocephala	White-crowned Pigeon
Patagioenas flavirostris	Red-billed Pigeon
Patagioenas inornata	Plain Pigeon
Patagioenas fasciata	Band-tailed Pigeon
Streptopelia orientalis	Oriental Turtle-Dove
Alopecoenas stairi	Shy Ground Dove
Alopecoenas xanthonurus	White-throated Ground Dove
Columbina inca	Inca Dove
Columbina passerina	Common Ground Dove
Columbina talpacoti	Ruddy Ground Dove
Geotrygon montana	Ruddy Quail-Dove
Geotrygon chrysia	Key West Quail-Dove
Geotrygon mystacea	Bridled Quail-Dove
Leptotila verreauxi	White-tipped Dove
Zenaida asiatica	White-winged Dove

continued on next page

TABLE C.1—*continued*

Zenaida aurita	Zenaida Dove
Zenaida macroura	Mourning Dove
Ptilinopus perousii	Many-colored Fruit-Dove
Ptilinopus porphyraceus	Crimson-crowned Fruit-Dove
Ptilinopus roseicapilla	Mariana Fruit-Dove
Ducula pacifica	Pacific Imperial-Pigeon
(v) Order Cuculiformes	
FAMILY CUCULIDAE	
(1) SUBFAMILY CROTOPHAGINAE	
Crotophaga ani	Smooth-billed Ani
Crotophaga sulcirostris	Groove-billed Ani
(2) SUBFAMILY NEOMORPHINAE	
X *Geococcyx californianus*	Greater Roadrunner
(3) SUBFAMILY CUCULINAE	
Urodynamis taitensis	Long-tailed Koel
Hierococcyx nisicolor	Hodgson's Hawk-Cuckoo
Cuculus canorus	Common Cuckoo
Cuculus optatus	Oriental Cuckoo
Clamator coromandus	Chestnut-winged Cuckoo
Coccyzus melacoryphus	Dark-billed Cuckoo
Coccyzus americanus	Yellow-billed Cuckoo
Coccyzus minor	Mangrove Cuckoo
Coccyzus erythropthalmus	Black-billed Cuckoo
Coccyzus vieilloti	Puerto Rican Lizard-Cuckoo
(vi) Order Caprimulgiformes	
FAMILY CAPRIMULGIDAE	
(1) SUBFAMILY CHORDEILINAE	
Chordeiles acutipennis	Lesser Nighthawk
Chordeiles minor	Common Nighthawk
Chordeiles gundlachii	Antillean Nighthawk
(2) SUBFAMILY CAPRIMULGINAE	
Nyctidromus albicollis	Common Pauraque
Phalaenoptilus nuttallii	Common Poorwill

continued on next page

TABLE C.1—*continued*

Antrostomus carolinensis	Chuck-will's-widow
Antrostomus ridgwayi	Buff-collared Nightjar
Antrostomus vociferus	Eastern Whip-poor-will
Antrostomus arizonae	Mexican Whip-poor-will
Antrostomus noctitherus	Puerto Rican Nightjar
Hydropsalis cayennensis	White-tailed Nightjar
Caprimulgus jotaka	Gray Nightjar
(vii) Order Apodiformes	
(A) FAMILY APODIDAE	
(1) SUBFAMILY CYPSELOIDINAE	
Cypseloides niger	Black Swift
Streptoprocne zonaris	White-collared Swift
(2) SUBFAMILY CHAETURINAE	
Chaetura pelagica	Chimney Swift
Chaetura vauxi	Vaux's Swift
Chaetura brachyura	Short-tailed Swift
Hirundapus caudacutus	White-throated Needletail
Aerodramus spodiopygius	White-rumped Swiftlet
Aerodramus bartschi	Mariana Swiftlet
(3) SUBFAMILY APODINAE	
Apus apus	Common Swift
Apus pacificus	Fork-tailed Swift
Apus melba	Alpine Swift
Aeronautes saxatalis	White-throated Swift
Tachornis phoenicobia	Antillean Palm-Swift
(B) FAMILY TROCHILIDAE	
SUBFAMILY TROCHILINAE	
Colibri thalassinus	Mexican Violetear
Anthracothorax prevostii	Green-breasted Mango
Anthracothorax aurulentus	Puerto Rican Mango
Anthracothorax viridis	Green Mango
Eulampis jugularis	Purple-throated Carib
Eulampis holosericeus	Green-throated Carib
Eugenes fulgens	Rivoli's Hummingbird

continued on next page

TABLE C.1—*continued*

Heliomaster constantii	Plain-capped Starthroat
Lampornis amethystinus	Amethyst-throated Mountain-gem
X *Lampornis clemenciae*	Blue-throated Mountain-gem
Calothorax lucifer	Lucifer Hummingbird
X *Archilochus colubris*	Ruby-throated Hummingbird
Archilochus alexandri	Black-chinned Hummingbird
Mellisuga minima	Vervain Hummingbird
Nesophlox evelynae	Bahama Woodstar
Calypte anna	Anna's Hummingbird
Calypte costae	Costa's Hummingbird
Selasphorus calliope	Calliope Hummingbird
X *Selasphorus rufus*	Rufous Hummingbird
Selasphorus sasin	Allen's Hummingbird
Selasphorus platycercus	Broad-tailed Hummingbird
Selasphorus heloisa	Bumblebee Hummingbird
Riccordia maugaeus	Puerto Rican Emerald
Cynanthus latirostris	Broad-billed Hummingbird
Basilinna leucotis	White-eared Hummingbird
Basilinna xantusii	Xantus's Hummingbird
Orthorhyncus cristatus	Antillean Crested Hummingbird
Ramosomyia violiceps	Violet-crowned Hummingbird
Saucerottia beryllina	Berylline Hummingbird
Amazilia rutila	Cinnamon Hummingbird
Amazilia yucatanensis	Buff-bellied Hummingbird
(viii) Order Gruiformes	
(A) FAMILY RALLIDAE	
Gallirallus philippensis	Buff-banded Rail
Gallirallus owstoni	Guam Rail
Neocrex erythrops	Paint-billed Crake
Pardirallus maculatus	Spotted Rail
Aramides axillaris	Rufous-necked Wood-Rail
Rallus obsoletus	Ridgway's Rail
Rallus elegans	King Rail

continued on next page

TABLE C.1—*continued*

Rallus crepitans	Clapper Rail
Rallus limicola	Virginia Rail
Crex crex	Corn Crake
Porzana carolina	Sora
Gallinula galeata	Common Gallinule
Gallinula chloropus	Eurasian Moorhen
Fulica atra	Eurasian Coot
Fulica alai	Hawaiian Coot
Fulica americana	American Coot
Porphyrio martinicus	Purple Gallinule
Porphyrio flavirostris	Azure Gallinule
Porphyrio porphyrio	Purple Swamphen
Porzana tabuensis	Spotless Crake
Coturnicops noveboracensis	Yellow Rail
Hapalocrex flaviventer	Yellow-breasted Crake
Laterallus jamaicensis	Black Rail
(B) FAMILY ARAMIDAE	
Aramus guarauna	Limpkin
(C) FAMILY GRUIDAE	
SUBFAMILY GRUINAE	
Antigone canadensis	Sandhill Crane
Grus grus	Common Crane
Grus monacha	Hooded Crane
Grus americana	Whooping Crane
(ix) Order Charadriiformes	
(A) FAMILY RECURVIROSTRIDAE	
Himantopus himantopus	Black-winged Stilt
Himantopus mexicanus	Black-necked Stilt
Recurvirostra americana	American Avocet
(B) FAMILY HAEMATOPODIDAE	
Haematopus ostralegus	Eurasian Oystercatcher
Haematopus palliatus	American Oystercatcher
Haematopus bachmani	Black Oystercatcher

continued on next page

TABLE C.1—*continued*

(C) FAMILY CHARADRIIDAE	
(1) SUBFAMILY VANELLINAE	
Vanellus	Northern Lapwing
(2) SUBFAMILY CHARADRIINAE	
Pluvialis squatarola	Black-bellied Plover
Pluvialis apricaria	European Golden-Plover
Pluvialis dominica	American Golden-Plover
Pluvialis fulva	Pacific Golden-Plover
Charadrius morinellus	Eurasian Dotterel
Charadrius vociferus	Killdeer
Charadrius hiaticula	Common Ringed Plover
Charadrius semipalmatus	Semipalmated Plover
Charadrius melodus	Piping Plover
Charadrius dubius	Little Ringed Plover
Charadrius mongolus	Lesser Sand-Plover
Charadrius leschenaultii	Greater Sand-Plover
Charadrius wilsonia	Wilson's Plover
Charadrius collaris	Collared Plover
Charadrius alexandrinus	Kentish Plover
Charadrius montanus	Mountain Plover
Charadrius nivosus	Snowy Plover
(D) FAMILY JACANIDAE	
Jacana spinosa	Northern Jacana
(E) FAMILY SCOLOPACIDAE	
(1) SUBFAMILY NUMENIINAE	
Bartramia longicauda	Upland Sandpiper
Numenius tahitiensis	Bristle-thighed Curlew
Numenius phaeopus	Whimbrel
Numenius minutus	Little Curlew
Numenius borealis	Eskimo Curlew
Numenius americanus	Long-billed Curlew
Numenius madagascariensis	Far Eastern Curlew
Numenius arquata	Eurasian Curlew

continued on next page

TABLE C.1—*continued*

(2) SUBFAMILY LIMOSINAE	
Limosa lapponica	Bar-tailed Godwit
Limosa limosa	Black-tailed Godwit
Limosa haemastica	Hudsonian Godwit
Limosa fedoa	Marbled Godwit
(3) SUBFAMILY ARENARIINAE	
Arenaria interpres	Ruddy Turnstone
Arenaria melanocephala	Black Turnstone
Calidris tenuirostris	Great Knot
Calidris canutus	Red Knot
Calidris virgata	Surfbird
Calidris pugnax	Ruff
Calidris falcinellus	Broad-billed Sandpiper
Calidris acuminata	Sharp-tailed Sandpiper
Calidris himantopus	Stilt Sandpiper
Calidris ferruginea	Curlew Sandpiper
Calidris temminckii	Temminck's Stint
Calidris subminuta	Long-toed Stint
Calidris pygmea	Spoon-billed Sandpiper
Calidris ruficollis	Red-necked Stint
Calidris alba	Sanderling
Calidris alpina	Dunlin
Calidris ptilocnemis	Rock Sandpiper
Calidris maritima	Purple Sandpiper
Calidris bairdii	Baird's Sandpiper
Calidris minuta	Little Stint
Calidris minutilla	Least Sandpiper
Calidris fuscicollis	White-rumped Sandpiper
Calidris subruficollis	Buff-breasted Sandpiper
Calidris melanotos	Pectoral Sandpiper
Calidris pusilla	Semipalmated Sandpiper
Calidris mauri	Western Sandpiper
(4) SUBFAMILY SCOLOPACINAE	
Limnodromus griseus	Short-billed Dowitcher
Limnodromus scolopaceus	Long-billed Dowitcher

continued on next page

TABLE C.1—*continued*

Lymnocryptes minimus	Jack Snipe
Scolopax rusticola	Eurasian Woodcock
Scolopax minor	American Woodcock
Gallinago solitaria	Solitary Snipe
Gallinago stenura	Pin-tailed Snipe
Gallinago megala	Swinhoe's Snipe
Gallinago gallinago	Common Snipe
Gallinago delicata	Wilson's Snipe

(5) SUBFAMILY TRINGINAE

Xenus cinereus	Terek Sandpiper
Actitis hypoleucos	Common Sandpiper
Actitis macularius	Spotted Sandpiper
Tringa ochropus	Green Sandpiper
Tringa solitaria	Solitary Sandpiper
Tringa brevipes	Gray-tailed Tattler
Tringa incana	Wandering Tattler
Tringa flavipes	Lesser Yellowlegs
Tringa semipalmata	Willet
Tringa erythropus	Spotted Redshank
Tringa nebularia	Common Greenshank
Tringa guttifer	Nordmann's Greenshank
Tringa melanoleuca	Greater Yellowlegs
Tringa totanus	Common Redshank
Tringa glareola	Wood Sandpiper
Tringa stagnatilis	Marsh Sandpiper
Phalaropus tricolor	Wilson's Phalarope
Phalaropus lobatus	Red-necked Phalarope
Phalaropus fulicarius	Red Phalarope

(F) FAMILY STERCORARIIDAE

Stercorarius skua	Great Skua
Stercorarius maccormicki	South Polar Skua
Stercorarius pomarinus	Pomarine Jaeger
Stercorarius parasiticus	Parasitic Jaeger
Stercorarius longicaudus	Long-tailed Jaeger

continued on next page

TABLE C.1—*continued*

(G) FAMILY ALCIDAE	
Alle alle	Dovekie
Uria aalge	Common Murre
Uria lomvia	Thick-billed Murre
Alca torda	Razorbill
Cepphus grylle	Black Guillemot
Cepphus columba	Pigeon Guillemot
Brachyramphus perdix	Long-billed Murrelet
Brachyramphus marmoratus	Marbled Murrelet
Brachyramphus brevirostris	Kittlitz's Murrelet
Synthliboramphus scrippsi	Scripps's Murrelet
Synthliboramphus hypoleucus	Guadalupe Murrelet
Synthliboramphus craveri	Craveri's Murrelet
Synthliboramphus antiquus	Ancient Murrelet
Ptychoramphus aleuticus	Cassin's Auklet
Aethia psittacula	Parakeet Auklet
Aethia pusilla	Least Auklet
Aethia pygmaea	Whiskered Auklet
Aethia cristatella	Crested Auklet
Cerorhinca monocerata	Rhinoceros Auklet
Fratercula arctica	Atlantic Puffin
Fratercula corniculata	Horned Puffin
Fratercula cirrhata	Tufted Puffin
(H) FAMILY LARIDAE	
(1) SUBFAMILY LARINAE	
Creagrus furcatus	Swallow-tailed Gull
Rissa tridactyla	Black-legged Kittiwake
Rissa brevirostris	Red-legged Kittiwake
Pagophila eburnea	Ivory Gull
Xema sabini	Sabine's Gull
Chroicocephalus philadelphia	Bonaparte's Gull
Chroicocephalus cirrocephalus	Gray-hooded Gull
Chroicocephalus ridibundus	Black-headed Gull
Hydrocoloeus minutus	Little Gull

continued on next page

TABLE C.1—*continued*

Rhodostethia rosea	Ross's Gull
Leucophaeus atricilla	Laughing Gull
Leucophaeus pipixcan	Franklin's Gull
Ichthyaetus ichthyaetus	Pallas's Gull
Larus belcheri	Belcher's Gull
Larus crassirostris	Black-tailed Gull
Larus heermanni	Heermann's Gull
Larus canus	Common Gull
Larus brachyrhynchus	Short-billed Gull
Larus delawarensis	Ring-billed Gull
Larus occidentalis	Western Gull
Larus livens	Yellow-footed Gull
Larus californicus	California Gull
Larus argentatus	Herring Gull
Larus michahellis	Yellow-legged Gull
Larus glaucoides	Iceland Gull
Larus fuscus	Lesser Black-backed Gull
Larus schistisagus	Slaty-backed Gull
Larus glaucescens	Glaucous-winged Gull
Larus hyperboreus	Glaucous Gull
Larus marinus	Great Black-backed Gull
Larus dominicanus	Kelp Gull

(2) SUBFAMILY STERNINAE

Anous stolidus	Brown Noddy
Anous minutus	Black Noddy
Anous ceruleus	Blue-gray Noddy
Gygis alba	White Tern
Onychoprion fuscatus	Sooty Tern
Onychoprion lunatus	Gray-backed Tern
Onychoprion anaethetus	Bridled Tern
Onychoprion aleuticus	Aleutian Tern
Sternula albifrons	Little Tern
Sternula antillarum	Least Tern
Phaetusa simplex	Large-billed Tern

continued on next page

TABLE C.1—*continued*

Gelochelidon nilotica	Gull-billed Tern
Hydroprogne caspia	Caspian Tern
Larosterna inca	Inca Tern
Chlidonias niger	Black Tern
Chlidonias leucopterus	White-winged Tern
Chlidonias hybrida	Whiskered Tern
Sterna dougallii	Roseate Tern
Sterna sumatrana	Black-naped Tern
Sterna hirundo	Common Tern
Sterna paradisaea	Arctic Tern
Sterna forsteri	Forster's Tern
Thalasseus maximus	Royal Tern
Thalasseus bergii	Great Crested Tern
Thalasseus sandvicensis	Sandwich Tern
Thalasseus elegans	Elegant Tern
(3) Subfamily Rynchopinae	
Rynchops niger	Black Skimmer
(x) Order Phaethontiformes	
Family Phaethontidae	
Phaethon lepturus	White-tailed Tropicbird
Phaethon aethereus	Red-billed Tropicbird
Phaethon rubricauda	Red-tailed Tropicbird
(xi) Order Gaviiformes	
Family Gaviidae	
Gavia stellata	Red-throated Loon
Gavia arctica	Arctic Loon
Gavia pacifica	Pacific Loon
Gavia immer	Common Loon
Gavia adamsii	Yellow-billed Loon
(xii) Order Procellariiformes	
(A) Family Diomedeidae	
Thalassarche chlororhynchos	Yellow-nosed Albatross
Thalassarche cauta	White-capped Albatross
Thalassarche eremita	Chatham Albatross

continued on next page

TABLE C.1—*continued*

Thalassarche salvini	Salvin's Albatross
Thalassarche melanophris	Black-browed Albatross
Phoebetria palpebrata	Light-mantled Albatross
Diomedea exulans	Wandering Albatross
Phoebastria immutabilis	Laysan Albatross
Phoebastria nigripes	Black-footed Albatross
Phoebastria albatrus	Short-tailed Albatross
(B) FAMILY OCEANITIDAE	
FAMILY PHAETHONTIDAE	
Oceanites oceanicus	Wilson's Storm-Petrel
Pelagodroma marina	White-faced Storm-Petrel
Fregetta grallaria	White-bellied Storm-Petrel
Fregetta tropica	Black-bellied Storm-Petrel
Nesofregetta fuliginosa	Polynesian Storm-Petrel
(C) FAMILY HYDROBATIDAE	
Hydrobates pelagicus	European Storm-Petrel
Hydrobates furcatus	Fork-tailed Storm-Petrel
Hydrobates hornbyi	Ringed Storm-Petrel
Hydrobates monorhis	Swinhoe's Storm-Petrel
Hydrobates leucorhous	Leach's Storm-Petrel
Hydrobates socorroensis	Townsend's Storm-Petrel
Hydrobates homochroa	Ashy Storm-Petrel
Hydrobates castro	Band-rumped Storm-Petrel
Hydrobates tethys	Wedge-rumped Storm-Petrel
Hydrobates melania	Black Storm-Petrel
Hydrobates matsudairae	Matsudaira's Storm-Petrel
Hydrobates tristrami	Tristram's Storm-Petrel
Hydrobates microsoma	Least Storm-Petrel
(D) FAMILY PROCELLARIIDAE	
Macronectes halli	Northern Giant-Petrel
Fulmarus glacialis	Northern Fulmar
Pterodroma gouldi	Gray-faced Petrel
Pterodroma solandri	Providence Petrel

continued on next page

TABLE C.1—*continued*

Pterodroma neglecta	Kermadec Petrel
Pterodroma arminjoniana	Trindade Petrel
Pterodroma heraldica	Herald Petrel
Pterodroma ultima	Murphy's Petrel
Pterodroma inexpectata	Mottled Petrel
Pterodroma cahow	Bermuda Petrel
Pterodroma hasitata	Black-capped Petrel
Pterodroma externa	Juan Fernandez Petrel
Pterodroma sandwichensis	Hawaiian Petrel
Pterodroma cervicalis	White-necked Petrel
Pterodroma hypoleuca	Bonin Petrel
Pterodroma nigripennis	Black-winged Petrel
Pterodroma feae	Fea's Petrel
Pterodroma madeira	Zino's Petrel
Pterodroma cookii	Cook's Petrel
Pterodroma leucoptera	Gould's Petrel
Pterodroma longirostris	Stejneger's Petrel
Pterodroma alba	Phoenix Petrel
Pseudobulweria rostrata	Tahiti Petrel
Bulweria bulwerii	Bulwer's Petrel
Bulweria fallax	Jouanin's Petrel
Procellaria aequinoctialis	White-chinned Petrel
Procellaria parkinsoni	Parkinson's Petrel
Calonectris leucomelas	Streaked Shearwater
Calonectris diomedea	Cory's Shearwater
Calonectris edwardsii	Cape Verde Shearwater
Ardenna pacifica	Wedge-tailed Shearwater
Ardenna bulleri	Buller's Shearwater
Ardenna tenuirostris	Short-tailed Shearwater
Ardenna grisea	Sooty Shearwater
Ardenna gravis	Great Shearwater
Ardenna creatopus	Pink-footed Shearwater
Ardenna carneipes	Flesh-footed Shearwater
Puffinus nativitatis	Christmas Shearwater

continued on next page

TABLE C.1—*continued*

Puffinus puffinus	Manx Shearwater
Puffinus newelli	Newell's Shearwater
Puffinus bryani	Bryan's Shearwater
Puffinus opisthomelas	Black-vented Shearwater
Puffinus lherminieri	Audubon's Shearwater
Puffinus baroli	Barolo Shearwater
(xiii) Order Ciconiiformes	
FAMILY CICONIIDAE	
Jabiru mycteria	Jabiru
Mycteria americana	Wood Stork
(xiv) Order Suliformes	
(A) FAMILY FREGATIDAE	
Fregata ariel	Lesser Frigatebird
Fregata magnificens	Magnificent Frigatebird
Fregata minor	Great Frigatebird
(B) FAMILY SULIDAE	
Sula dactylatra	Masked Booby
Sula granti	Nazca Booby
Sula nebouxii	Blue-footed Booby
Sula leucogaster	Brown Booby
Sula sula	Red-footed Booby
Papasula abbotti	Abbott's Booby
Morus bassanus	Northern Gannet
(C) FAMILY ANHINGIDAE	
Anhinga anhinga	Anhinga
(D) FAMILY PHALACROCORACIDAE	
Microcarbo melanoleucos	Little Pied Cormorant
Urile penicillatus	Brandt's Cormorant
Urile urile	Red-faced Cormorant
Urile pelagicus	Pelagic Cormorant
Phalacrocorax carbo	Great Cormorant
Nannopterum auritum	Double-crested Cormorant
Nannopterum brasilianum	Neotropic Cormorant
(xv) Order Pelecaniformes	

continued on next page

TABLE C.1—*continued*

(A) FAMILY PELECANIDAE	
Pelecanus erythrorhynchos	American White Pelican
Pelecanus occidentalis	Brown Pelican

(B) FAMILY ARDEIDAE	
Botaurus lentiginosus	American Bittern
Ixobrychus sinensis	Yellow Bittern
Ixobrychus exilis	Least Bittern
Ixobrychus eurhythmus	Schrenck's Bittern
Ixobrychus flavicollis	Black Bittern
Tigrisoma mexicanum	Bare-throated Tiger-Heron
X *Ardea herodias*	Great Blue Heron
Ardea cinerea	Gray Heron
Ardea alba	Great Egret
Ardea intermedia	Intermediate Egret
Egretta eulophotes	Chinese Egret
Egretta garzetta	Little Egret
Egretta sacra	Pacific Reef-Heron
Egretta gularis	Western Reef-Heron
Egretta thula	Snowy Egret
Egretta caerulea	Little Blue Heron
Egretta tricolor	Tricolored Heron
Egretta rufescens	Reddish Egret
Bubulcus ibis	Cattle Egret
Ardeola bacchus	Chinese Pond-Heron
Butorides virescens	Green Heron
Nycticorax nycticorax	Black-crowned Night-Heron
Nycticorax caledonicus	Nankeen Night-Heron
Nyctanassa violacea	Yellow-crowned Night-Heron
Gorsachius goisagi	Japanese Night-Heron
Gorsachius melanolophus	Malayan Night-Heron

(C) FAMILY THRESKIORNITHIDAE	
(1) SUBFAMILY THRESKIORNITHINAE	
Eudocimus albus	White Ibis
Eudocimus ruber	Scarlet Ibis

continued on next page

TABLE C.1—*continued*

Plegadis falcinellus	Glossy Ibis
Plegadis chihi	White-faced Ibis
(2) SUBFAMILY PLATALEINAE	
Platalea ajaja	Roseate Spoonbill
(xvi) Order Carthartiformes	
FAMILY CATHARTIDAE	
Gymnogyps californianus	California Condor
Coragyps atratus	Black Vulture
Cathartes aura	Turkey Vulture
(xvii) Order Accipitriformes	
(A) FAMILY PANDIONIDAE	
X *Pandion haliaetus*	Osprey
(B) FAMILY ACCIPITRIDAE	
(1) SUBFAMILY ELANINAE	
Elanus leucurus	White-tailed Kite
(2) SUBFAMILY GYPAETINAE	
Chondrohierax uncinatus	Hook-billed Kite
Elanoides forficatus	Swallow-tailed Kite
(3) SUBFAMILY ACCIPITRINAE	
X *Aquila chrysaetos*	Golden Eagle
Harpagus bidentatus	Double-toothed Kite
Circus hudsonius	Northern Harrier
Circus spilonotus	Eastern Marsh-Harrier
Accipiter soloensis	Chinese Sparrowhawk
Accipiter gularis	Japanese Sparrowhawk
Accipiter striatus	Sharp-shinned Hawk
X *Accipiter cooperii*	Cooper's Hawk
Accipiter gentilis	Northern Goshawk
(4) SUBFAMILY BUTEONINAE	
Milvus migrans	Black Kite
X *Haliaeetus leucocephalus*	Bald Eagle
Haliaeetus albicilla	White-tailed Eagle
Haliaeetus pelagicus	Steller's Sea-Eagle
Ictinia mississippiensis	Mississippi Kite

continued on next page

TABLE C.1—*continued*

Butastur indicus	Gray-faced Buzzard
Geranospiza caerulescens	Crane Hawk
Rostrhamus sociabilis	Snail Kite
Buteogallus anthracinus	Common Black Hawk
Buteogallus urubitinga	Great Black Hawk
Rupornis magnirostris	Roadside Hawk
X *Parabuteo unicinctus*	Harris's Hawk
Geranoaetus albicaudatus	White-tailed Hawk
Buteo plagiatus	Gray Hawk
Buteo lineatus	Red-shouldered Hawk
Buteo platypterus	Broad-winged Hawk
Buteo solitarius	Hawaiian Hawk
Buteo brachyurus	Short-tailed Hawk
Buteo swainsoni	Swainson's Hawk
Buteo albonotatus	Zone-tailed Hawk
X *Buteo jamaicensis*	Red-tailed Hawk
Buteo lagopus	Rough-legged Hawk
Buteo regalis	Ferruginous Hawk
Buteo rufinus	Long-legged Buzzard
(xviii) Order Strigiformes	
(A) FAMILY TYTONIDAE	
X *Tyto alba*	Barn Owl
(B) FAMILY STRIGIDAE	
Otus sunia	Oriental Scops-Owl
Psiloscops flammeolus	Flammulated Owl
Gymnasio nudipes	Puerto Rican Owl
Megascops trichopsis	Whiskered Screech-Owl
Megascops kennicottii	Western Screech-Owl
Megascops asio	Eastern Screech-Owl
X *Bubo virginianus*	Great Horned Owl
Bubo scandiacus	Snowy Owl
Surnia ulula	Northern Hawk Owl
Glaucidium gnoma	Northern Pygmy-Owl
Glaucidium brasilianum	Ferruginous Pygmy-Owl

continued on next page

TABLE C.1—*continued*

Micrathene whitneyi	Elf Owl
Athene cunicularia	Burrowing Owl
Strix occidentalis	Spotted Owl
Strix varia	Barred Owl
Strix virgata	Mottled Owl
Strix nebulosa	Great Gray Owl
Asio otus	Long-eared Owl
Asio stygius	Stygian Owl
Asio flammeus	Short-eared Owl
Aegolius funereus	Boreal Owl
Aegolius acadicus	Northern Saw-whet Owl
Ninox japonica	Northern Boobook
(xix) Order Trogoniformes	
FAMILY TROGONIDAE	
SUBFAMILY TROGONINAE	
Trogon elegans	Elegant Trogon
Euptilotis neoxenus	Eared Quetzal
(xx) Order Upupiformes	
FAMILY UPUPIDAE	
Upupa epops	Eurasian Hoopoe
(xxi) Order Coraciiformes	
FAMILY ALCEDINIDAE	
(1) SUBFAMILY ALCEDININAE	
Alcedo atthis	Common Kingfisher
(2) SUBFAMILY HALCYONINAE	
Todiramphus sacer	Pacific Kingfisher
Todiramphus cinnamominus	Guam Kingfisher
Todiramphus albicilla	Mariana Kingfisher
(3) SUBFAMILY CERYLINAE	
Megaceryle torquata	Ringed Kingfisher
Megaceryle alcyon	Belted Kingfisher
Chloroceryle amazona	Amazon Kingfisher
Chloroceryle americana	Green Kingfisher

continued on next page

TABLE C.1—*continued*

(xxii) Order Piciformes	
FAMILY PICIDAE	
(1) SUBFAMILY JYNGINAE	
Jynx torquilla	Eurasian Wryneck
(2) SUBFAMILY PICINAE	
Melanerpes lewis	Lewis's Woodpecker
Melanerpes portoricensis	Puerto Rican Woodpecker
X *Melanerpes erythrocephalus*	Red-headed Woodpecker
X *Melanerpes formicivorus*	Acorn Woodpecker
Melanerpes uropygialis	Gila Woodpecker
Melanerpes aurifrons	Golden-fronted Woodpecker
Melanerpes carolinus	Red-bellied Woodpecker
Sphyrapicus thyroideus	Williamson's Sapsucker
Sphyrapicus varius	Yellow-bellied Sapsucker
Sphyrapicus nuchalis	Red-naped Sapsucker
Sphyrapicus ruber	Red-breasted Sapsucker
Picoides dorsalis	American Three-toed Woodpecker
Picoides arcticus	Black-backed Woodpecker
Dendrocopos major	Great Spotted Woodpecker
X *Dryobates pubescens*	Downy Woodpecker
Dryobates nuttallii	Nuttall's Woodpecker
Dryobates scalaris	Ladder-backed Woodpecker
Dryobates borealis	Red-cockaded Woodpecker
X *Dryobates villosus*	Hairy Woodpecker
Dryobates albolarvatus	White-headed Woodpecker
X *Dryobates arizonae*	Arizona Woodpecker
X *Colaptes auratus*	Northern Flicker
X *Colaptes chrysoides*	Gilded Flicker
Dryocopus pileatus	Pileated Woodpecker
Campephilus principalis	Ivory-billed Woodpecker

continued on next page

TABLE C.1—*continued*

(xxiii) Order Falconiformes	
FAMILY FALCONIDAE	
(1) SUBFAMILY HERPETOTHERINAE	
Micrastur semitorquatus	Collared Forest-Falcon
(2) SUBFAMILY FALCONINAE	
Caracara plancus	Crested Caracara
Falco tinnunculus	Eurasian Kestrel
Falco sparverius	American Kestrel
Falco vespertinus	Red-footed Falcon
Falco amurensis	Amur Falcon
Falco columbarius	Merlin
Falco subbuteo	Eurasian Hobby
X *Falco femoralis*	Aplomado Falcon
Falco rusticolus	Gyrfalcon
X *Falco peregrinus*	Peregrine Falcon
X *Falco mexicanus*	Prairie Falcon
(xxiv) Order Passeriformes	
(A) FAMILY TITYRIDAE	
Tityra semifasciata	Masked Tityra
Pachyramphus major	Gray-collared Becard
Pachyramphus aglaiae	Rose-throated Becard
(B) FAMILY TYRANNIDAE	
(1) SUBFAMILY ELAENIINAE	
Camptostoma imberbe	Northern Beardless-Tyrannulet
Myiopagis viridicata	Greenish Elaenia
Elaenia martinica	Caribbean Elaenia
Elaenia albiceps	White-crested Elaenia
Elaenia parvirostris	Small-billed Elaenia
(2) SUBFAMILY TYRANNINAE	
Myiarchus tuberculifer	Dusky-capped Flycatcher
Myiarchus cinerascens	Ash-throated Flycatcher
Myiarchus nuttingi	Nutting's Flycatcher
Myiarchus crinitus	Great Crested Flycatcher

continued on next page

TABLE C.1—*continued*

Myiarchus tyrannulus	Brown-crested Flycatcher
Myiarchus sagrae	La Sagra's Flycatcher
Myiarchus antillarum	Puerto Rican Flycatcher
Pitangus sulphuratus	Great Kiskadee
Myiozetetes similis	Social Flycatcher
Myiodynastes luteiventris	Sulphur-bellied Flycatcher
Legatus leucophaius	Piratic Flycatcher
Empidonomus varius	Variegated Flycatcher
Empidonomus aurantioatrocristatus	Crowned Slaty Flycatcher
Tyrannus melancholicus	Tropical Kingbird
Tyrannus couchii	Couch's Kingbird
Tyrannus vociferans	Cassin's Kingbird
Tyrannus crassirostris	Thick-billed Kingbird
Tyrannus verticalis	Western Kingbird
Tyrannus tyrannus	Eastern Kingbird
Tyrannus dominicensis	Gray Kingbird
Tyrannus caudifasciatus	Loggerhead Kingbird
Tyrannus forficatus	Scissor-tailed Flycatcher
Tyrannus savana	Fork-tailed Flycatcher

(3) SUBFAMILY FLUVICOLINAE

Mitrephanes phaeocercus	Tufted Flycatcher
Contopus cooperi	Olive-sided Flycatcher
Contopus pertinax	Greater Pewee
Contopus sordidulus	Western Wood-Pewee
Contopus virens	Eastern Wood-Pewee
Contopus caribaeus	Cuban Pewee
Contopus hispaniolensis	Hispaniolan Pewee
Contopus latirostris	Lesser Antillean Pewee
Empidonax flaviventris	Yellow-bellied Flycatcher
Empidonax virescens	Acadian Flycatcher
Empidonax alnorum	Alder Flycatcher
Empidonax traillii	Willow Flycatcher
Empidonax minimus	Least Flycatcher
Empidonax hammondii	Hammond's Flycatcher

continued on next page

TABLE C.1—*continued*

Empidonax wrightii	Gray Flycatcher
Empidonax oberholseri	Dusky Flycatcher
Empidonax affinis	Pine Flycatcher
Empidonax difficilis	Pacific-slope Flycatcher
Empidonax occidentalis	Cordilleran Flycatcher
Empidonax fulvifrons	Buff-breasted Flycatcher
Sayornis nigricans	Black Phoebe
Sayornis phoebe	Eastern Phoebe
Sayornis saya	Say's Phoebe
Pyrocephalus rubinus	Vermilion Flycatcher

X (C) FAMILY VIREONIDAE

Vireo atricapilla	Black-capped Vireo
Vireo griseus	White-eyed Vireo
Vireo crassirostris	Thick-billed Vireo
Vireo gundlachii	Cuban Vireo
Vireo latimeri	Puerto Rican Vireo
Vireo bellii	Bell's Vireo
X *Vireo vicinior*	Gray Vireo
Vireo huttoni	Hutton's Vireo
Vireo flavifrons	Yellow-throated Vireo
Vireo cassinii	Cassin's Vireo
Vireo solitarius	Blue-headed Vireo
Vireo plumbeus	Plumbeous Vireo
Vireo philadelphicus	Philadelphia Vireo
Vireo gilvus	Warbling Vireo
Vireo olivaceus	Red-eyed Vireo
Vireo flavoviridis	Yellow-green Vireo
Vireo altiloquus	Black-whiskered Vireo
Vireo magister	Yucatan Vireo

(D) FAMILY LANIIDAE

Lanius cristatus	Brown Shrike
Lanius ludovicianus	Loggerhead Shrike
Lanius borealis	Northern Shrike

continued on next page

TABLE C.1—*continued*

X (E) Family Corvidae	
Perisoreus canadensis	Canada Jay
Psilorhinus morio	Brown Jay
X *Cyanocorax yncas*	Green Jay
X *Gymnorhinus cyanocephalus*	Pinyon Jay
X *Cyanocitta stelleri*	Steller's Jay
X *Cyanocitta cristata*	Blue Jay
Aphelocoma coerulescens	Florida Scrub-Jay
Aphelocoma insularis	Island Scrub-Jay
X *Aphelocoma californica*	California Scrub-Jay
Aphelocoma woodhouseii	Woodhouse's Scrub-Jay
X *Aphelocoma wollweberi*	Mexican Jay
Nucifraga columbiana	Clark's Nutcracker
X *Pica hudsonia*	Black-billed Magpie
X *Pica nuttalli*	Yellow-billed Magpie
Corvus monedula	Eurasian Jackdaw
Corvus kubaryi	Mariana Crow
X *Corvus brachyrhynchos*	American Crow
Corvus leucognaphalus	White-necked Crow
Corvus imparatus	Tamaulipas Crow
Corvus ossifragus	Fish Crow
Corvus hawaiiensis	Hawaiian Crow
X *Corvus cryptoleucus*	Chihuahuan Raven
X *Corvus corax*	Common Raven
(F) Family Remizidae	
Auriparus flaviceps	Verdin
(G) Family Paridae	
Poecile carolinensis	Carolina Chickadee
Poecile atricapillus	Black-capped Chickadee
Poecile gambeli	Mountain Chickadee
Poecile sclateri	Mexican Chickadee
Poecile rufescens	Chestnut-backed Chickadee

continued on next page

TABLE C.1—*continued*

Poecile hudsonicus	Boreal Chickadee
Poecile cinctus	Gray-headed Chickadee
Baeolophus wollweberi	Bridled Titmouse
Baeolophus inornatus	Oak Titmouse
Baeolophus ridgwayi	Juniper Titmouse
Baeolophus bicolor	Tufted Titmouse
Baeolophus atricristatus	Black-crested Titmouse
(H) FAMILY ALAUDIDAE	
Alauda arvensis	Eurasian Skylark
Eremophila alpestris	Horned Lark
(I) FAMILY ACROCEPHALIDAE	
Arundinax aedon	Thick-billed Warbler
Acrocephalus luscinius	Nightingale Reed Warbler
Acrocephalus hiwae	Saipan Reed Warbler
Acrocephalus nijoi	Aguiguan Reed Warbler
Acrocephalus yamashinae	Pagan Reed Warbler
Acrocephalus familiaris	Millerbird
Acrocephalus schoenobaenus	Sedge Warbler
Acrocephalus dumetorum	Blyth's Reed Warbler
(J) FAMILY LOCUSTELLIDAE	
Helopsaltes certhiola	Pallas's Grasshopper Warbler
Helopsaltes ochotensis	Middendorff's Grasshopper Warbler
Locustella lanceolata	Lanceolated Warbler
Locustella fluviatilis	River Warbler
(K) FAMILY HIRUNDINIDAE	
SUBFAMILY HIRUNDININAE	
Riparia riparia	Bank Swallow
Tachycineta bicolor	Tree Swallow
Tachycineta cyaneoviridis	Bahama Swallow
Tachycineta thalassina	Violet-green Swallow
Tachycineta albilinea	Mangrove Swallow
Pygochelidon cyanoleuca	Blue-and-white Swallow
Stelgidopteryx serripennis	Northern Rough-winged Swallow

continued on next page

TABLE C.1—*continued*

Progne tapera	Brown-chested Martin
Progne subis	Purple Martin
Progne elegans	Southern Martin
Progne chalybea	Gray-breasted Martin
Progne cryptoleuca	Cuban Martin
Progne dominicensis	Caribbean Martin
Hirundo rustica	Barn Swallow
Delichon urbicum	Common House-Martin
Petrochelidon pyrrhonota	Cliff Swallow
Petrochelidon fulva	Cave Swallow
(L) FAMILY AEGITHALIDAE	
Psaltriparus minimus	Bushtit
(M) FAMILY PHYLLOSCOPIDAE	
Phylloscopus trochilus	Willow Warbler
Phylloscopus collybita	Common Chiffchaff
Phylloscopus sibilatrix	Wood Warbler
Phylloscopus fuscatus	Dusky Warbler
Phylloscopus proregulus	Pallas's Leaf Warbler
Phylloscopus inornatus	Yellow-browed Warbler
Phylloscopus borealis	Arctic Warbler
Phylloscopus examinandus	Kamchatka Leaf Warbler
(N) FAMILY SYLVIIDAE	
Sylvia curruca	Lesser Whitethroat
Chamaea fasciata	Wrentit
(O) FAMILY REGULIDAE	
Corthylio calendula	Ruby-crowned Kinglet
Regulus satrapa	Golden-crowned Kinglet
(P) FAMILY BOMBYCILLIDAE	
Bombycilla garrulus	Bohemian Waxwing
Bombycilla cedrorum	Cedar Waxwing
(Q) FAMILY PTILIOGONATIDAE	
Ptiliogonys cinereus	Gray Silky-flycatcher
Phainopepla nitens	Phainopepla

continued on next page

TABLE C.1—*continued*

(R) FAMILY SITTIDAE	
SUBFAMILY SITTINAE	
Sitta canadensis	Red-breasted Nuthatch
Sitta carolinensis	White-breasted Nuthatch
Sitta pygmaea	Pygmy Nuthatch
Sitta pusilla	Brown-headed Nuthatch
(S) FAMILY CERTHIIDAE	
SUBFAMILY CERTHIINAE	
Certhia americana	Brown Creeper
(T) FAMILY POLIOPTILIDAE	
Polioptila caerulea	Blue-Gray Gnatcatcher
Polioptila melanura	Black-tailed Gnatcatcher
Polioptila californica	California Gnatcatcher
Polioptila nigriceps	Black-capped Gnatcatcher
X (U) FAMILY TROGLODYTIDAE	
Salpinctes obsoletus	Rock Wren
Catherpes mexicanus	Canyon Wren
Thryophilus sinaloa	Sinaloa Wren
X *Campylorhynchus brunneicapillus*	Cactus Wren
Thryomanes bewickii	Bewick's Wren
Thryothorus ludovicianus	Carolina Wren
Troglodytes aedon	House Wren
Troglodytes pacificus	Pacific Wren
Troglodytes hiemalis	Winter Wren
Cistothorus stellaris	Sedge Wren
Cistothorus palustris	Marsh Wren
(V) FAMILY MIMIDAE	
Melanotis caerulescens	Blue Mockingbird
Melanoptila glabrirostris	Black Catbird
Dumetella carolinensis	Gray Catbird
Margarops fuscatus	Pearly-eyed Thrasher
Toxostoma curvirostre	Curve-billed Thrasher

continued on next page

TABLE C.1—*continued*

Toxostoma rufum	Brown Thrasher
Toxostoma longirostre	Long-billed Thrasher
Toxostoma bendirei	Bendire's Thrasher
Toxostoma redivivum	California Thrasher
Toxostoma lecontei	LeConte's Thrasher
Toxostoma crissale	Crissal Thrasher
Oreoscoptes montanus	Sage Thrasher
Mimus gundlachii	Bahama Mockingbird
Mimus polyglottos	Northern Mockingbird
(W) FAMILY STURNIDAE	
Agropsar philippensis	Chestnut-cheeked Starling
Spodiopsar cineraceus	White-cheeked Starling
(X) FAMILY CINCLIDAE	
Cinclus mexicanus	American Dipper
X (Y) FAMILY TURDIDAE	
X *Sialia sialis*	Eastern Bluebird
X *Sialia mexicana*	Western Bluebird
X *Sialia currucoides*	Mountain Bluebird
Myadestes townsendi	Townsend's Solitaire
Myadestes occidentalis	Brown-backed Solitaire
Myadestes myadestinus	Kāma'o
Myadestes lanaiensis	Oloma'o
Myadestes obscurus	ʻŌma'o
Myadestes palmeri	Puaiohi
Catharus aurantiirostris	Orange-billed Nightingale-Thrush
Catharus mexicanus	Black-headed Nightingale-Thrush
Catharus fuscescens	Veery
Catharus minimus	Gray-cheeked Thrush
Catharus bicknelli	Bicknell's Thrush
Catharus ustulatus	Swainson's Thrush
Catharus guttatus	Hermit Thrush
Hylocichla mustelina	Wood Thrush
Turdus obscurus	Eyebrowed Thrush

continued on next page

TABLE C.1—*continued*

Turdus eunomus	Dusky Thrush
Turdus naumanni	Naumann's Thrush
Turdus pilaris	Fieldfare
Turdus iliacus	Redwing
Turdus grayi	Clay-colored Thrush
Turdus assimilis	White-throated Thrush
Turdus rufopalliatus	Rufous-backed Robin
Turdus migratorius	American Robin
Turdus plumbeus	Red-legged Thrush
Ixoreus naevius	Varied Thrush
Ridgwayia pinicola	Aztec Thrush
(Z) FAMILY MUSCICAPIDAE	
Muscicapa griseisticta	Gray-streaked Flycatcher
Muscicapa dauurica	Asian Brown Flycatcher
Muscicapa striata	Spotted Flycatcher
Muscicapa sibirica	Dark-sided Flycatcher
Erithacus rubecula	European Robin
Larvivora cyane	Siberian Blue Robin
Larvivora sibilans	Rufous-tailed Robin
Cyanecula svecica	Bluethroat
Calliope calliope	Siberian Rubythroat
Tarsiger cyanurus	Red-flanked Bluetail
Ficedula narcissina	Narcissus Flycatcher
Ficedula mugimaki	Mugimaki Flycatcher
Ficedula albicilla	Taiga Flycatcher
Phoenicurus phoenicurus	Common Redstart
Saxicola maurus	Asian Stonechat
Oenanthe oenanthe	Northern Wheatear
Oenanthe pleschanka	Pied Wheatear
Monticola solitarius	Blue Rock-Thrush
(AA) FAMILY PEUCEDRAMIDAE	
Peucedramus taeniatus	Olive Warbler
(BB) FAMILY PRUNELLIDAE	
Prunella montanella	Siberian Accentor

continued on next page

TABLE C.1—*continued*

(CC) FAMILY MOTACILLIDAE	
Motacilla tschutschensis	Eastern Yellow Wagtail
Motacilla citreola	Citrine Wagtail
Motacilla cinerea	Gray Wagtail
Motacilla alba	White Wagtail
Anthus trivialis	Tree Pipit
Anthus hodgsoni	Olive-backed Pipit
Anthus gustavi	Pechora Pipit
Anthus cervinus	Red-throated Pipit
Anthus rubescens	American Pipit
Anthus spragueii	Sprague's Pipit
(DD) FAMILY FRINGILLIDAE	
(1) SUBFAMILY FRINGILLINAE	
Fringilla coelebs	Common Chaffinch
Fringilla montifringilla	Brambling
(2) SUBFAMILY EUPHONIINAE	
Chlorophonia musica	Antillean Euphonia
(3) SUBFAMILY CARDUELINAE	
Coccothraustes vespertinus	Evening Grosbeak
Coccothraustes coccothraustes	Hawfinch
Carpodacus erythrinus	Common Rosefinch
Carpodacus roseus	Pallas's Rosefinch
Melamprosops phaeosoma	Po'ouli
Oreomystis bairdi	'Akikiki
Paroreomyza maculata	O'ahu 'Alauahio
Paroreomyza flammea	Kākāwahie
Paroreomyza montana	Maui 'Alauahio
Loxioides bailleui	Palila
Telespiza cantans	Laysan Finch
Telespiza ultima	Nihoa Finch
Palmeria dolei	'Akohekohe
Himatione fraithii	Laysan Honeycreeper
Himatione sanguinea	'Apapane

continued on next page

TABLE C.1—*continued*

Drepanis coccinea	'I'iwi
Psittirostra psittacea	'Ō'ū
Pseudonestor xanthophrys	Maui Parrotbill
Hemignathus hanapepe	Kauai Nukupu'u
Hemignathus lucidus	O'ahu Nukupu'u
Hemignathus affinis	Maui Nukupu'u
Hemignathus wilsoni	'Akiapola'au
Akialoa stejnegeri	Kauai 'Akialoa
Akialoa ellisiana	O'ahu 'Akialoa
Akialoa lanaiensis	Maui Nui 'Akialoa
Magumma parva	'Anianiau
Chlorodrepanis virens	Hawaii 'Amakihi
Chlorodrepanis flava	O'ahu 'Amakihi
Chlorodrepanis stejnegeri	Kaua'i 'Amakihi
Loxops mana	Hawaii Creeper
Loxops caeruleirostris	'Akeke'e
Loxops wolstenholmei	O'ahu 'Akepa
Loxops ochraceus	Maui 'Akepa
Loxops coccineus	Hawaii 'Akepa
Pinicola enucleator	Pine Grosbeak
Pyrrhula pyrrhula	Eurasian Bullfinch
Leucosticte arctoa	Asian Rosy-Finch
Leucosticte tephrocotis	Gray-crowned Rosy-Finch
Leucosticte atrata	Black Rosy-Finch
Leucosticte australis	Brown-capped Rosy-Finch
Haemorhous mexicanus	House Finch
Haemorhous purpureus	Purple Finch
Haemorhous cassinii	Cassin's Finch
Chloris sinica	Oriental Greenfinch
Acanthis flammea	Common Redpoll
Acanthis hornemanni	Hoary Redpoll
Loxia curvirostra	Red Crossbill
Loxia sinesciuris	Cassia Crossbill

continued on next page

TABLE C.1—*continued*

Loxia leucoptera	White-winged Crossbill
Spinus spinus	Eurasian Siskin
Spinus pinus	Pine Siskin
Spinus psaltria	Lesser Goldfinch
Spinus lawrencei	Lawrence's Goldfinch
Spinus tristis	American Goldfinch
(EE) FAMILY CALCARIIDAE	
Calcarius lapponicus	Lapland Longspur
Calcarius ornatus	Chestnut-collared Longspur
Calcarius pictus	Smith's Longspur
Rhynchophanes mccownii	Thick-billed Longspur
Plectrophenax nivalis	Snow Bunting
Plectrophenax hyperboreus	McKay's Bunting
(FF) FAMILY EMBERIZIDAE	
Emberiza leucocephalos	Pine Bunting
Emberiza chrysophrys	Yellow-browed Bunting
Emberiza pusilla	Little Bunting
Emberiza rustica	Rustic Bunting
Emberiza elegans	Yellow-throated Bunting
Emberiza aureola	Yellow-breasted Bunting
Emberiza variabilis	Gray Bunting
Emberiza pallasi	Pallas's Bunting
Emberiza schoeniclus	Reed Bunting
(GG) FAMILY PASSERELLIDAE	
Peucaea carpalis	Rufous-winged Sparrow
Peucaea botterii	Botteri's Sparrow
Peucaea cassinii	Cassin's Sparrow
Peucaea aestivalis	Bachman's Sparrow
Ammodramus savannarum	Grasshopper Sparrow
Arremonops rufivirgatus	Olive Sparrow
Amphispizopsis quinquestriata	Five-striped Sparrow
Amphispiza bilineata	Black-throated Sparrow

continued on next page

TABLE C.1—*continued*

Chondestes grammacus	Lark Sparrow
Calamospiza melanocorys	Lark Bunting
Spizella passerina	Chipping Sparrow
Spizella pallida	Clay-colored Sparrow
Spizella atrogularis	Black-chinned Sparrow
Spizella pusilla	Field Sparrow
Spizella breweri	Brewer's Sparrow
Spizella wortheni	Worthen's Sparrow
Passerella iliaca	Fox Sparrow
Spizelloides arborea	American Tree Sparrow
Junco hyemalis	Dark-eyed Junco
Junco phaeonotus	Yellow-eyed Junco
Zonotrichia leucophrys	White-crowned Sparrow
Zonotrichia atricapilla	Golden-crowned Sparrow
Zonotrichia querula	Harris's Sparrow
Zonotrichia albicollis	White-throated Sparrow
Artemisiospiza nevadensis	Sagebrush Sparrow
Artemisiospiza belli	Bell's Sparrow
Pooecetes gramineus	Vesper Sparrow
Ammospiza leconteii	LeConte's Sparrow
Ammospiza maritima	Seaside Sparrow
Ammospiza nelsoni	Nelson's Sparrow
Ammospiza caudacuta	Saltmarsh Sparrow
Centronyx bairdii	Baird's Sparrow
Centronyx henslowii	Henslow's Sparrow
Passerculus sandwichensis	Savannah Sparrow
Melospiza melodia	Song Sparrow
Melospiza lincolnii	Lincoln's Sparrow
Melospiza georgiana	Swamp Sparrow
Melozone fusca	Canyon Towhee
Melozone aberti	Abert's Towhee
Melozone crissalis	California Towhee
Aimophila ruficeps	Rufous-crowned Sparrow

continued on next page

TABLE C.1—*continued*

Pipilo chlorurus	Green-tailed Towhee
Pipilo maculatus	Spotted Towhee
Pipilo erythrophthalmus	Eastern Towhee
(HH) FAMILY NESOSPINGIDAE	
Nesospingus speculiferus	Puerto Rican Tanager
(II) FAMILY SPINDALIDAE	
Spindalis zena	Western Spindalis
Spindalis portoricensis	Puerto Rican Spindalis
(JJ) FAMILY ICTERIDAE	
Icteria virens	Yellow-breasted Chat
(1) SUBFAMILY XANTHOCEPHALINAE	
Xanthocephalus xanthocephalus	Yellow-headed Blackbird
(2) SUBFAMILY DOLICHONYCHINAE	
Dolichonyx oryzivorus	Bobolink
(3) SUBFAMILY STURNELLINAE	
Sturnella lilianae	Chihuahuan Meadowlark
Sturnella magna	Eastern Meadowlark
Sturnella neglecta	Western Meadowlark
(4) SUBFAMILY ICTERINAE	
Icterus portoricensis	Puerto Rican Oriole
Icterus wagleri	Black-vented Oriole
Icterus spurius	Orchard Oriole
Icterus cucullatus	Hooded Oriole
Icterus pustulatus	Streak-backed Oriole
Icterus bullockii	Bullock's Oriole
Icterus gularis	Altamira Oriole
Icterus graduacauda	Audubon's Oriole
Icterus galbula	Baltimore Oriole
Icterus abeillei	Black-backed Oriole
Icterus parisorum	Scott's Oriole
(5) SUBFAMILY AGELAIINAE	
Agelaius phoeniceus	Red-winged Blackbird
Agelaius tricolor	Tricolored Blackbird

continued on next page

TABLE C.1—*continued*

Agelaius humeralis	Tawny-shouldered Blackbird
Agelaius xanthomus	Yellow-shouldered Blackbird
Molothrus bonariensis	Shiny Cowbird
Molothrus aeneus	Bronzed Cowbird
Molothrus ater	Brown-headed Cowbird
Euphagus carolinus	Rusty Blackbird
Euphagus cyanocephalus	Brewer's Blackbird
Quiscalus quiscula	Common Grackle
Quiscalus major	Boat-tailed Grackle
Quiscalus mexicanus	Great-tailed Grackle
Quiscalus niger	Greater Antillean Grackle
(KK) FAMILY PARULIDAE	
Seiurus aurocapilla	Ovenbird
Helmitheros vermivorum	Worm-eating Warbler
Parkesia motacilla	Louisiana Waterthrush
Parkesia noveboracensis	Northern Waterthrush
Vermivora bachmanii	Bachman's Warbler
Vermivora chrysoptera	Golden-winged Warbler
Vermivora cyanoptera	Blue-winged Warbler
Mniotilta varia	Black-and-white Warbler
Protonotaria citrea	Prothonotary Warbler
Limnothlypis swainsonii	Swainson's Warbler
Oreothlypis superciliosa	Crescent-chested Warbler
Leiothlypis peregrina	Tennessee Warbler
Leiothlypis celata	Orange-crowned Warbler
Leiothlypis crissalis	Colima Warbler
Leiothlypis luciae	Lucy's Warbler
Leiothlypis ruficapilla	Nashville Warbler
Leiothlypis virginiae	Virginia's Warbler
Oporornis agilis	Connecticut Warbler
Geothlypis poliocephala	Gray-crowned Yellowthroat
Geothlypis tolmiei	MacGillivray's Warbler
Geothlypis philadelphia	Mourning Warbler

continued on next page

TABLE C.1—*continued*

Geothlypis formosa	Kentucky Warbler
Geothlypis trichas	Common Yellowthroat
Setophaga angelae	Elfin-woods Warbler
Setophaga citrina	Hooded Warbler
Setophaga ruticilla	American Redstart
Setophaga kirtlandii	Kirtland's Warbler
Setophaga tigrina	Cape May Warbler
Setophaga cerulea	Cerulean Warbler
Setophaga americana	Northern Parula
Setophaga pitiayumi	Tropical Parula
Setophaga magnolia	Magnolia Warbler
Setophaga castanea	Bay-breasted Warbler
Setophaga fusca	Blackburnian Warbler
Setophaga petechia	Yellow Warbler
Setophaga pensylvanica	Chestnut-sided Warbler
Setophaga striata	Blackpoll Warbler
Setophaga caerulescens	Black-throated Blue Warbler
Setophaga palmarum	Palm Warbler
Setophaga pinus	Pine Warbler
Setophaga coronata	Yellow-rumped Warbler
Setophaga dominica	Yellow-throated Warbler
Setophaga discolor	Prairie Warbler
Setophaga adelaidae	Adelaide's Warbler
Setophaga graciae	Grace's Warbler
Setophaga nigrescens	Black-throated Gray Warbler
Setophaga townsendi	Townsend's Warbler
Setophaga occidentalis	Hermit Warbler
Setophaga chrysoparia	Golden-cheeked Warbler
Setophaga virens	Black-throated Green Warbler
Basileuterus lachrymosus	Fan-tailed Warbler
Basileuterus rufifrons	Rufous-capped Warbler
Basileuterus culicivorus	Golden-crowned Warbler
Cardellina canadensis	Canada Warbler

continued on next page

TABLE C.1—*continued*

Cardellina pusilla	Wilson's Warbler
Cardellina rubrifrons	Red-faced Warbler
Myioborus pictus	Painted Redstart
Myioborus miniatus	Slate-throated Redstart
X (LL) FAMILY CARDINALIDAE	
Piranga flava	Hepatic Tanager
Piranga rubra	Summer Tanager
Piranga olivacea	Scarlet Tanager
Piranga ludoviciana	Western Tanager
Piranga bidentata	Flame-colored Tanager
Rhodothraupis celaeno	Crimson-collared Grosbeak
X *Cardinalis cardinalis*	Northern Cardinal
Cardinalis sinuatus	Pyrrhuloxia
Pheucticus chrysopeplus	Yellow Grosbeak
Pheucticus ludovicianus	Rose-breasted Grosbeak
Pheucticus melanocephalus	Black-headed Grosbeak
X *Cyanocompsa parellina*	Blue Bunting
Passerina caerulea	Blue Grosbeak
Passerina amoena	Lazuli Bunting
X *Passerina cyanea*	Indigo Bunting
Passerina versicolor	Varied Bunting
Passerina ciris	Painted Bunting
Spiza americana	Dickcissel
(MM) FAMILY THRAUPIDAE	
(1) SUBFAMILY DACNINAE	
Cyanerpes cyaneus	Red-legged Honeycreeper
(2) SUBFAMILY COEREBINAE	
Coereba flaveola	Bananaquit
Tiaris olivaceus	Yellow-faced Grassquit
Melopyrrha portoricensis	Puerto Rican Bullfinch
Melanospiza bicolor	Black-faced Grassquit
(3) SUBFAMILY SPOROPHILINAE	
Sporophila morelleti	Morelet's Seedeater

Appendix D

Convention on International Trade in Endangered Species of Wild Fauna and Flora

Signed at Washington, DC, on 3 March 1973

Amended at Bonn, on 22 June 1979

Amended at Gaborone, on 30 April 1983

The Contracting States,

Recognizing that wild fauna and flora in their many beautiful and varied forms are an irreplaceable part of the natural systems of the earth which must be protected for this and the generations to come;

Conscious of the ever-growing value of wild fauna and flora from aesthetic, scientific, cultural, recreational and economic points of view;

Recognizing that peoples and States are and should be the best protectors of their own wild fauna and flora;

Recognizing, in addition, that international co-operation is essential for the protection of certain species of wild fauna and flora against over-exploitation through international trade;

Convinced of the urgency of taking appropriate measures to this end;

Have agreed as follows:

https://doi.org/10.5876/9781646427543.c011

Article I

DEFINITIONS

For the purpose of the present Convention, unless the context otherwise requires:

(a) "Species" means any species, subspecies, or geographically separate population thereof;

(b) "Specimen" means:

(i) any animal or plant, whether alive or dead;

(ii) in the case of an animal: for species included in Appendices I and II, any readily recognizable part or derivative thereof; and for species included in Appendix III, any readily recognizable part or derivative thereof specified in Appendix III in relation to the species; and

(iii) in the case of a plant: for species included in Appendix I, any readily recognizable part or derivative thereof; and for species included in Appendices II and III, any readily recognizable part or derivative thereof specified in Appendices II and III in relation to the species;

(c) "Trade" means export, re-export, import and introduction from the sea;

(d) "Re-export" means export of any specimen that has previously been imported;

(e) "Introduction from the sea" means transportation into a State of specimens of any species which were taken in the marine environment not under the jurisdiction of any State;

(f) "Scientific Authority" means a national scientific authority designated in accordance with Article IX;

(g) "Management Authority" means a national management authority designated in accordance with Article IX;

(h) "Party" means a State for which the present Convention has entered into force.

Article II

FUNDAMENTAL PRINCIPLES

1. Appendix I shall include all species threatened with extinction which are or may be affected by trade. Trade in specimens of these species must be

subject to particularly strict regulation in order not to endanger further their survival and must only be authorized in exceptional circumstances.

2. Appendix II shall include:

(a) all species which although not necessarily now threatened with extinction may become so unless trade in specimens of such species is subject to strict regulation in order to avoid utilization incompatible with their survival; and

(b) other species which must be subject to regulation in order that trade in specimens of certain species referred to in sub-paragraph (a) of this paragraph may be brought under effective control.

3. Appendix III shall include all species which any Party identifies as being subject to regulation within its jurisdiction for the purpose of preventing or restricting exploitation, and as needing the co-operation of other Parties in the control of trade.

4. The Parties shall not allow trade in specimens of species included in Appendices I, II and III except in accordance with the provisions of the present Convention.

Article III

REGULATION OF TRADE IN SPECIMENS OF SPECIES INCLUDED IN APPENDIX I

1. All trade in specimens of species included in Appendix I shall be in accordance with the provisions of this Article.

2. The export of any specimen of a species included in Appendix I shall require the prior grant and presentation of an export permit. An export permit shall only be granted when the following conditions have been met:

(a) a Scientific Authority of the State of export has advised that such export will not be detrimental to the survival of that species;

(b) a Management Authority of the State of export is satisfied that the specimen was not obtained in contravention of the laws of that State for the protection of fauna and flora;

(c) a Management Authority of the State of export is satisfied that any living specimen will be so prepared and shipped as to minimize the risk of injury, damage to health or cruel treatment; and

(d) a Management Authority of the State of export is satisfied that an import permit has been granted for the specimen.

3. The import of any specimen of a species included in Appendix I shall require the prior grant and presentation of an import permit and either an export permit or a re-export certificate. An import permit shall only be granted when the following conditions have been met:

(a) a Scientific Authority of the State of import has advised that the import will be for purposes which are not detrimental to the survival of the species involved;

(b) a Scientific Authority of the State of import is satisfied that the proposed recipient of a living specimen is suitably equipped to house and care for it; and

(c) a Management Authority of the State of import is satisfied that the specimen is not to be used for primarily commercial purposes.

4. The re-export of any specimen of a species included in Appendix I shall require the prior grant and presentation of a re-export certificate. A re-export certificate shall only be granted when the following conditions have been met:

(a) a Management Authority of the State of re-export is satisfied that the specimen was imported into that State in accordance with the provisions of the present Convention;

(b) a Management Authority of the State of re-export is satisfied that any living specimen will be so prepared and shipped as to minimize the risk of injury, damage to health or cruel treatment; and

(c) a Management Authority of the State of re-export is satisfied that an import permit has been granted for any living specimen.

5. The introduction from the sea of any specimen of a species included in Appendix I shall require the prior grant of a certificate from a Management Authority of the State of introduction. A certificate shall only be granted when the following conditions have been met:

(a) a Scientific Authority of the State of introduction advises that the introduction will not be detrimental to the survival of the species involved;

(b) a Management Authority of the State of introduction is satisfied that the proposed recipient of a living specimen is suitably equipped to house and care for it; and

(c) a Management Authority of the State of introduction is satisfied that the specimen is not to be used for primarily commercial purposes.

Article IV

REGULATION OF TRADE IN SPECIMENS OF SPECIES INCLUDED IN
APPENDIX II

1. All trade in specimens of species included in Appendix II shall be in
accordance with the provisions of this Article.

2. The export of any specimen of a species included in Appendix II shall
require the prior grant and presentation of an export permit. An export
permit shall only be granted when the following conditions have been met:

(a) a Scientific Authority of the State of export has advised that such
export will not be detrimental to the survival of that species;

(b) a Management Authority of the State of export is satisfied that the
specimen was not obtained in contravention of the laws of that
State for the protection of fauna and flora; and

(c) a Management Authority of the State of export is satisfied that any
living specimen will be so prepared and shipped as to minimize the
risk of injury, damage to health or cruel treatment.

3. A Scientific Authority in each Party shall monitor both the export
permits granted by that State for specimens of species included in
Appendix II and the actual exports of such specimens. Whenever a
Scientific Authority determines that the export of specimens of any such
species should be limited in order to maintain that species throughout
its range at a level consistent with its role in the ecosystems in which
it occurs and well above the level at which that species might become
eligible for inclusion in Appendix I, the Scientific Authority shall advise
the appropriate Management Authority of suitable measures to be taken
to limit the grant of export permits for specimens of that species.

4. The import of any specimen of a species included in Appendix II shall
require the prior presentation of either an export permit or a re-export
certificate.

5. The re-export of any specimen of a species included in Appendix II shall
require the prior grant and presentation of a re-export certificate. A re-
export certificate shall only be granted when the following conditions
have been met:

(a) a Management Authority of the State of re-export is satisfied that
the specimen was imported into that State in accordance with the
provisions of the present Convention; and

(b) a Management Authority of the State of re-export is satisfied that any living specimen will be so prepared and shipped as to minimize the risk of injury, damage to health or cruel treatment.

6. The introduction from the sea of any specimen of a species included in Appendix II shall require the prior grant of a certificate from a Management Authority of the State of introduction. A certificate shall only be granted when the following conditions have been met:

(a) a Scientific Authority of the State of introduction advises that the introduction will not be detrimental to the survival of the species involved; and

(b) a Management Authority of the State of introduction is satisfied that any living specimen will be so handled as to minimize the risk of injury, damage to health or cruel treatment.

7. Certificates referred to in paragraph 6 of this Article may be granted on the advice of a Scientific Authority, in consultation with other national scientific authorities or, when appropriate, international scientific authorities, in respect of periods not exceeding one year for total numbers of specimens to be introduced in such periods.

Article V

REGULATION OF TRADE IN SPECIMENS OF SPECIES INCLUDED IN
APPENDIX III

1. All trade in specimens of species included in Appendix III shall be in accordance with the provisions of this Article.

2. The export of any specimen of a species included in Appendix III from any State which has included that species in Appendix III shall require the prior grant and presentation of an export permit. An export permit shall only be granted when the following conditions have been met:

(a) a Management Authority of the State of export is satisfied that the specimen was not obtained in contravention of the laws of that State for the protection of fauna and flora; and

(b) a Management Authority of the State of export is satisfied that any living specimen will be so prepared and shipped as to minimize the risk of injury, damage to health or cruel treatment.

3. The import of any specimen of a species included in Appendix III shall require, except in circumstances to which paragraph 4 of this Article applies, the prior presentation of a certificate of origin and, where the import is from a State which has included that species in Appendix III, an export permit.

4. In the case of re-export, a certificate granted by the Management Authority of the State of re-export that the specimen was processed in that State or is being re-exported shall be accepted by the State of import as evidence that the provisions of the present Convention have been complied with in respect of the specimen concerned.

Article VI

PERMITS AND CERTIFICATES

1. Permits and certificates granted under the provisions of Articles III, IV, and V shall be in accordance with the provisions of this Article.

2. An export permit shall contain the information specified in the model set forth in Appendix IV, and may only be used for export within a period of six months from the date on which it was granted.

3. Each permit or certificate shall contain the title of the present Convention, the name and any identifying stamp of the Management Authority granting it and a control number assigned by the Management Authority.

4. Any copies of a permit or certificate issued by a Management Authority shall be clearly marked as copies only and no such copy may be used in place of the original, except to the extent endorsed thereon.

5. A separate permit or certificate shall be required for each consignment of specimens.

6. A Management Authority of the State of import of any specimen shall cancel and retain the export permit or re-export certificate and any corresponding import permit presented in respect of the import of that specimen.

7. Where appropriate and feasible a Management Authority may affix a mark upon any specimen to assist in identifying the specimen. For these purposes "mark" means any indelible imprint, lead seal or other suitable means of identifying a specimen, designed in such a way as to render its imitation by unauthorized persons as difficult as possible.

Article VII

EXEMPTIONS AND OTHER SPECIAL PROVISIONS RELATING TO TRADE

1. The provisions of Articles III, IV and V shall not apply to the transit or transhipment of specimens through or in the territory of a Party while the specimens remain in Customs control.

2. Where a Management Authority of the State of export or re-export is satisfied that a specimen was acquired before the provisions of the present Convention applied to that specimen, the provisions of Articles III, IV and V shall not apply to that specimen where the Management Authority issues a certificate to that effect.

3. The provisions of Articles III, IV and V shall not apply to specimens that are personal or household effects. This exemption shall not apply where:

(a) in the case of specimens of a species included in Appendix I, they were acquired by the owner outside his State of usual residence, and are being imported into that State; or

(b) in the case of specimens of species included in Appendix II:

(i) they were acquired by the owner outside his State of usual residence and in a State where removal from the wild occurred;

(ii) they are being imported into the owner's State of usual residence; and

(iii) the State where removal from the wild occurred requires the prior grant of export permits before any export of such specimens; unless a Management Authority is satisfied that the specimens were acquired before the provisions of the present Convention applied to such specimens.

4. Specimens of an animal species included in Appendix I bred in captivity for commercial purposes, or of a plant species included in Appendix I artificially propagated for commercial purposes, shall be deemed to be specimens of species included in Appendix II.

5. Where a Management Authority of the State of export is satisfied that any specimen of an animal species was bred in captivity or any specimen of a plant species was artificially propagated, or is a part of such an animal or plant or was derived therefrom, a certificate by that Management Authority to that effect shall be accepted in lieu of any of the permits or certificates required under the provisions of Article III, IV or V.

6. The provisions of Articles III, IV and V shall not apply to the non-commercial loan, donation or exchange between scientists or scientific institutions registered by a Management Authority of their State, of herbarium specimens, other preserved, dried or embedded museum specimens, and live plant material which carry a label issued or approved by a Management Authority.

7. A Management Authority of any State may waive the requirements of Articles III, IV and V and allow the movement without permits or certificates of specimens which form part of a travelling zoo, circus, menagerie, plant exhibition or other travelling exhibition provided that:

   (a) the exporter or importer registers full details of such specimens with that Management Authority;

   (b) the specimens are in either of the categories specified in paragraph 2 or 5 of this Article; and

   (c) the Management Authority is satisfied that any living specimen will be so transported and cared for as to minimize the risk of injury, damage to health or cruel treatment.

Article VIII

MEASURES TO BE TAKEN BY THE PARTIES

1. The Parties shall take appropriate measures to enforce the provisions of the present Convention and to prohibit trade in specimens in violation thereof. These shall include measures:

   (a) to penalize trade in, or possession of, such specimens, or both; and

   (b) to provide for the confiscation or return to the State of export of such specimens.

2. In addition to the measures taken under paragraph 1 of this Article, a Party may, when it deems it necessary, provide for any method of internal reimbursement for expenses incurred as a result of the confiscation of a specimen traded in violation of the measures taken in the application of the provisions of the present Convention.

3. As far as possible, the Parties shall ensure that specimens shall pass through any formalities required for trade with a minimum of delay. To facilitate such passage, a Party may designate ports of exit and ports of entry at which specimens must be presented for clearance. The Parties shall ensure further that all living specimens, during any period of

transit, holding or shipment, are properly cared for so as to minimize the risk of injury, damage to health or cruel treatment.

4. Where a living specimen is confiscated as a result of measures referred to in paragraph 1 of this Article:

(a) the specimen shall be entrusted to a Management Authority of the State of confiscation;

(b) the Management Authority shall, after consultation with the State of export, return the specimen to that State at the expense of that State, or to a rescue centre or such other place as the Management Authority deems appropriate and consistent with the purposes of the present Convention; and

(c) the Management Authority may obtain the advice of a Scientific Authority, or may, whenever it considers it desirable, consult the Secretariat in order to facilitate the decision under sub-paragraph (b) of this paragraph, including the choice of a rescue centre or other place.

5. A rescue centre as referred to in paragraph 4 of this Article means an institution designated by a Management Authority to look after the welfare of living specimens, particularly those that have been confiscated.

6. Each Party shall maintain records of trade in specimens of species included in Appendices I, II and III which shall cover:

(a) the names and addresses of exporters and importers; and

(b) the number and type of permits and certificates granted; the States with which such trade occurred; the numbers or quantities and types of specimens, names of species as included in Appendices I, II and III and, where applicable, the size and sex of the specimens in question.

7. Each Party shall prepare periodic reports on its implementation of the present Convention and shall transmit to the Secretariat:

(a) an annual report containing a summary of the information specified in sub-paragraph (b) of paragraph 6 of this Article; and

(b) a biennial report on legislative, regulatory and administrative measures taken to enforce the provisions of the present Convention.

8. The information referred to in paragraph 7 of this Article shall be available to the public where this is not inconsistent with the law of the Party concerned.

Article IX

MANAGEMENT AND SCIENTIFIC AUTHORITIES

1. Each Party shall designate for the purposes of the present Convention:

    (a) one or more Management Authorities competent to grant permits or certificates on behalf of that Party; and

    (b) one or more Scientific Authorities.

2. A State depositing an instrument of ratification, acceptance, approval or accession shall at that time inform the Depositary Government of the name and address of the Management Authority authorized to communicate with other Parties and with the Secretariat.

3. Any changes in the designations or authorizations under the provisions of this Article shall be communicated by the Party concerned to the Secretariat for transmission to all other Parties.

4. Any Management Authority referred to in paragraph 2 of this Article shall, if so requested by the Secretariat or the Management Authority of another Party, communicate to it impression of stamps, seals or other devices used to authenticate permits or certificates.

Article X

TRADE WITH STATES NOT PARTY TO THE CONVENTION

Where export or re-export is to, or import is from, a State not a Party to the present Convention, comparable documentation issued by the competent authorities in that State which substantially conforms with the requirements of the present Convention for permits and certificates may be accepted in lieu thereof by any Party.

Article XI

CONFERENCE OF THE PARTIES

1. The Secretariat shall call a meeting of the Conference of the Parties not later than two years after the entry into force of the present Convention.

2. Thereafter the Secretariat shall convene regular meetings at least once every two years, unless the Conference decides otherwise, and extraordinary meetings at any time on the written request of at least one-third of the Parties.

3. At meetings, whether regular or extraordinary, the Parties shall review the implementation of the present Convention and may:

(a) make such provision as may be necessary to enable the Secretariat to carry out its duties, and adopt financial provisions;

(b) consider and adopt amendments to Appendices I and II in accordance with Article XV;

(c) review the progress made towards the restoration and conservation of the species included in Appendices I, II and III;

(d) receive and consider any reports presented by the Secretariat or by any Party; and

(e) where appropriate, make recommendations for improving the effectiveness of the present Convention.

4. At each regular meeting, the Parties may determine the time and venue of the next regular meeting to be held in accordance with the provisions of paragraph 2 of this Article.

5. At any meeting, the Parties may determine and adopt rules of procedure for the meeting.

6. The United Nations, its Specialized Agencies and the International Atomic Energy Agency, as well as any State not a Party to the present Convention, may be represented at meetings of the Conference by observers, who shall have the right to participate but not to vote.

7. Any body or agency technically qualified in protection, conservation or management of wild fauna and flora, in the following categories, which has informed the Secretariat of its desire to be represented at meetings of the Conference by observers, shall be admitted unless at least one-third of the Parties present object:

(a) international agencies or bodies, either governmental or non-governmental, and national governmental agencies and bodies; and

(b) national non-governmental agencies or bodies which have been approved for this purpose by the State in which they are located. Once admitted, these observers shall have the right to participate but not to vote.

Article XII

THE SECRETARIAT

1. Upon entry into force of the present Convention, a Secretariat shall be provided by the Executive Director of the United Nations

Environment Programme. To the extent and in the manner
he considers appropriate, he may be assisted by suitable inter-
governmental or non-governmental international or national agencies
and bodies technically qualified in protection, conservation and
management of wild fauna and flora.

2. The functions of the Secretariat shall be:

(a) to arrange for and service meetings of the Parties;

(b) to perform the functions entrusted to it under the provisions of
Articles XV and XVI of the present Convention;

(c) to undertake scientific and technical studies in accordance with
programmes authorized by the Conference of the Parties as will
contribute to the implementation of the present Convention,
including studies concerning standards for appropriate preparation
and shipment of living specimens and the means of identifying
specimens;

(d) to study the reports of Parties and to request from Parties such
further information with respect thereto as it deems necessary to
ensure implementation of the present Convention;

(e) to invite the attention of the Parties to any matter pertaining to the
aims of the present Convention;

(f) to publish periodically and distribute to the Parties current editions
of Appendices I, II and III together with any information which
will facilitate identification of specimens of species included in
those Appendices;

(g) to prepare annual reports to the Parties on its work and on the
implementation of the present Convention and such other reports
as meetings of the Parties may request;

(h) to make recommendations for the implementation of the aims and
provisions of the present Convention, including the exchange of
information of a scientific or technical nature;

(i) to perform any other function as may be entrusted to it by the Parties.

Article XIII

INTERNATIONAL MEASURES

1. When the Secretariat in the light of information received is satisfied
that any species included in Appendix I or II is being affected adversely

by trade in specimens of that species or that the provisions of the present Convention are not being effectively implemented, it shall communicate such information to the authorized Management Authority of the Party or Parties concerned.

2. When any Party receives a communication as indicated in paragraph 1 of this Article, it shall, as soon as possible, inform the Secretariat of any relevant facts insofar as its laws permit and, where appropriate, propose remedial action. Where the Party considers that an inquiry is desirable, such inquiry may be carried out by one or more persons expressly authorized by the Party.

3. The information provided by the Party or resulting from any inquiry as specified in paragraph 2 of this Article shall be reviewed by the next Conference of the Parties which may make whatever recommendations it deems appropriate.

Article XIV

EFFECT ON DOMESTIC LEGISLATION AND INTERNATIONAL CONVENTIONS

1. The provisions of the present Convention shall in no way affect the right of Parties to adopt:

   (a) stricter domestic measures regarding the conditions for trade, taking, possession or transport of specimens of species included in Appendices I, II and III, or the complete prohibition thereof; or

   (b) domestic measures restricting or prohibiting trade, taking, possession or transport of species not included in Appendix I, II or III.

2. The provisions of the present Convention shall in no way affect the provisions of any domestic measures or the obligations of Parties deriving from any treaty, convention, or international agreement relating to other aspects of trade, taking, possession or transport of specimens which is in force or subsequently may enter into force for any Party including any measure pertaining to the Customs, public health, veterinary or plant quarantine fields.

3. The provisions of the present Convention shall in no way affect the provisions of, or the obligations deriving from, any treaty, convention or international agreement concluded or which may be concluded between States creating a union or regional trade agreement

establishing or maintaining a common external Customs control and removing Customs control between the parties thereto insofar as they relate to trade among the States members of that union or agreement.

4. A State party to the present Convention, which is also a party to any other treaty, convention or international agreement which is in force at the time of the coming into force of the present Convention and under the provisions of which protection is afforded to marine species included in Appendix II, shall be relieved of the obligations imposed on it under the provisions of the present Convention with respect to trade in specimens of species included in Appendix II that are taken by ships registered in that State and in accordance with the provisions of such other treaty, convention or international agreement.

5. Notwithstanding the provisions of Articles III, IV and V, any export of a specimen taken in accordance with paragraph 4 of this Article shall only require a certificate from a Management Authority of the State of introduction to the effect that the specimen was taken in accordance with the provisions of the other treaty, convention or international agreement in question.

6. Nothing in the present Convention shall prejudice the codification and development of the law of the sea by the United Nations Conference on the Law of the Sea convened pursuant to Resolution 2750 C (XXV) of the General Assembly of the United Nations nor the present or future claims and legal views of any State concerning the law of the sea and the nature and extent of coastal and flag State jurisdiction.

Article XV

AMENDMENTS TO APPENDICES I AND II

1. The following provisions shall apply in relation to amendments to Appendices I and II at meetings of the Conference of the Parties:

(a) Any Party may propose an amendment to Appendix I or II for consideration at the next meeting. The text of the proposed amendment shall be communicated to the Secretariat at least 150 days before the meeting. The Secretariat shall consult the other Parties and interested bodies on the amendment in accordance with the provisions of sub-paragraphs (b) and (c) of paragraph 2 of this Article and shall communicate the response to all Parties not later than 30 days before the meeting.

(b) Amendments shall be adopted by a two-thirds majority of Parties present and voting. For these purposes "Parties present and voting" means Parties present and casting an affirmative or negative vote. Parties abstaining from voting shall not be counted among the two-thirds required for adopting an amendment.

(c) Amendments adopted at a meeting shall enter into force 90 days after that meeting for all Parties except those which make a reservation in accordance with paragraph 3 of this Article.

2. The following provisions shall apply in relation to amendments to Appendices I and II between meetings of the Conference of the Parties:

(a) Any Party may propose an amendment to Appendix I or II for consideration between meetings by the postal procedures set forth in this paragraph.

(b) For marine species, the Secretariat shall, upon receiving the text of the proposed amendment, immediately communicate it to the Parties. It shall also consult inter-governmental bodies having a function in relation to those species especially with a view to obtaining scientific data these bodies may be able to provide and to ensuring co-ordination with any conservation measures enforced by such bodies. The Secretariat shall communicate the views expressed and data provided by these bodies and its own findings and recommendations to the Parties as soon as possible.

(c) For species other than marine species, the Secretariat shall, upon receiving the text of the proposed amendment, immediately communicate it to the Parties, and, as soon as possible thereafter, its own recommendations.

(d) Any Party may, within 60 days of the date on which the Secretariat communicated its recommendations to the Parties under sub-paragraph (b) or (c) of this paragraph, transmit to the Secretariat any comments on the proposed amendment together with any relevant scientific data and information.

(e) The Secretariat shall communicate the replies received together with its own recommendations to the Parties as soon as possible.

(f) If no objection to the proposed amendment is received by the Secretariat within 30 days of the date the replies and recommendations were communicated under the provisions of sub-paragraph (e) of this paragraph, the amendment shall enter into force 90 days later for all Parties except those which make a reservation in accordance with paragraph 3 of this Article.

(g) If an objection by any Party is received by the Secretariat, the proposed amendment shall be submitted to a postal vote in accordance with the provisions of sub-paragraphs (h), (i) and (j) of this paragraph.

(h) The Secretariat shall notify the Parties that notification of objection has been received.

(i) Unless the Secretariat receives the votes for, against or in abstention from at least one-half of the Parties within 60 days of the date of notification under sub-paragraph (h) of this paragraph, the proposed amendment shall be referred to the next meeting of the Conference for further consideration.

(j) Provided that votes are received from one-half of the Parties, the amendment shall be adopted by a two-thirds majority of Parties casting an affirmative or negative vote.

(k) The Secretariat shall notify all Parties of the result of the vote.

(l) If the proposed amendment is adopted it shall enter into force 90 days after the date of the notification by the Secretariat of its acceptance for all Parties except those which make a reservation in accordance with paragraph 3 of this Article.

3. During the period of 90 days provided for by sub-paragraph (c) of paragraph 1 or sub-paragraph (l) of paragraph 2 of this Article any Party may by notification in writing to the Depositary Government make a reservation with respect to the amendment. Until such reservation is withdrawn the Party shall be treated as a State not a Party to the present Convention with respect to trade in the species concerned.

Article XVI

APPENDIX III AND AMENDMENTS THERETO

1. Any Party may at any time submit to the Secretariat a list of species which it identifies as being subject to regulation within its jurisdiction for the purpose mentioned in paragraph 3 of Article II. Appendix III shall include the names of the Parties submitting the species for inclusion therein, the scientific names of the species so submitted, and any parts or derivatives of the animals or plants concerned that are

specified in relation to the species for the purposes of sub-paragraph (b) of Article I.

2. Each list submitted under the provisions of paragraph 1 of this Article shall be communicated to the Parties by the Secretariat as soon as possible after receiving it. The list shall take effect as part of Appendix III 90 days after the date of such communication. At any time after the communication of such list, any Party may by notification in writing to the Depositary Government enter a reservation with respect to any species or any parts or derivatives, and until such reservation is withdrawn, the State shall be treated as a State not a Party to the present Convention with respect to trade in the species or part or derivative concerned.

3. A Party which has submitted a species for inclusion in Appendix III may withdraw it at any time by notification to the Secretariat which shall communicate the withdrawal to all Parties. The withdrawal shall take effect 30 days after the date of such communication.

4. Any Party submitting a list under the provisions of paragraph 1 of this Article shall submit to the Secretariat a copy of all domestic laws and regulations applicable to the protection of such species, together with any interpretations which the Party may deem appropriate or the Secretariat may request. The Party shall, for as long as the species in question is included in Appendix III, submit any amendments of such laws and regulations or any interpretations as they are adopted.

Article XVII

AMENDMENT OF THE CONVENTION

1. An extraordinary meeting of the Conference of the Parties shall be convened by the Secretariat on the written request of at least one-third of the Parties to consider and adopt amendments to the present Convention. Such amendments shall be adopted by a two-thirds majority of Parties present and voting. For these purposes "Parties present and voting" means Parties present and casting an affirmative or negative vote. Parties abstaining from voting shall not be counted among the two-thirds required for adopting an amendment.

2. The text of any proposed amendment shall be communicated by the Secretariat to all Parties at least 90 days before the meeting.

3. An amendment shall enter into force for the Parties which have accepted it 60 days after two-thirds of the Parties have deposited an instrument of acceptance of the amendment with the Depositary Government. Thereafter, the amendment shall enter into force for any other Party 60 days after that Party deposits its instrument of acceptance of the amendment.

Article XVIII

RESOLUTION OF DISPUTES

1. Any dispute which may arise between two or more Parties with respect to the interpretation or application of the provisions of the present Convention shall be subject to negotiation between the Parties involved in the dispute.

2. If the dispute can not be resolved in accordance with paragraph 1 of this Article, the Parties may, by mutual consent, submit the dispute to arbitration, in particular that of the Permanent Court of Arbitration at The Hague, and the Parties submitting the dispute shall be bound by the arbitral decision.

Article XIX

SIGNATURE

The present Convention shall be open for signature at Washington until 30th April 1973 and thereafter at Berne until 31st December 1974.

Article XX

RATIFICATION, ACCEPTANCE, APPROVAL

The present Convention shall be subject to ratification, acceptance or approval. Instruments of ratification, acceptance or approval shall be deposited with the Government of the Swiss Confederation which shall be the Depositary Government.

Article XXI

ACCESSION

1. The present Convention shall be open indefinitely for accession. Instruments of accession shall be deposited with the Depositary Government.

2. This Convention shall be open for accession by regional economic integration organizations constituted by sovereign States which have competence in respect of the negotiation, conclusion and implementation of international agreements in matters transferred to them by their Member States and covered by this Convention.

3. In their instruments of accession, such organizations shall declare the extent of their competence with respect to the matters governed by the Convention. These organizations shall also inform the Depositary Government of any substantial modification in the extent of their competence. Notifications by regional economic integration organizations concerning their competence with respect to matters governed by this Convention and modifications thereto shall be distributed to the Parties by the Depositary Government.

4. In matters within their competence, such regional economic integration organizations shall exercise the rights and fulfil the obligations which this Convention attributes to their Member States, which are Parties to the Convention. In such cases the Member States of the organizations shall not be entitled to exercise such rights individually.

5. In the fields of their competence, regional economic integration organizations shall exercise their right to vote with a number of votes equal to the number of their Member States which are Parties to the Convention. Such organizations shall not exercise their right to vote if their Member States exercise theirs, and vice versa.

6. Any reference to "Party" in the sense used in Article I (h) of this Convention to "State"/"States" or to "State Party"/"State Parties" to the Convention shall be construed as including a reference to any regional economic integration organization having competence in respect of the negotiation, conclusion and application of international agreements in matters covered by this Convention.

Article XXII

ENTRY INTO FORCE

1. The present Convention shall enter into force 90 days after the date of deposit of the tenth instrument of ratification, acceptance, approval or accession, with the Depositary Government.

2. For each State which ratifies, accepts or approves the present Convention or accedes thereto after the deposit of the tenth instrument of

ratification, acceptance, approval or accession, the present Convention shall enter into force 90 days after the deposit by such State of its instrument of ratification, acceptance, approval or accession.

Article XXIII

RESERVATIONS

1. The provisions of the present Convention shall not be subject to general reservations. Specific reservations may be entered in accordance with the provisions of this Article and Articles XV and XVI.

2. Any State may, on depositing its instrument of ratification, acceptance, approval or accession, enter a specific reservation with regard to:

   (a) any species included in Appendix I, II or III; or

   (b) any parts or derivatives specified in relation to a species included in Appendix III.

3. Until a Party withdraws its reservation entered under the provisions of this Article, it shall be treated as a State not a Party to the present Convention with respect to trade in the particular species or parts or derivatives specified in such reservation.

Article XXIV

DENUNCIATION

Any Party may denounce the present Convention by written notification to the Depositary Government at any time. The denunciation shall take effect twelve months after the Depositary Government has received the notification.

Article XXV

DEPOSITARY

1. The original of the present Convention, in the Chinese, English, French, Russian and Spanish languages, each version being equally authentic, shall be deposited with the Depositary Government, which shall transmit certified copies thereof to all States that have signed it or deposited instruments of accession to it.

2. The Depositary Government shall inform all signatory and acceding States and the Secretariat of signatures, deposit of instruments of ratification, acceptance, approval or accession, entry into force of the

present Convention, amendments thereto, entry and withdrawal of reservations and notifications of denunciation.

3. As soon as the present Convention enters into force, a certified copy thereof shall be transmitted by the Depositary Government to the Secretariat of the United Nations for registration and publication in accordance with Article 102 of the Charter of the United Nations.

In witness whereof the undersigned Plenipotentiaries, being duly authorized to that effect, have signed the present Convention.

Done at Washington this third day of March, One Thousand Nine Hundred and Seventy-three.

Notes

1. Another, smaller project in southern Arizona provided feathers to people among the Tohono O'odham and at one or two Second Mesa Hopi villages.

2. It must be noted, however, that some of the reduction in print advertisements was replaced by advertisements on the internet, and sales of macaw and parrot feathers were relatively common on such internet auction sites as eBay, though the number of sellers seems to have declined. Some Pueblo men reported buying feathers on the internet.

3. Taos, Picuris, Okay Owingeh (San Juan), Pojoaque, Santa Clara, San Ildefonso, Nambe, Tesuque, Cochití, Santo Domingo, San Felipe, Jemez, Zia, Santa Ana, Sandia, Isleta, Laguna, Acoma, Zuni, Polacca, Walpi, Sichomovi, Hano (Tewa), Shungopovi, Mishongnovi, Sipaulovi, Kykotsmovi, Oraibi, Hotevilla, Bacavi, Upper Moencopi, and Lower Moencopi.

4. I remain unconvinced by the current dating of Paquimé, because of questions about the dendrochronology and also because the archaeology there and at Ancestral Pueblo sites at Chaco Canyon and elsewhere, with regard to macaws, does not fit well with the new chronology at Paquimé. This latest chronology, specifically for the Medio Period at Paquimé (table 1.1), means the site could not have been the source for Scarlet Macaws and Military Macaws found at Chaco Canyon, Wupatki, and other sites. But if Paquimé, with its 504 remains of macaws, was not the source, what site or sites were? No other site or sites have been suggested. This remains an open and troubling question, which might be resolved if DNA analyses of macaw skeletal materials from Pueblo Bonito, Pueblo del Arroyo, Wupatki, Point of Pines, and other Southwestern sites could be compared

with macaw skeletal DNA from Paquimé specimens. If the individual macaws could be shown to come from a common breeding population, then the revised chronology would be unlikely because the Southwestern macaws could not pre-date the Paquimé population. If, however, the populations are different, then the revised chronology would be more secure, and we must seek another source for the pre–Medio Period macaws in the Southwest.

The last I knew, the macaw skeletons and eggshells from Paquimé are housed in the laboratory and storage facility at the site. Macaw skeletal remains from the Southwest, if still extant (a question for those excavated from Pueblo Bonito by the Hyde Exploring Expedition from 1896 to 1899), were or are housed at the American Museum of Natural History, the Smithsonian, the Arizona State Museum, and perhaps the School for Advanced Research (formerly the School of American Research), Salmon Ruin, the Maxwell Museum of Anthropology and the University of New Mexico, the Museum of Northern Arizona, and the National Park Service Western Archaeological Research Center. It is possible to test at least some of these skeletal materials for DNA, but whether the sample size is sufficient remains to be determined.

5. The Earth moves around the sun, but from the perspective of the Earth's surface, the sun appears to move along the horizons, to rise and set and pass overhead, during the course of the days and years.

6. This section is derived substantially from Reyman 1995b, with revisions resulting from research in the intervening years and information learned from the Feather Distribution Project. It is followed in chapter 2 by material taken from Reyman 2008, which revised and expanded upon the 1995b publication and which itself is revised on the basis of research and information learned since 2008.

7. Plumed Serpent representations are still found today in all Pueblos.

8. *Pochteca* are also sometimes referred to as *trocadores* (Kelley 1980) or "mobile merchants" (Kelley 1986) in the literature. Kelley first suggested *trocadores* to replace *pochteca* because *trocadores*, a more general term for the concept of Mesoamerican traders in the Southwest, indicated their presence preceded the pochteca, who were an Aztec-specific group. Kelley later substituted "mobile merchants" "in order to avoid use of overly loaded and controversial terms" (Kelley 1986:82), i.e., *pochteca* and *trocadores*.

9. For more information, see http://www.wingwise.com/feather.htm.

10. One cannot always be certain about the identification of psittacines in murals, in rock art, and on ceramics and other artifacts. All macaws (which are parrots) found at archaeological sites in the Southwest have much longer tail feathers than either the Thick-billed Parrot or the two species of Amazon parrots found there. The bird depicted inside the cage has its tail against the left edge of the container, so the bird could be a macaw; but the general overall proportions are somewhat more suggestive of a parrot.

Using the criterion of tail length, there are many more images of macaws than of parrots on artifacts. The predominance of macaw images is supported by the fact that skeletal remains of macaws are far more common at Southwestern archaeological sites than are the skeletal remains of parrots—several hundred versus a dozen or so (McKusick 2001). Surprisingly, although the Thick-billed Parrot was indigenous to the Southwest, it is not frequently found in archaeological sites there. Furthermore, while macaw feathers and objects with feathers have been recovered archaeologically, few, if any, parrot feathers have been found.

11. The degree to which turkeys and other birds were used for food is debatable. Ladd (1972:12) states, "Generally speaking, birds were never an important part of the Zuni diet." McKusick (2001:123) states: "Turkeys were so valuable for their production of raw materials for feather-cord robes and feathers for a variety of other purposes, that most were probably kept for this purpose. . . . Cuts made on dead bone . . . suggest that tool stock was removed from dead turkeys before they were consigned to the trash dump." Lange (1959:112–113) also makes the point that while turkeys were eaten, they were much more valuable for their feathers.

12. Santo Domingo Pueblo has long been noted for its commercial activities.

13. I have found no evidence that Judd complied with this request.

14. One can also see long macaw center tail feathers sticking out from the ball atop the pole carried during the Rio Grande Pueblos' Corn Dance, most often at Feast Day ceremonies. The feathers are most commonly from the Scarlet Macaw (*Ara macao*) and the Blue-and-Yellow Macaw (*Ara ararauna*), though I have occasionally observed center tails from other macaws such as the Greenwing Macaw (*Ara chloroptera*).

15. It is unclear what species the term "parakeet" refers to, but Tyler (1979:18) suggests that it might refer to the Orange-fronted Parakeet (*Eupsittula caniculari*) or the Green Parakeet (*Psittacara holochlora*), both of which occur in Mexico. However, as far as I am aware, no actual parakeets of either species nor skeletal remains from them have been found in Southwestern sites. Tyler (1979:44) also references Stephen (1936:216) in this context, and Stephen does use the term "Parroquet," but the Hopi term he provides (*gyarz-ñúna*) is one of the standard Hopi terms for parrot, as in the Parrot Katsina mentioned earlier in this volume.

16. This section on the meeting at Cochití Pueblo and on obtaining feathers from the Hillside Pet Shop in Ottawa, Illinois, is based on Reyman 2003.

17. A number of Pueblo men have inquired about obtaining their own macaw or parrot, most often an Amazon parrot. We actively dissuaded them from acquiring parrots, not because we don't want to provide twice as many feathers to bird owners but because of the purchase expense, the high cost of maintenance (cage, food, toys, veterinary visits, etc.), and the high maintenance required in time and care to keep the bird well socialized. Macaws and parrots are generally social animals which live in flocks, and in

captivity, humans become their flock. Failure to provide sufficient intellectual stimulus and social care (handling and play) usually results in feather plucking, screaming, and other negative behaviors. We've even pointed out that, as much as we discourage commercial purchase of feathers, this is preferable to bird ownership where the bird doesn't receive the care and attention it needs and deserves in order to be happy and well-adjusted to captive life. So far, our cautions have worked, but we are less sanguine about what will occur now that the Project has ended.

18. There is a certain irony to this. The Pueblos are among the most conservative Native American groups, yet they readily seem to embrace new technology to fill the ancient requirements for feathers in the sacred, and often secretive, aspects of their lives. One Pueblo religious official is so computer-savvy that he has sent JPEG images of wild turkeys and macaws marked with Xs for the specific feathers he wants, or more recently an Adobe Flash video clip of the bird moving the part from which he wants feathers—tail, wing, breast, etc. Pueblo conservatism in religious matters extends just so far. But as I argued long ago (Reyman 1970, 1971), Pueblo conservatism in something of a misconception, i.e., the Pueblos are "conservative" when it is in their best interests and for reasons of self-preservation but "progressive" when their best interests are served by adapting to new ideas and practices: in this case, including wireless communication technology to request feathers.

19. So swift was the reaction, that two of the calls arrived while the man was selling the feathers in an outside visitor's area in the village.

20. An exception to this occurred more than a decade ago when we received a donation of thousands of chicken feathers dyed almost every color imaginable, but especially in psychedelic yellow, green, red, and orange hues. These were neither feathers nor colors for which we had ever received a single request, nor could we imagine they would be used in a traditional context. We offered them to the American Indian Dance Theatre in New York City, who accepted them to use as "flash" in costumes, and to powwow dancers in Chicago, who accepted them for the same purpose. We never had another such donation.

21. Similar public art programs were "The Trail of Painted Ponies" and one in Springfield, Illinois, using oversize replicas of Abraham Lincoln's iconic top hat.

22. The cow sculpture can be seen by entering the following URL into a search engine: http://www.gatewayparrotclub.org/events/programs/featherdistribution/Images/Cow-Mingled.jpg.

23. Curiously, some Pueblo men do *not* want the longest center tails but specifically request shorter ones. One Zuni man, for example, requests Greenwing Macaw tails of 16–18 inches.

24. 494 U.S. 872. See http://en.wikipedia.org/wiki/Employment_Division,_Department_of_Human_Resources_of_Oregon_v._Smith.

25. Generally, we would not have had access to hornbill feathers. A project to collect them started several years earlier among zoos in the US to provide tail and wing feathers, especially from the Rhino Hornbill, to peoples in Malaysia and elsewhere in Southeast Asia in order to stop the hunting of the birds for their feathers. For various reasons, the project had stalled, but feathers continued to accumulate. We were offered the feathers by the lead zoo and accepted them to distribute among Native American Church members in the US for peyote fans.

26. Fred Cordero served as a distributor for the Project within Cochití, i.e., we would send large numbers of feathers to him, and he would distribute them to others. In December 1989, it was apparent that Fred, then in his eighties, was gradually losing physical strength, although he was still mentally acute. So I asked, when he no longer needed feathers, to whom should I give them to distribute in the village? He replied, "There's a kid I know. Next time you're here, you can meet him." On my next trip to Cochití in March 1990, Fred introduced me to the "kid." Jose Dolores Pecos, also known as Joe or J. D., was almost seventy. "Kid" is obviously a relative term in some Pueblos.

27. Since the Project began in 1982, a number of Pueblo friends have died, some young (thirty-four, fifty-eight) and some older (in their seventies and eighties), including several who distributed feathers for us within their villages. Each time this happens, we must find someone to take over the work. In one case, the village has a Department of Natural Resources (DNR) that has now served this purpose for five years. At another village, we tried to make the same arrangement, but their DNR official died before the program could be finalized, and the replacement hasn't been willing to undertake the work.

28. As noted earlier, when I first visited Fred Cordero to deliver feathers, his wife, Helen, left the house before the actual delivery took place.

29. The total number of duck feathers distributed by the Project is probably fewer than two thousand.

30. Honoraria or reimbursements for travel expenses were accepted and put into an Illinois State Museum Society account to pay for Project expenses, especially postage.

31. It would have been much more, except that a substantial amount was saved because we were often invited to stay in Pueblo homes and to take meals with the families, rather than living in motels and eating at restaurants.

References

Bandelier, Adolph F. 1890. "Contributions to the History of the Southwestern Portion of the United States." *Papers of the Archaeological Institute of America, American Series* 5 (2): 24–67.

Bandelier, Adolph F. 1890–1892. *Final Report of Investigations Among the Indians of the Southwestern United States, Carried on Mainly in the Years from 1880 to 1885*, parts 1 and 2. Papers of the Archaeological Institute of America, American Series, nos. 3–4. Cambridge: John Wilson and Son.

Bandelier, Adolph F. 1892. "An Outline of the Documentary History of the Zuñi Tribe." *Journal of American Ethnology and Archaeology*, no. 3, 1–115.

Benedict, Ruth. 1935. *Zuni Mythology*. Vol. 2. New York: Columbia University Press.

Borhegyi, Stephan F. de. 1965. "Archaeological Synthesis of the Guatemalan Highlands." In *Handbook of Middle American Indians*, vol. 2 of *Archaeology of Southern Mesoamerica*, part 1, edited by Gordon R. Willey, 3–58. Austin: University of Texas Press.

Bourke, John G. 1884. *The Snake-Dance of the Moquis of Arizona*. New York: Scribner.

Brand, Donald D., Florence M. Hawley, Frank C. Hibben, Donvan Senter, Wesley Bliss, Robert Lister, James Spuhler, et al. 1937. *Tseh So, A Small House Ruin, Chaco Canyon, New Mexico: Preliminary Report*. University of New Mexico Bulletin, whole number 308, vol. 2, no. 2 of Anthropological Series.

Braniff C., Beatriz. 1986. "Ojo de Agua, Sonora and Casas Grandes, Chihuahua: A Suggested Chronology." In *Ripples in the Chichimec Sea*, edited by Frances Joan

Mathien and Randall C. McGuire, 70–80. Carbondale: Southern Illinois University Press.

Breitburg, Emanuel. 1988. "Prehistoric New World Turkey Domestication: Origins, Developments, and Consequences." PhD diss., Southern Illinois University, Carbondale.

Brody, J. J. 1977. *Mimbres Painted Pottery*. Santa Fe: School of American Research; Albuquerque: University of New Mexico Press.

Brody, J. J., Catherine J. Scott, Steven A. LeBlanc, and Tony Berlant. 1983. *Mimbres Pottery: Ancient Art of the American Southwest*. New York: Hudson Hills Press.

Bunzel, Ruth L. 1932a. "Introduction to Zuñi Ceremonialism." In *Bureau of American Ethnology, 47th Annual Report*, 467–835. Washington, DC: Government Printing Office.

Bunzel, Ruth L. 1932b. "Zuñi Katcinas." In *Bureau of American Ethnology, 47th Annual Report*, 837–1108. Washington, DC: Government Printing Office.

Bunzel, Ruth L. 1932c. "Zuñi Ritual Poetry." In *Bureau of American Ethnology, 47th Annual Report*, 611–835. Washington, DC: Government Printing Office.

Burland, Cottie, and Werner Forman. 1975. *Feathered Serpent and Smoking Mirror*. London: Orbis Publishing.

Canby, Thomas Y. 1982. "The Anasazi Riddles in Ruins." *National Geographic* 162 (4): 562–592.

Clark, Tiffany C. 2007. "An Assessment of the Archaeofaunal Remains from Pottery Mound." In *New Perspectives on Pottery Mound Pueblo*, edited by Polly Schaafsma, 207–227. Albuquerque: University of New Mexico Press.

Colton, Harold S. 1949. *Hopi Kachina Dolls, with a Key to Their Identification*. Albuquerque: University of New Mexico Press.

Cordell, Linda S. 1984. *Prehistory of the Southwest*. New York: Academic Press.

Creel, Darrell, and Charmion McKusick. 1994. "Prehistoric Macaws and Parrots in the Mimbres Area, New Mexico." *American Antiquity* 59 (3): 510–524.

Crown, Patricia. 2016a. "Just Macaws: A Review for the U.S. Southwest / Mexican Northwest." *Kiva* 82 (4): 331–363.

Crown, Patricia. 2016b. "The Scarlet Macaws of Arroyo Hondo Pueblo." In *Arroyo Hondo Pueblo Project: A Comprehensive Review and Evaluation*. Santa Fe: School of Advanced Research. http://www.arroyohondo.org/broader-current-perspectives/scarlet-macaws -arroyyo-hondo-pueblo.

Cushing, Frank Hamilton. 1882. "My Adventures in Zuñi." *Century Illustrated Monthly Magazine*, no. 25, 191–207.

Cushing, Frank Hamilton. 1883. "My Adventures in Zuñi." *Century Illustrated Monthly Magazine*, no. 26, 28–47.

Diaz, Gisele, and Alan Rogers. 1993. *The Codex Borgia: A Full-Color Restoration of the Ancient Mexican Manuscript*. New York: Dover Fine Art.

Dibble, Charles E., and Arthur J. O. Anderson. 1959. *Florentine Codex: General History of the Things of New Spain*, by Fray Bernardino de Sahagun, *Book 9—The Merchants*. Monographs of the School of American Research and the Museum of New Mexico, no. 14, part 10. Santa Fe: School of American Research; Logan: University of Utah.

Di Peso, Charles C., John B. Rinaldo, and Gloria J. Fenner. 1974. *Casas Grandes: A Fallen Trading Center of the Gran Chichimeca*, vols. 2, 4–8. Dragoon, AZ: Amerind Foundation; Flagstaff, AZ: Northland Press.

Dozier, Edward P. 1970. *The Pueblo Indians of North America*. New York: Holt, Rinehart, and Winston.

Dutton, Bertha P. 1963. *Sun Father's Way: The Kiva Murals of Kuaua, a Pueblo Ruin, Coronado State Monument, New Mexico*. Albuquerque: University of New Mexico Press; Santa Fe: School of American Research.

Eggan, Fred. 1950. *Social Organization of the Western Pueblos*. Chicago: University of Chicago Press.

Ellis, Florence Hawley. 1968. "An Interpretation of Prehistoric Death Customs in Terms of Modern Southwestern Parallels." In *Collected Papers in Honor of Lyndon Lane Hargrave*, edited by Albert H. Schroeder, 57–74. Papers of the Archaeological Society of New Mexico, no. 1. Santa Fe: Museum of New Mexico Press.

Emslie, Steven D. 1981. "Prehistoric Agricultural Systems: Avifauna from Pottery Mound, New Mexico." *American Antiquity* 86 (4): 853–861.

Ferdon, Edwin. 1955. *A Trial Survey of Mexican-Southwestern Architectural Parallels*. Monograph 21 of the School of American Research. Santa Fe: School of American Research.

Fox, Robin. 1967. *The Keresan Bridge: A Problem in Pueblo Ethnology*. New York: Humanities Press.

George, Richard J., Stephen Plog, Adam S. Watson, et al. 2018. "Archaeogenomic Evidence from the Southwestern US Points to a Pre-Hispanic Scarlet Macaw Breeding Colony." *Proceedings of the National Academy of Sciences of the United States of America* 115 (35): 8740–8745.

Hammond, George P., and Agapito Rey. 1940. *Narratives of the Coronado Expedition 1540–1542*. Albuquerque: University of New Mexico Press.

Hargrave, Lyndon L. 1970. *Mexican Macaws: Comparative Osteology and Survey of Remains from the Southwest*. Anthropological Papers of the University of Arizona, no. 20. Tucson: University of Arizona.

Hargrave, Lyndon L. 1979. "A Macaw Artifact from Southeastern Utah." *Southwestern Lore* 45 (4):1–6.

Haury, Emil W. 1976. *The Hohokam, Desert Farmers and Craftsmen: Excavations at Snaketown, 1964–1965*. Tucson: University of Arizona Press.

Henderson, Junius, and John Peabody Harrington. 1914. *Ethnozoology of the Tewa Indians*. Bureau of American Ethnology Bulletin 56. Washington, DC: Government Printing Office.

Hibben, Frank C. 1975. *Kiva Art of the Anasazi at Pottery Mound*. Las Vegas, NV: KC Publications.

Hill, W. W. 1982. *An Ethnography of Santa Clara Pueblo New Mexico*, edited and annotated by Charles H. Lange. Albuquerque: University of New Mexico Press.

Hodge, Frederick Webb. 1896. "Pueblo Indian Clans." *American Anthropologist* (o.s.) 9 (10): 345–352.

Hughte, Phil. 1994. *A Zuni Artist Looks at Frank Hamilton Cushing: Cartoons by Phil Hughte*. Zuni, NM: Pueblo of Zuni Arts and Crafts; A:shiwi A:Wan Museum and Heritage Center.

Judd, Neil M. 1954. *The Material Culture of Pueblo Bonito*. Smithsonian Miscellaneous Collections, Volume 124. Washington, DC: Government Printing Office.

Judd, Neil M. 1959. *Pueblo del Arroyo, Chaco Canyon*. Smithsonian Miscellaneous Collections, Volume 138, number 1. Washington, DC: Government Printing Office.

Judd, Neil M. 1964. *The Architecture of Pueblo Bonito*. Smithsonian Miscellaneous Collections, Volume 147, number 1. Washington, DC: Government Printing Office.

Juniper, Tony, and Mike Parr. 1998. *Parrots: A Guide to Parrots of the World*. New Haven, CT: Yale University Press.

Kelley, J. Charles. 1980. "Discussion of Papers by Fred Plog, David Doyel, and Carroll Riley." In *Current Issues in Hohokam Prehistory, Proceedings of a Symposium*, edited by David Doyel and Fred Plog, 49–71. Arizona State University Anthropological Research Papers, Number 23. Tucson: University of Arizona Press.

Kelley, J. Charles. 1986. "The Mobile Merchants of Molino." In *Ripples in the Chichimec Sea*, edited by Frances Joan Mathien and Randall H. McGuire, 81–104. Carbondale: Southern Illinois University Press.

Kroeber, Alfred L. 1917. *Zuñi Kin and Clan*. Anthropological Papers of the American Museum of Natural History, Vol. 18, pt. 2. New York: American Museum of Natural History.

La Barre, Weston. 2012. *The Peyote Cult*. 5th enlarged ed. Norman: University of Oklahoma Press.

Ladd, Edmund J. 1963. "Zuni Ethno-Ornithology." MS thesis, University of New Mexico, Albuquerque.

Ladd, Edmund J. 1972. "Avifaunal Usage Among the Zuni." In *Southwest Birds of Sacrifice*, by Charmion R. McKusick, 11–13. Arizona Archaeologist, no. 31. Tucson: Arizona Archaeological Society.

Lang, Richard W., and Arthur H. Harris. 1984. *The Faunal Remains from Arroyo Hondo Pueblo, New Mexico: A Study in Short-Term Subsistence Change*. Arroyo Hondo Archaeological Series, no. 5. Santa Fe, NM: School of American Research.

Lange, Charles H. 1959. *Cochiti: A New Mexico Pueblo, Past and Present*. Austin: University of Texas Press.

Lange, Frederick W. 1986. "Central America and the Southwest: A Comparison of Mesoamerica's Two Peripheries." In *Research and Reflections in Archaeology and History: Essays in Honor of Doris Stone*, edited by E. Wyllys Andrews V, 159–177. New Orleans: Middle American Research Institute.

LeBlanc, Steven A. 1980. "The Dating of Casas Grandes." *American Antiquity* 45 (4):799–806.

Lekson, Stephen H. 1984. "Dating of Casas Grandes." *The Kiva* 50 (1): 55–60.

Lekson, Stephen H. 1997. "Rewriting Southwestern Prehistory." *Archaeology* (January–February): 55.

Maca, Allan L., Jonathan E. Reyman, and William J. Folan, eds. 2010. *Prophet, Pariah, and Pioneer: Walter W. Taylor and Dissension in American Archaeology*. Boulder: University Press of Colorado.

McGregor, John C. 1943. "Burial of an Early American Magician." *Proceedings of the American Philosophical Society* 86 (2): 270–295.

McGuire, Randall H., and Dean Saitta. 1996. "Although They Have Petty Captains, They Obey Them Badly: The Dialectics of Prehispanic Western Pueblo Social Organization." *American Antiquity* 61 (2): 197–216.

McKusick, Charmion R. 1974. "The Casas Grandes Avian Report." In *Casas Grandes: A Fallen Trading Center of the Gran Chichimeca*, edited by Charles C. Di Peso, John B. Rinaldo, and Gloria J. Fenner, vol. 8, 273–284. Dragoon, AZ: Amerind Foundation.

McKusick, Charmion R. 2001. *Southwest Birds of Sacrifice*. Arizona Archaeologist, no. 31. Tucson: Arizona Archaeological Society.

Moorehead, Warren K. 1906. *A Narrative of Explorations in New Mexico, Arizona, Indiana, etc., Together with a Brief History of the Department*. Department of Archaeology Bulletin, no. 3. Andover, MA: Andover Press.

Morris, Earl H. 1919. *The Aztec Ruin*. Anthropological Papers of the American Museum of Natural History, vol. 26, part 1.

Naranjo, Tessie. 2024. "Review of Millions of Gifts for the Gods: The Feather Distribution Project." Typescript in possession of the author.

Nelson, Richard H. 1986. "Pochtecas and Prestige: Mesoamerican Artifacts in Hohokam Sites." In *Ripples in the Chichimec Sea*, edited by Frances Joan Mathien and Randall H. McGuire, 155–182. Carbondale: Southern Illinois University Press.

Nequatewa, Edmund. 1936. *Truth of a Hopi: Stories Relating to the Origin, Myths, and Clan Histories of the Hopi*, edited by Mary-Russell F. Colton. Bulletin No. 8. Flagstaff: Northern Arizona Society of Science and Art.

Nilsson, Greta. 1981. *The Bird Business: A Study of the Commercial Cage Bird Trade*. 2nd ed. Washington, DC: Animal Welfare Institute.

Olsen, Stanley J. 1968. "Fish, Amphibians, and Reptile Remains from Archaeological Sites. Part I, Southeastern and Southwestern United States. Appendix: The Osteology of the Wild Turkey." *Papers of the Peabody Museum of Archaeology and Ethnology* 47 (2): 193–466.

Parsons, Elsie Clews. 1932. "Isleta, New Mexico." In *Bureau of American Ethnology, 47th Annual Report*, 193–466. Washington, DC: Government Printing Office.

Parsons, Elsie Clews. 1939. *Pueblo Indian Religion*. 2 vols. Chicago: University of Chicago Press.

Pepper, George H. 1905. "Ceremonial Objects and Ornaments from Pueblo Bonito, New Mexico." *American Anthropologist* (n.s.) 7 (2): 182–197.

Pepper, George H. 1909. "Exploration of a Burial-Room in Pueblo Bonito, New Mexico." In *Putnam Anniversary Volume*, 196–252. New York: G. P. Stechert.

Pepper, George H. 1920. *Pueblo Bonito*. Anthropological Papers of the American Museum of Natural History, vol. 27. New York: American Museum of Natural History.

Peterson, Roger Tory. 1990. *A Field Guide to Western Birds*, 3rd ed., rev. and enlarged. Boston: Houghton Mifflin Company.

Pinkley, Jean M. 1965. "The Pueblos and the Turkey: Who Domesticated Whom?" *American Antiquity* 31 (2): 70–72.

Plog, Fred, Steadman Upham, and Phil C. Weigand. 1982. "A Perspective on Mogollon-Mesoamerican Interaction." In *Mogollon Archaeology, Proceedings of the 1980 Mogollon Conference*, edited by Patrick H. Beckett and Kira Silverbird, 227–238. Ramona, CA: Acoma Books.

Ravesloot, John C., Jeffrey S. Dean, and Michael S. Foster. 1995. "A New Perspective on the Casas Grandes Tree-Ring Dates." In *The Gran Chichimeca: Essays on the Archaeology and Ethnohistory of Northern Mesoamerica*, edited by Jonathan E. Reyman, 240–251. Worldwide Archaeology Series #12. Aldershot: Avebury Press.

Rea, Amadeo M. 1980. "Late Pleistocene and Holocene Turkeys in the Southwest." In *Papers in Avian Paleontology Honoring Hildegarde Howard*, edited by Kenneth E. Campbell Jr., 209–224. Los Angeles: Natural History Museum of Los Angeles County.

Reyman, Jonathan E. 1970. "Southwestern Pueblo Conservatism: A New Look at an Old Myth." Paper presented at 35th Annual Meeting of the Society for American Archaeology, Mexico City.

Reyman, Jonathan E. 1971. "Mexican Influence on Southwestern Ceremonialism." PhD diss., Southern Illinois University, Carbondale.

Reyman, Jonathan E. 1976a. "Astronomy, Architecture, and Adaptation at Pueblo Bonito." *Science* 193 (4257): 957–962.

Reyman, Jonathan E. 1976b. "Mexican-Southwestern Interaction: The Puebloan Ethnographic Evidence." In *Archaeological Frontiers: Papers on New World High Cultures in Honor of J. Charles Kelley*, edited by Robert B. Pickering, 87–128. University Museum Studies, Research Records, no. 4. Carbondale: University Museum; Southern Illinois University Press.

Reyman, Jonathan E. 1978. "*Pochteca* Burials at Anasazi Sites?" In *Across the Chichimec Sea: Papers in Honor of J. Charles Kelley*, edited by C. L. Riley and B. C. Hedrick, 242–259, 273 (ff. 14–16). Carbondale: Southern Illinois University Press.

Reyman, Jonathan E. 1980. "The Predictive Dimension of Priestly Power (With a Note on Solar and Lunar Cycles by Harold J. Born)." In *New Frontiers in the Archaeology and Ethnohistory of the Greater Southwest*, edited by Carroll L. Riley and Basil C. Hedrick, 40–59. *Transactions of the Illinois Academy of Science* 72 (4): 40–59.

Reyman, Jonathan E. 1985. "A Re-Evaluation of Bi-Wall and Tri-Wall Structures in the Anasazi Area." In *Archaeological Frontiers: Papers on New World High Cultures in Honor of J. Charles Kelley*, edited by William J. Folan, 293–334. Carbondale: Southern Illinois University Press.

Reyman, Jonathan E. 1990a. "The Feather Distribution Project: An Example of Applied Archaeology." *Living Museum* 52 (2): 19–22.

Reyman, Jonathan E. 1990b. "The Macaw Feather Project." *Cultural Survival* 14 (4): 77–79.

Reyman, Jonathan E. 1995a. "*Pala'tkwabi*: The Red Land of the South." In *The Gran Chichimeca: Essays on the Archaeology and Ethnohistory of Northern Mesoamerica*, edited by Jonathan E. Reyman, 320–335. Worldwide Archaeology Series, no. 12. Aldershot: Avebury Press.

Reyman, Jonathan E. 1995b. "Value in Mesoamerican-Southwestern Trade." In *The Gran Chichimeca: Essays on the Archaeology and Ethnohistory of Northern Mesoamerica*, edited by Jonathan E. Reyman, 271–280. Worldwide Archaeology Series, no. 12. Aldershot: Avebury Press.

Reyman, Jonathan E. 1999. "Preserving Tradition and Native Bird Populations: The Feather Distribution Project." *AFA Watchbird* 26 (1): 10–15.

Reyman, Jonathan E. 2003. "Conserving Culture, Preserving Birds: The Feather Distribution Project." *Living Museum* 65 (4): 3–7.

Reyman, Jonathan E. 2008. "Feathers and Ceremonialism in the American Southwest, Past and Present." *Journal of the West* 47 (3): 16–22.

Reyman, Jonathan E. 2009. "Millions of Gifts for the Gods." *PsittaScene* 21 (4): 6–9.

Riley, Carroll L. 1963. "Color-Direction Symbolism: An Example of Mesoamerican Southwestern Contacts." *America Indigena*, no. 23, 49–60.

Riley, Carroll L. 1974. "Mesoamerican Indians in the Early Southwest." *Ethnohistory* 22 (1): 25–36.

Roberts, Frank H. H., Jr. 1932. "Unpublished Field Notes." National Anthropological Archives.

Roberts, Frank H. H., Jr. 1933. "Unpublished Field Notes." National Anthropological Archives.

Roberts, Frank H. H., Jr. 1939. *Archaeological Remains in the Whitewater District, Eastern Arizona*, Part I: *House Types*. Bureau of American Ethnology Bulletin 121. Washington, DC: Government Printing Office.

Roberts, Frank H. H., Jr. 1940a. *Archaeological Remains in the Whitewater District, Eastern Arizona*, Part II: *Artifacts and Burials*. Bureau of American Ethnology Bulletin 126. Washington, DC: Government Printing Office.

Roberts, Frank H. H., Jr. 1940b. "Unpublished Field Notes." National Anthropological Archives.

Rubinstein, Robert A. 1991. "A Conversation with Sol Tax." *Current Anthropology* 32 (2): 175–183.

Schorger, A. W. 1966. *The Wild Turkey: Its History and Domestication*. Norman: University of Oklahoma Press.

Schroeder, Albert H. 1968. "Birds and Feathers in Documents Relating to Indians of the Southwest." In *Collected Papers in Honor of Lyndon Lane Hargrave*, edited by Albert H. Schroeder, 95–114. Papers of the Archaeological Society of New Mexico, no. 1. Santa Fe: Museum of New Mexico Press.

Schwartz, Christopher W., Stephen Plog, and Patricia A. Gilman. 2022. *Birds of the Sun: Macaws and People in the U.S. Southwest and Mexican Northwest*. Tucson: University of Arizona Press.

Seowtewa, Octavius. 2022. "Zuni Use of Macaws." In *Birds of the Sun: Macaws and People in the U.S. Southwest and Mexican Northwest*, 58–59. Tucson: University of Arizona Press.

Shaw, Harley G. 2002. "Merriam Turkey Prehistory: A Biologist's Perspective." In *Culture and Environment in the American Southwest: Essays in Honor of Robert C. Euler*, edited by David A. Phillips Jr. and John A. Ware, 69–78. SWCA Anthropological Research Paper, no. 8. Phoenix: SWCA.

Smith, Watson. 1952. *Kiva Mural Decorations at Awatovi and Kawaika-a*. Papers of the Peabody Museum of American Archaeology and Ethnology, Harvard University, Vol. XXXVII, Reports of the Awatovi Expedition, Report No. 5.

Stephen, Alexander M. 1936. *Hopi Journal*. Edited by Elsie Clews Parsons. New York: Columbia University Press,

Stevenson, Matilda Coxe. 1904. "The Zuñi Indians: Their Mythology, Esoteric Fraternities, and Ceremonies." *Bureau of American Ethnology, 23rd Annual Report*. Washington, DC: Government Printing Office.

Suina, Joseph. 2024. "Review of Millions of Gifts for the Gods: The Feather Distribution Project." Typescript in possession of the author.

Tax, Sol. 1952. "Action Anthropology." *América Indigena*, no. 12, 103–106.

Tax, Sol. 1975. "Action Anthropology." *Current Anthropology* 16 (4): 514–517.

Thornton, Erin Kennedy, Kitty F. Emery, David W. Steadman, Camilla Speller, Ray Matheny, and Dongya Yang. 2012. "Earliest Mexican Turkeys (*Meleagris gallopavo*) in the Maya Region: Implications for Pre-Hispanic Animal Trade and the Timing of Turkey Domestication." *PLoS ONE*. http://journals.plos.org/plosone/article?id=10 .1371/journal.pone.0042630.

Turner, Christy G., II, and Jacqueline A. Turner. 1999. *Man Corn: Cannibalism and Violence in the Prehistoric American Southwest*. Salt Lake City: University of Utah Press.

Tyler, Hamilton A. 1979. *Pueblo Birds and Myths*. Norman: University of Oklahoma Press.

Vaillant, George C. 1950. *Aztecs of Mexico*. Garden City, NY: Doubleday and Company.

Vivian, R. Gwinn, Dulce N. Dodgen, and Gayle H. Hartmann. 1978. *Wooden Ritual Artifacts from Chaco Canyon, New Mexico. The Chetro Ketl Collection*. Submitted in fulfillment of Contract 4940P21004. Chaco Archive 2017, NPS Chaco Culture NHP Museum Archive, University of New Mexico, Albuquerque.

Vivian, R. Gwinn, and Bruce Hilpert. 2012. *The Chaco Handbook: An Encyclopedic Guide*. Salt Lake City: University of Utah Press.

Watson, Adam S., Stephen Plog, Brendan J. Culleton, et al. 2015. "Early Procurement of Scarlet Macaws and the Emergence of Social Complexity in Chaco Canyon, NM." *Proceedings of the National Academy of Science* 112 (25). http://www.pnas.org/content /early/2015/06/17/15098225112.full.pdf ?sid=f9ba6a66-78db-4fc4-ba92-ba99aee54646.

White, Leslie A. 1932. "The Acoma Indians." In *Bureau of American Ethnology, 47th Annual Report*, 17–192. Washington, DC: Government Printing Office.

Wilcox, David R. 1986. "A Historical Analysis of the Problem of Mexican-Southwestern Connections." In *Ripples in the Chichimec Sea*, edited by Frances Joan Mathien and Randall H. McGuire, 9–44. Carbondale: Southern Illinois University Press.

Winship, George P. 1896. "The Coronado Expedition, 1540–1542." *Bureau of American Ethnology, 14th Annual Report*, part 1, 329–613. Washington, DC: Government Printing Office.

Wyllys, Rufus Kay. 1931. "Padre Luis Velarde's Relacion of Pimeria Alta, 1716." *New Mexico Historical Review* 6 (2): 111–157.

Index

Page numbers followed by f indicate a figure, and page numbers followed by t indicate a table.

About the Author

Jonathan E. Reyman is a retired professor of anthropology from Illinois State University. He served for more than a decade as curator of the American Southwest, Mesoamerican, and South American archaeological and ethnographic collections at the Illinois State Museum. He is the author of *Pueblo Bonito and Chaco Canyon Revisited*, along with several other books.

www.ingramcontent.com/pod-product-compliance
Lightning Source LLC
Chambersburg PA
CBHW051257020426
42333CB00026B/3237